ADVERTISING

What it is and how to do it

Third edition

ADVERTISING
What it is and how to do it

Third Edition

Roderick White

Planning Director
Lansdown Conquest

The McGraw-Hill Companies

London · New York · St Louis · San Francisco · Auckland · Bogotá · Caracas
Lisbon · Madrid · Mexico · Milan · Montreal · New Delhi · Panama · Paris
San Juan · São Paulo · Singapore · Sydney · Tokyo · Toronto

Published by
McGraw-Hill Publishing Company
Shoppenhangers Road, Maidenhead, Berkshire, SL6 2QL, England
Telephone 01628 23432 Fax 01628 770224

British Library Cataloguing in Publication Data
White, Roderick
   Advertising: what it is and how to do it.
   –3 Rev. ed
   I. Title
   659.1
   ISBN 0–07–707764–4

Library of Congress Cataloging-in-Publication Data
White, Roderick
   Advertising: what it is and how to do it/Roderick White—3rd ed.
   p.   cm.
   Includes bibliographical references and index.
      1. Advertising.   I. Title.
HF5823.W468   1993   92–46380 CIP
659.1   dc20

ISBN 0–07–707764–4

First published 1980

McGraw-Hill

A Division of The McGraw-Hill Companies

   45 CUP 96

Typeset by Goodfellow & Egan Phototypesetting Ltd, Cambridge
and printed and bound in Great Britain at the University Press, Cambridge
Printed on permanent paper in compliance with ISO Standard 9706

Contents

Note: the plates will be found between pages 54 and 55.

Foreword

Good books about advertising are amazingly rare. The many great tomes on advertising that litter the shelves of company libraries are all too often the product of academics, or others from the world of learning, whose knowledge may be extensive but which very rarely seems to extend to a proper appreciation of life in the trenches of the advertising world. Another great swathe of books about advertising are rendered nearly valueless to anyone anxious to understand how advertising works in Britain, by being about American advertising practices or by using American terms, which often have little similarity to those encountered in Europe.

This book is different. It is obviously written by a practitioner. By someone who has lived and breathed for many years in the hot-house world of advertising, and who consequently knows his subject very well indeed. As a result, this is a very good, immensely practical guide for anyone about to get involved in the world of advertising. Roderick White explains, in simple, jargon-free, clear language, the basic concepts and techniques which the beginner needs to know about to avoid confusion in what is a fairly complex business. The author strikes a splendid balance between over-simplification and unnecessary detail for a book of this nature.

It is consequently an ideal book for the businessman or businesswoman about to get involved in advertising for the first time, for people in a first job in advertising or marketing, and for teachers or students requiring a straightforward but reasonably detailed introduction to the subject.

In addition, the book describes the advertising business in sufficient depth to be of use to specialists actually working in advertising who would like a broader knowledge of the business in which they work.

Now in its third edition, the book has once again been comprehensively updated, with more weight now given to the increasingly important subjects of international advertising and direct marketing. In addition, a new and very useful chapter on campaign planning has been added by the author.

M.J. Waterson
Director of Research
The Advertising Association

Acknowledgements

This book owes its origins to Mike Waterson, and its contents to a host of colleagues and clients with whom I have worked over the years, at JWT and Lansdown Conquest, formerly LansdownEuro.

A vast number of people have—whether they believe it or not—contributed their ideas, wisdom, knowledge and experience, which I have happily exploited.

The fact that we have arrived at a third edition is proof of the value of their contributions—and of the tolerance of my colleagues, family and my various editors at McGraw-Hill, most recently Kate Allen. My thanks to all of them.

Specifically, I would like to thank the various companies who have kindly allowed me to reproduce their advertisements: Allied-Maples Group Ltd, DeBeers Consolidated Mines Ltd, Ferrero (UK) Ltd, Gallaher Tobacco UK Ltd, Guinness Brewing Worldwide Ltd, Häagen Dazs UK Ltd, Lloyds Bank plc, Loretta Cigars (London) Ltd and EBAS International BV, Mercedes-Benz (UK) Ltd, Peugeot Talbot Motor Company Ltd, Prestige & Collections (UK) Ltd, J Sainsbury plc, Société des Products Nestlé SA, Sun Life Assurance Company, and Triumph International Ltd.

Finally—last but no means least—my thanks to Hatik Ahmed, who usually succeeds in translating my hieroglyphics into typescript.

Roderick White

1 Introduction

Everyone knows all about advertising. This is particularly true of everyone who works in, or with, the advertising business, but it is also true of economists, politicians, sociologists, and consumerists. It is even true of consumers, though this is not believed by economists, politicians, and consumerists. The evidence for this is everywhere, especially on the bookshelves of business libraries, but also in the media and even in the bars of pubs many miles north of Watford, where London-based advertising agency staff are never seen, or so it is said. It is, evidently, very easy to have opinions, at length, about advertising, and to persuade publishers to go to the trouble of printing and distributing them.

It is, equally, perfectly clear that no one knows everything about advertising. The mechanics of the process of producing and placing advertisements, and the business of running an agency, or of working out and maintaining the relationship between an agency and a client, are, on the face of it, fairly straightforward. The only problem is that for an advertisement to work, to help a product sell, requires an idea. It is, as all the researchers in all the R&D departments all over the world have found, rather difficult to have successful ideas. What is more, in an advertisement, when someone has had an idea, it can be quite difficult to decide whether it is a good idea, or a bad idea, or merely a run-of-the-mill idea, which is what the vast majority turn out to be. Since a really good idea appears to be able to make a vast difference to a brand's sales, this obviously introduces a small element of uncertainty into the whole process. It is this uncertainty that makes advertising, as a business, exciting, challenging, frustrating, impossible, stimulating, mad, tough, chaotic, controversial, and, sometimes, rewarding.

Some 30 years ago, when I first stumbled into the agency business, still wet behind the ears, I fairly quickly decided that books about advertising were not very helpful, and I vowed that I would never write one, because it was impossible to get it right. It is still, I believe, impossible to get it right, but it is difficult to resist temptation, and someone put temptation in my way. The old Adam duly yielded.

What I have tried to do is to provide a reasonably straightforward guide to the state of the art as it is today, and to point out the main pitfalls that face the unwary and the over-confident—and most people in or near the advertising business are one or the other, usually the latter. I have not tried to include

1

even the kitchen sink (I could not remember the brand name), so there are, undoubtedly, gaps. In particular, I have concentrated almost entirely on consumer advertising, to the virtual exclusion of the industrial and financial sections of the business. Most of the principles, however, apply just as much to these activities as to consumer advertising: the role of advertising in the overall marketing activity of the industrial marketer may be smaller and slightly different in character, but the process of arriving at the key decisions is, or should be, still the same. In practice, advertising is simply one part of a company's communications, all of which should meet the same brand strategy.

Obviously, what is essentially an introduction to the business has to skate rather quickly over many subjects, and plenty of issues are only discussed very superficially. You will, I hope, want to know more, and I have therefore provided at the end of the book a very brief guide to finding out more about many aspects of the business. The best educator, though, is experience— experience going hand in hand with an open mind and endless curiosity.

Advertisements: not just 'advertising'

This is a book about how to make and use advertisements. This means that it is not mainly about that weird abstract noun 'advertising', which is a convenient political whipping boy for a wide variety of social, psychological, and economic theories. When I talk about 'advertising', I shall be using the word, as far as possible, to mean, precisely, the act of using advertisements to sell goods.

The reason for this is very simple. 'Advertising', as it is too often used, is a blanket term covering everything from the postcard in a newsagent's window selling a secondhand pram to an expensively produced commercial appearing five times a night on national TV. To say, therefore, that 'advertising does this', or 'advertising causes that', is nonsense. Even when one is talking, as most of this book is, about the use of advertisements to sell goods or services to large numbers of customers, it is still difficult to generalize about the process.

There is a further difficulty, too. An advertisement is not necessarily a commercial on TV, or a page in the *Daily Express*. In a sense, any piece of material produced by a company is a form of advertisement—even if it is only an invoice. Much of this material is not likely to come into the usual media arguments about advertising—nor, indeed, into many textbooks about advertising or marketing. It is, however, all part of the way in which a company presents itself to the public and calls attention to what it has to sell.

This book, then, is a basic guide to how to advertise: what it involves, what it can achieve and how to get it done.

Although it is basically a 'how to' book, it cannot give all the answers. Devising advertisements is an imaginative and chancy business, and no one has ever produced a foolproof technique for having imaginative ideas—let alone the right imaginative ideas. The business of advertising is, too, a changing and developing one. Some of the most successful advertisers have been those who have, in effect, rewritten the rule book. I can provide a more or less comprehensive toolkit and instruction on how to use it, but it is up to the reader to work at becoming the expert cabinet-maker. Practice and experience are, in the last resort, essential to successful advertising.

Advertisements and your business

'It pays to advertise.' This nice simple-minded slogan used to appear on poster sites up and down the country some 30 years ago—with no further explanation. To the poster proprietors who put it on their (empty) sites, it seemed self-evident. Perhaps it does to you.

If you are running a business, it may not be so simple. There are plenty of businesses, in all sectors of the economy, which advertise either very little or, indeed, not at all. You still do not see many advertisements for Marks & Spencer, and few for British Home Stores—though, of course, their shop windows are their own ads. The fact is that advertisements are just one of the many tools available to help a firm to sell what it has to offer, and it may well be that advertising is, quite simply, not appropriate for the firm's particular circumstances. Before going on in the next chapter to consider how a business should decide whether or not to advertise, and why it might do so, it is important to consider, in fairly general terms, how advertising fits into a company's activities, and what it can do to contribute to the selling effort.

At its simplest, a business buys resources, which can be raw materials, parts and components, the brains and muscles of its employees, or even money, turns them into some form of product or service, and sells them to its customers at a profit. To do this, it requires working capital, employees, premises, potential customers, and a means of reaching them. This applies pretty well to any kind of business. The process of identifying, reaching, and selling to the potential customers is, nowadays, called marketing, which is rather more than just the jumped-up name for 'selling' that it is sometimes thought to be.

People involved in marketing, who for some reason are often rather defensive about it, spend a great deal of time trying to invent better definitions of their task, in order to make clear to everyone else what it is all about. This is not a very helpful process, as the definitions tend to be ingenious but obscure. Very simply, the idea of marketing is that a business ought, as far as possible, to start with its customers; and it should gear all its efforts to giving the customers what they want—at a profit, of course. This means, for example, that customers should somehow have some say in the design of the product; and that it should be made as easy as possible for the customer to buy and use.

The process of marketing, then, includes a whole range of activities relating to selling the product—actual selling, decisions on pricing and distribution policy, advertising and other forms of promotion—and, indeed, at least part of the specification of the product. It involves, therefore, the market research and intelligence on which the necessary understanding of the customer must be based. This collection of activities is usually called, in marketing jargon, the 'marketing mix'.

The marketing mix

It is useful to look at the marketing mix from two points of view. The first is a simple, practical analysis of how it fits into the operations of the business. Bearing in mind that marketing should have contributed, through market research, to the specification of the product, it is easiest to see it as filling the time and space between when the product comes off the end of the production line and when the ultimate customer buys it. (In fact, if you are making a complex piece of machinery, or selling insurance, it goes beyond this, into after-sales service.)

It is the task of people in business to plan how best to fill the gap, in terms of making the best use of available resources to achieve sufficient sales, profitably, to satisfied customers.

If you look at the costs of a hypothetical manufacturing company, you will find a picture which looks, basically, rather like the one shown in Table 1.1.

Table 1.1   P/L statement for hypothetical manufacturing company (£'000s)

	1. Value of sales		100
	Less		
	2. Cost of materials		35
	3. Labour and related costs		10
	4. Overheads		10
=	5. Gross margin	45	
	Less		
	6. Selling and distribution costs		30
=	7. Net profit (pre-tax)	15	

To all intents and purposes, item 6 is the marketing mix in this simple trading statement. For the manager with a sales target to meet and a planned gross margin of 45 per cent, the problem is how to use as little as possible of that margin to achieve the sales target, to have a continuing, viable business and, still, to make a satisfactory profit.

The second way to look at the marketing mix is to consider what the mix is actually doing to the relationship between the product and its purchasers. In a way, the key to this lies in what I have just said. Most businesses are looking for continuing success. They achieve this, basically, through satisfied customers—and they have to do it in the face of their competitors.

Through the elements of the marketing mix, the business sets out to build and maintain its competitive position. In most cases, the most effective way to protect this position is through successfully *branding* its products. The distinction between a product and a brand is important, as it explains much of what marketing tries to do, and much of the use of advertisements.

A product, in these terms, is quite simply something which is offered to potential buyers and which, while it may be very good of its kind, is not systematically presented in a way which differentiates it from its competitors. A brand, on the other hand, is a product whose producer has set out deliberately and consistently to use every element in its presentation to make it uniquely desirable to its potential buyers. If this is done successfully, it makes the brand extremely difficult to compete with—not necessarily because it is physically that much better than its competitors, but because it has acquired an aura (a 'brand image') which makes it appear that much better. Perhaps *the* classic example of this in Britain is Heinz Baked Beans.

A brand is created by all the elements in the marketing mix working together, consistently, to create a clear prejudice in its favour among its customers. In other words, a brand has a place in people's minds, as a brand, whereas a mere product is simply a way of fulfilling a physical need. In a competitive economy, there is a clear theoretical advantage in being a brand.

Diagrammatically, being a brand is quite a simple concept. All the parts of the marketing mix, as a consistent group, contribute their share to the product, so as to help build up a favourable prejudice among its actual and potential customers—roughly as shown in Figure 1.1. Of course, it may not be necessary to use all the elements in the diagram to build up a particular brand. The possible combinations are numerous.

The role of advertising
How does advertising fit in with all this? Obviously, it can be one of the elements which contribute to the character and reputation of the brand. It can,

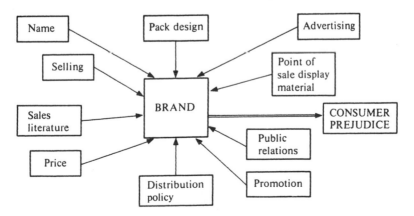

Fig 1.1   How a brand fits together

clearly, be a very important part of getting to the customer, in order to create that favourable prejudice. Ultimately though, its role is, very simply, to sell: if it fails to do that, in one way or another, there is little point in it.

Once you accept that advertisements have to sell, it is clear that you do not automatically *need* to advertise. Advertising is not the only available method for making sales, nor can it, usually, do the whole job—unless you are selling solely by direct mail or through direct response advertising, you will be using salespeople to sell direct to the public, or to distribute your product through the wholesale and retail trade. If, like the majority of consumer goods manufacturers, you are selling through the distributive trade, you have, first, to sell to them. At least at the wholesale level, you probably do this by personal selling—and you probably sell direct to major retailers, too. This process may be helped by advertising to the trade, to announce your intentions and to show that you mean business: but you do not necessarily need to do this, and you will meet plenty of people both in advertising agencies and their client companies who say that it is generally a waste of money to do so.

In the same way, you *need* not advertise to the consumer: you can rely on the retailer to sell your product for you. This has become extremely difficult in fast-moving consumer goods (fmcg) markets, since the major multiple retailers who dominate the sale of these products have become increasingly selective in their choice of brands, and now put such emphasis on their own private label products. In these markets, the many small and unadvertised brands that exist are, usually, struggling for marginal distribution and competing almost wholly on price. In some durable markets, however, especially in furniture and furnishings, and also in fashion, there are numerous small and often successful brands with little or no consumer advertising support. It is noticeable, however, that in recent years these markets, too, have begun to see more advertising activity, and this has put increased competitive pressure on the unadvertised brands.

So is there any point in advertising, when the retail shelf can do the job for you? Almost certainly the answer to this question is 'Yes—if you can afford it'. In these days of self-service, no retailer is going to do much of a job to *sell* your product to the consumer: and even if it is sold through the sort of shop where a customer can actually get advice, the retailer will only be able to talk to a few people about it. Increasingly, retailers *expect* products to be advertised, as part of the overall business of selling them to the consumer.

A postcard to every home?

Advertising gives the opportunity of speaking, remarkably cheaply, to a great many people. As Procter & Gamble pointed out in their evidence to the Monopolies Commission inquiry on detergents in the mid-sixties, their multi-million pound expenditure enabled them to speak to virtually every household in the country on TV for 30 seconds or more, several times a year—all for the cost of sending every home just one postcard.

If, like P & G, you can afford a massive advertising budget, the economies of scale in speaking to people are enormous. But even for the small advertiser, they are still there. A 30-second radio spot on Capital Radio might reach 5 per cent of London's adults—an audience of over 480 000—for only £1800. A 25 cm × 4 col ad in the *Daily Express* reaches a circulation of 1.6 million (and more than two readers per copy) for £9700. In both cases, the cost per thousand contacts with the public is tiny—£3.75 and £2.57 respectively. A thousand postcards will cost £180 on postage, let alone the cost of the cards themselves and of printing and addressing them.

It is all very well deciding to send the equivalent of several postcards to a lot of people 'out there': but what for? Clearly, to sell to them; to tell them why they should want what it is that you have to offer, among the thousands of other possible ways of spending their money. If they do not know about your product, they may come on it by accident but they certainly will not go looking for it; and when they find it, they may not realize how good or useful or new it is. When Emerson said 'If a man build a better mousetrap. . . the world will beat a path to his door' he seems to have ignored the need for communication—or he was putting a lot of faith in word-of-mouth, which is far the best form of advertising, but difficult to organize.

Building a reputation
Advertising, then, can help to sell. It does this, to a substantial extent, by giving information—what the product is, what it does, where it can be found. This is its primary role for a new product, and a continuing role, in introducing the product to people who have never tried it, for an established one. In addition to this, however, it can do more: it can begin to develop a reputation for your product, and for your company as the makers of the product. By advertising, or rather by the way you do it, you can begin to give your product a reputation for good quality. Obviously it helps if the product is genuinely the best available, but this is objectively true of few products (whatever their producers may think): in most competitive markets, the differences between competing products are fairly marginal, and an established reputation can make the difference between market leader and also ran. If you look at brands which have been successful for 30, 40, 50, or more years, like Persil, Oxo, Bisto, Black Magic, Bovril, Walls. . . they have been consistently advertised—and they have also been consistently improved to live up to their reputation as technology has developed. The advertising which can develop a strong reputation is not a reliable safeguard against superior product developments by competitors, but it can certainly fight off equals and buy time for the brand's own product development.

Supporting and motivating distributors
I said earlier that if you once get a product on the shelves of a supermarket, it will probably sell. The same applies, up to a point, in most other channels of distribution, as long as the distributor is adequately informed of the product's merits, so that it is displayed (advertising again!) or sold verbally.

However, in most distributive operations these days it is increasingly unlikely that a trade buyer will buy a new product from any supplier, except to be sold under the trader's own brand name, without the promise of either advertising support or other forms of promotion. Usually, too, part of any promotion is expected to be in advertising—even if it is only in-store display material, or a contribution to the retailer's own advertising.

One element, then, in the task to be performed by an advertising programme is to support or gain the cooperation of the distributive trade. This can be done formally in the shape of promotional support, or less directly through the advertising of the product to the consumer. In many cases, from cars to fashion, this advertising will often include lists of stores or dealers selling the products, to make sure that would-be buyers can find them. Often this reflects the fragmented nature of the markets, both in terms of brands and of retailers, and the advertising is part of a sort of mutual support system for manufacturer and retailer.

For the retailer, conversely, the existence of the advertising for the products being handled is not merely a form of support and encouragement from the producer. It is, in fact, a valuable part of the retailer's own promotion of his or her store. To potential customers it is an important sign about the store that it should be associated with particular types of brand and the reputations these brands have. On a more mundane, day-to-day level, a major element in the success of the big grocery multiples during the price war that raged from 1977 to about 1982, was their ability to promote by cutting the prices of major advertised brands. Even Sainsbury, with nearly two-thirds of its sales in private label, concentrated the weight of its price advertising on manufacturers' brands.

Direct response

In the circumstances I have been discussing so far, advertising interacts with distribution and with pricing and promotions. It can sell the product to the distributor and sell it to the consumer—which it does by getting the consumer into the distributor's shop or showroom or office.

But, of course, advertising does not need to have a distributor who is independent of the manufacturer in order to sell. It can, and does, work very effectively by selling direct to the customer. Direct response mail order advertising in newspapers, magazines and, more recently, on TV and radio has become increasingly important in the UK in recent years. Total direct response advertising in press and TV at card rates in 1991 was reported by *the Media Register* as £205 million, which represents 1.5 per cent of total display advertising. An almost infinite variety of goods can be, and is, sold by direct response.

More important, and of increasing significance for a wide range of goods and services, is direct mail advertising. According to figures compiled by the Advertising Association, direct mail now accounts for £1000 million of expenditure annually, 12 per cent of all advertising, and is the third most important medium, after press and TV. Because direct mail is essentially a 'private' medium, detailed evidence of success is rarely published, but expert practitioners such as Reader's Digest, who have a long and successful history of selling books and records direct, reckon to be able to get response rates as high as 20 or even 30 per cent for many of their mailings.

The beauty of direct mail, of course, is that you can advertise as little as you like, and have a precise measure of the response. This is rather less true of direct response, and hardly true at all of general media advertising, as we shall see in Chapter 9.

For companies that do not want to get involved in selling through the retail trade, these direct forms of advertising provide a superficially simple alternative. In terms of the marketing mix, you will see that they have eliminated the costs of selling to the retailers and distributing to them: instead, they have substituted what is, probably, a rather higher level of advertising in relation to sales, plus the cost of distributing goods to every individual customer. In addition, this process may add 'hidden' costs of carrying stocks which would normally have been sold to the wholesaler or retailer.

Advertising and competition

It should be clear from what I have already said that advertising is a weapon of competition as well as merely a way of achieving sales. It is a key way of helping to distinguish one brand from its competitors, and of making it stand out to potential buyers. You may argue as to whether Heineken lager's 'Refreshes the parts other beers cannot reach' is any sort of genuine claim for the product, but there is no doubt that it has made the brand clearly recognized and remembered, and associated with refreshment—a key quality of a lager, but one which is presumably pretty much a common characteristic of virtually all lager brands.

Of course, advertising can be a lot more directly competitive than that. Around the world the rules vary: in Germany it is illegal to make any comparison of your product with a competitor's in advertising, but in Britain and the USA things are different, and honest claims of superiority over named competitors can be made. It is a matter of debate whether this is necessarily a good strategy to adopt, and it can lead to expensive litigation, as has occurred in the USA between PepsiCo and Coca-Cola, if the basis of claims is disputed. Only the lawyers win that kind of fight.

Advertising is widely believed by academic economists to represent a barrier to market entry in markets where heavy advertising is the major method of competition. I do not think many large advertisers see it that way: they are usually advertising in order to protect their position against competitors already in the market, and to build up the size of the total market. Certainly, heavy advertising is no real barrier against significantly better, more reliable and better value products, as has been shown, for example, by Japanese cars, wherever they have been allowed to compete freely, over the past 15–20 years.

Keeping customers

Much of the time, even in competitive markets, advertising is used as a way of reminding customers that the brand exists, and retaining their confidence in its ability to meet their needs. This 'reminder' function is greatly misunderstood by many people outside the business world, who appear to believe that once a product has been announced to the public at large there is no need to advertise it further. For this school of thought, the whole task of advertising is to provide 'information', and there are periodically complex bouts of academic wrangling as to how much of a given advertisement or campaign or industry's advertising expenditure is 'information' and therefore somehow 'justifiable'. This is a peculiarly sterile argument.

The value of this 'reminder' advertising is actually very high to the business that uses it. Initial advertising when a product is launched may achieve a satisfactory level of awareness, understanding, and trial by consumers. It is very unlikely, however, that 100 per cent of potential buyers will have seen the advertising, and even among those who have, a significant proportion will not have been interested: perhaps they were not really paying attention; or they had just bought another brand; or they were not really in the market for this type of product at present. These are all people who will have to be reached again by the advertising (or by some other means) if they are to become purchasers of the product. If there is no more advertising, the product will have failed to approach its potential sale.

Then again, consider the people who saw the advertising and bought the product. Will they buy it again? Some of them, certainly, will consider they have been conned—or at least misled—and will not buy again. Others will become firmly converted, and determined to re-purchase. But for many the brand will go into a sort of mental 'bank' of acceptable products, which they have no compulsive urge to buy but which they are quite happy to consider when they want something of that type. If these people *do not* buy the brand again, its sales will be much lower than they would otherwise have been.

The facts of economic life are such that a higher level of sales will normally lead to greater economies of production—and also of buying and distribution—so that costs can be lower. As a result, either the customer gets a cheaper product, or the manufacturer a greater profit, or both—but only if sales are obtained. And advertising can be an important part of getting and *maintaining* those sales. This, of course, is especially true if your brand's competitors are also advertising, since by so doing they are greatly reducing the likelihood of customers buying your brand.

Summary

1. Advertising is merely part of the marketing mix. As such, it is not essential to the sales of a product or service, but can contribute, along with a variety of other activities, to them.
2. As such, it is part of the process of branding, which is a way of distinguishing

products from each other in consumers' minds.

3. It is, most particularly, a very cost-effective way of communicating to large numbers of people.

4. This involves both communicating information about the product and building its reputation: both selling to new buyers and reminding existing buyers to buy again.

5. Apart from talking to consumers, advertising has a role in supporting and stimulating the distributive trade.

6. Although the majority of advertising is designed to help sell goods through distributors, there is a substantial and growing business in direct marketing—direct mail advertising takes over the major role of selling in the marketing mix.

7. In all this, advertising is a weapon of competition:
   (a) it differentiates one brand from its competitors;
   (b) it is an aggressive, but sometimes expensive, weapon in a company's sales armoury;
   (c) by intensive use, it can discourage competitive entry into the market—but it cannot keep out a superior product;
   (d) it helps to keep loyal customers for the brand.

2 Should you advertise: and if so, how much?

Advertising, as I have said, is merely one element in the marketing mix. Like the rest of the elements in the mix, it is one which can be omitted, so long as something else is doing the necessary job. The decision whether or not to advertise is not, in fact, a simple one. It is much easier simply to take it for granted that you ought to advertise than to pick the reason, and the moment, to start doing so.

Ultimately, deciding to advertise should be the result of a careful and rational analysis of the prospects and possible objectives of the brand or business, and of the means by which these objectives can be achieved. In this process of analysis you may well find a role for advertising—or at least some form of general communication to your customers—which cannot readily be fulfilled by any other tool at your disposal. Then there is a case for considering advertising. It will still be an open question whether advertising will make sense for you in terms of its absolute cost and the return you can expect to get for that cost. There is probably a minimum size of business in any field below which it will be very difficult to afford sufficient advertising to generate enough additional business to justify the expenditure. In the long run, the decision to advertise is an economic one.

The economic task

The basic task of advertising, nine times out of ten, is to sell, or to assist sales. (In the case of much public service and Government advertising, and some corporate campaigns of a 'prestige' character, almost the only things being sold are ideas.) Advertising usually does this more or less indirectly, and works in conjunction with other parts of the marketing mix: only direct response advertising is pure selling by advertisement.

It follows, therefore, that if you can sell all you want to without advertising, you can do without it—unless you can see a way whereby advertising can save you some other cost. Usually, a new advertising campaign for a previously unadvertised brand is a straightforward addition to costs. This means, very crudely, that such a campaign has to be capable of generating additional sales and, more precisely, marginal profits sufficient to cover the added costs. What is more, it ought to be capable of doing this more cheaply than any alternative method—such as adding another half dozen people to the sales force, or opening up a wholly new distribution channel.

The one very fundamental reason for advertising, then, is to sell more, more profitably. This is, however, a very typical example of advertising language, since it begs the question: 'More than what?' Once you ask that question, the whole situation rapidly becomes rather complicated, instead of the apparently simple picture we have been looking at. If a brand has been on the market for some time, its sales may have started to decline: by means of advertising, the decline may be slowed. In this case, sales will be, say, 5 per cent down rather than the 10 per cent down which they would have been without the advertising. In other words, with advertising you will actually be selling *less*, but that 'less' is still more than the result which (you assume) would have been achieved without advertising—and this may be a major benefit to your overall profitability.

The roles of advertising
Clearly, in order to achieve these extra sales, advertising has to be working in some way in the marketplace. The market for a particular product consists, if you analyse it in detail, of a number of different groups of people, who can be categorized in terms of their relationship to the product:

Non-users of the product category
1. Those who do not and never will use these products.
2. Non-users who are possible future users but are unaware of our product.
3. Non-users who are possible future users and are aware of our product.

Users of the product category
1. Users of competitive brands, who are unaware of our product.
2. Users of competitive brands, who are aware of our product
   (a) Who have never tried our product.
   (b) Who have tried our product.
3. Users of both competitive brands and of our product.
4. Users of our product only
   (a) Who have never used another brand.
   (b) Who have used another brand.

Once you look at a market like this it becomes clear that the apparently simple task of using advertising to increase sales of our brand can be achieved by working against virtually any (or all) of the dozen or so different groups of people described. And to work against each of these groups the advertising may have to have a rather different effect: it can *remind* the brand's users to buy it—or to use it; it can try to *persuade* users of competitive brands that our brand is as good as or better than the one that they are using at present; it can *make aware* the ignorant about our brand's existence, and *inform* them about its virtues; it can, conceivably, *encourage* non-users to use the product category.

Now, these are all things that advertising can help to do: but it is not the only thing that can do this. Information about the product category, or about our brand, may best be disseminated through magazine and newspaper editorial copy obtained by means of public relations activity. Reminders to buy the brand may be provided by in-store display material; and to use it, by the pack design. The best way of persuading users of competitive brands to try ours may be through pricing policy or through a consumer promotion. The pack on the table or larder shelf may be the best thing to encourage users to use more.

Although advertising can do most of the things apparently necessary to achieve extra sales, it is not the only way to do this. And it can have little direct effect on what is often the best way of getting extra sales, which also has a less direct relationship to our classification of consumers—that is to say, extending our brand's distribution to new retail stockists. But here, too, it can have a specific role: the promise of consumer advertising support can encourage new retailers to handle the brand, and the advertising can announce to the consumer where the brand can be found, while trade press advertising, or direct mail, may help persuade new distributors to stock the brand.

Economies of scale

Now, obviously, once we look at a brand in terms of its consumers, and we start to think of large numbers of potential buyers with whom we may want to communicate for one of the reasons suggested in the previous section, it becomes rather more reasonable to think about advertising. As has already been said, advertising in mass media is a particularly cheap way, potentially at least, of talking to a great many people at once.

It is also, in many ways, more reliable than the alternatives suggested in the last section. A public relations effort cannot guarantee that the desired message will appear at all in the right media, let alone at the right time or in the form in which you want it. In-store display material is increasingly difficult to get placed in major stores, and the cost of achieving really broadscale use of display material is extremely high. Promotions are often difficult to arrange on a broadscale basis, and specific types of promotion often have a limited appeal to the consumer. Packaging can appear the wrong way up on a shop shelf, or the product be transferred to a different container in the home. At least with advertising it is possible to place the message you want in the media you require to reach your target audience—though it is up to the creative quality of the ads to ensure that notice is taken of them.

By reaching a very large audience of consumers through effective advertising you immediately introduce economies of scale in selling. Instead of having a large sales force calling on individuals, you can have a much smaller sales force calling on retailers or wholesalers: and the more effective your advertising, the less time each salesperson needs—at least in theory—to persuade the distributor to buy more. In the same way, this ability to sell very large volumes of a product consistently to a mass audience makes possible economies of scale in production, which serve both to keep prices down and to increase profitability.

This sounds, of course, very simple: almost as if all you have to do to increase sales and profits is switch on a large volume of advertising and cut your sales force. Unfortunately it is not as simple as that, for two key reasons. One is the question of the size of investment in advertising required to achieve this highly desirable result. The other is the time factor.

Considerations of the sums of money involved to achieve sufficient impact on enough people to begin to achieve scale economies may make the whole idea impractical. If you need to treble your sales volume to shift your basic production cost curve a notch or two down the scale, the required money to achieve this may be massive—whether you see it as a one-off expenditure or as a gradually built-up campaign. This is, really, another way of pointing to the time factor: it usually takes time for results to develop from advertising, and you may not be able to afford to wait for them.

The risk factor

In other words, a decision to advertise involves a risk—the risk that the advertising will not pay off to the extent planned. Because advertising involves putting money down now against future sales, it is a form of investment, and decisions to advertise are like decisions to invest. They are, however, more risky than the average investment, since the pay-off is peculiarly uncertain. What this means, therefore, is that a major advertising campaign should be approached with considerable caution and, ideally, a significant reserve of cash to tide you over if it fails to deliver. The idea of having a reserve in the advertising budget is a valuable one in any event, and should never be neglected.

Product quality

The other critical element in a decision to advertise is the ability of the product to support the advertising. If you know that your product can offer your customers clear and distinct advantages—which may be in performance, in price or purely in psychological satisfaction—over its competitors, you then have a property which is, on the face of it, worth advertising. This is, obviously, an ideal in a world which rarely provides ideals. In highly competitive markets like the US grocery market, a product can rarely maintain a genuine technical advantage over competition for more than a few months unless it is based on new, patented technology. Thus, it has to rely on temporary advantages in performance or price, and attempt to build itself a safe, long-term psychological advantage among its consumers. While it is quite easy to identify a technical advantage, it is much more difficult to be sure of a psychological one. It is very tempting to say 'Our product is as good as theirs: all we have to do is give it some added values in consumers' minds'. This, after all, is what a great deal of advertising sets out to do, and is the fundamental basis of brand marketing.

The preconditions for successful branding of a product are, nonetheless, fairly stringent, too. To be able to begin to give a product brand values the product has to be capable of offering a combination of factual qualities—its physical performance, its price in relation to performance, its appearance or design—sufficient for it to be potentially an effective competitor in its market. You cannot lift an inferior product to safety simply by advertising. (This is not to say that you cannot have 'cheap-and-cheerful' brands: you can, but they have to be recognizably value-for-money.)

If your product cannot stand up to competition, either you need to improve it physically before you try to advertise it, or you need to cut its price—and if you cut its price enough to re-establish it as value for money, you probably will not have enough margin left to advertise it. Of course, if you have a long-established product which has been over-taken by competitors, you may be justified in using advertising to try to maintain at least a part of its share of the market until you can reformulate it and relaunch it. But time will usually be against you.

Selling and branding: creating and sustaining sales

As can be seen from the preceding pages, it is quite likely that new advertisers will start, very simply, by using advertising to increase sales by bringing their product to the attention of the consumer. By so doing, they can generate the funds to advertise more, and they can generate the sales volume to reduce their overall costs—thus increasing profits, which they can use for further investment, enabling them to keep prices down.

Once they have started to reach this enviable position, the role of the advertising is liable to change. There is a point in most markets where it is going to be increasingly difficult to expand total sales, because all the likely buyers are buying all they could reasonably need; and where it will be increasingly difficult to increase market share, because you have either got 8o per cent of the market or you have come up against strong competitors who are able to match your efforts. By now a significant part of your marketing effort for this particular product is going to be devoted to maintaining your position and, if possible, improving profitability.

It is at this stage that the value of having successfully established brand values becomes clear. The better you have been able to differentiate your brand from its competition, whether by particular physical characteristics or by its overall appeal to the consumer, the easier it is to protect your franchise in the market. A brand whose users relate to it as if to some sort of close friend is much stronger than one which could be a more distant though familiar personality—perhaps the person who delivers the post or the milk. (This idea of treating a brand as a 'personality' is, in fact, a valuable research tool. Most people find it quite easy to describe a reasonably well-known brand as if it were a person, and these descriptions tend to be surprisingly consistent, and informative to agency creative people.)

It is easier to establish these sorts of brand values if you set out to do so right from the brand launch. This means, of course, that the name, the pack, the point-of-sale, and the advertising should all combine to contribute to and reflect a completely integrated brand personality. This integration of style and appearance is most evident in well thought-out retail concepts. Next Retail was a classic example of a brand idea, worked through to the last detail, which not only proved highly successful but sparked off a host of imitators. Conversely, the massive confectionery success of the early eighties, Cadbury's Wispa, was presented in such a powerful and coherent way that the brand appears stronger than what is—to me at least—a very ordinary product.

Offence and defence

It should be apparent from all this that a decision to advertise is a complex one, depending both on economic factors and on the competitive capability of the brand. It should be apparent, too, that advertising can be a weapon of either offence or defence. By effective advertising a brand can carve out for itself a new market or a significant share of an old one, at the expense of direct or indirect competitors. Often, it may do this by a direct assault on the weaknesses of vulnerable competitors. Alternatively, advertising may be one way in which a brand can be sustained at a high level of sales in the face of competition. Experience has shown that quite large brands can gradually lose sales and market share simply through failing to advertise—even if they increase their promotional activity instead. The classic case is probably that of the UK orange squash market, where the failure of the initially quite strong manufacturer brands to support their franchise with advertising enabled private label products to take over more than half the market. It may not always be possible to prevent this from happening, but the aggressive behaviour of Heinz in defence of their baked bean franchise demonstrates how it can be done extremely successfully.

Testing the water

The decision to advertise, whether for the first time or for an established brand, is evidently complex, and ultimately a matter of judgement rather than of science. When the decision seems totally impossible to weigh up, there is nearly always a compromise solution available. If you are not prepared to take the plunge to the full extent of the available resources, you can always do a test. The possibilities of achieving truly measurable results from a test are somewhat limited, and are discussed in greater detail in Chapter 9. Also the investment in a test will be disproportionately high, since you have to produce effectively the same advertising material for the test as for a much larger, full-scale operation, so that production costs—especially for film media—will loom high in your budget.

You can test advertising, in theory, in an area of the country, in a particular medium, or, perhaps, among a particular group of people. You can even test a sort of advertising in conjunction with 'mini-markets' run for test purposes by various market research companies. There are now also one or two modelling systems, of which Burke Marketing Research's BASES system is probably the best known, that use relatively simple consumer research techniques to provide predictions of a new brand's potential brand share of sales volume, on the basis of a combination of the advertising and product samples.

A marketplace test loses you time and may reveal your hand to competitors. But it can help you assess your prospects and it may save you money.

How much to spend

If we assume that you have decided that you will advertise, in spite of all the pitfalls and uncertainties facing you, the next, critical question is how much to spend. There is one simple and pretty unhelpful answer: 'At least 10 per cent less than you can afford'. It is unhelpful, because it is very difficult to decide how much you can afford, since advertising can, in theory, take money from other sales and marketing activities, as well as from profits. It is, however, sound advice, since the risks of over-reaching yourself are considerable.

Budgeting for advertising is a very uncertain art, and one on which theory and practice tend to be far apart.* The budget is something every agency wants to know at the start of its planning, but which in an ideal world would not be determined until the planning was complete: in an ideal world, the advertising task would be identified precisely, the various elements required for the campaign determined, the most effective ways of reaching the target group costed out, a schedule prepared and then—only—when this scientific process had been carried out, would a budget appear.

Unfortunately, it is not like that. Occasionally, with a new product, it may get near it, but there are too many variables to achieve certainty. The art of working out what is needed to reach quite precise advertising targets is still extremely imprecise, and the alternatives available are numerous. The creative quality of the ads is an unknown but powerful factor: some fairly experimental research has shown that one ad's effectiveness may exceed that of another by a factor as high as 15 or 20 times, or even more. Given the current state of the art of pre-testing ads (see Chapter 9), it is only after a campaign has been run that you can begin to decide whether your ad was a winner or a loser.

Not surprisingly, then, few advertisers use the 'task' method outlined above. In the real world, simpler ways have to prevail.

Methods of setting budgets used by advertisers cover three broad approaches:

– methods relating to sales;
– methods relating to competitors' activity;
– methods based on market theories.

On the whole, these methods, in practice, overlap.

---

*For a detailed discussion of budget-setting see Simon Broadbent's excellent book *The Advertising Budget* (NTC Publications, Henley, 1989).

Advertising-to-sales ratios

The simplest method—and the commonest—is to take a standard percentage of sales revenue as the basis for the budget. This has its basis, clearly, in the way in which products are costed, since it is quite easy to decide—even if only arbitrarily—that, given a particular level of gross margin, a certain proportion of this can be devoted to advertising. In many companies this proportion has become one of the laws of the Medes and Persians, which it is virtually impossible to change. Sometimes it has been derived as a result of at least some experimentation in the market. Sometimes it is purely arbitrary.

This method of setting the budget, or 'appropriation', as it is usually called, has the virtue of simplicity. It is, however, obviously fairly naive, since it has no obvious relation to what is happening in the rest of the market, in terms of either the market's dynamics or competitive activity. In some cases, indeed, the budget is based on a set proportion of the previous year's sales, rather than of the forecast sales for the year being budgeted. In any market where things are changing at all rapidly, this seems to be, to say the least, an odd way to plan.

The fact is that deciding on an advertising-to-sales ratio or 'A/S ratio' is far from easy, as it should depend both on the competitive character of the market and on the individual brand's position in the market. Numerous studies have shown clearly that A/S ratios vary quite markedly between different companies, different markets and different brands within markets. Some recent examples from the UK are given in Table 2.1.

Table 2.1: Estimated UK advertising-to-sales ratios 1985 and 1989

Public utilities	% 1985	% 1989		% 1985	% 1989
The Post Office	0.57	2.91	Shampoo	11.47	13.41
British Telecom	0.53	1.62	Breakfast cereals	9.73	11.97
British Rail	0.55	0.94	Coffee	5.39	7.87
British Gas	0.24	0.17	Cat food	5.20	3.97
			Tea	4.44	3.32
			Chocolates	3.54	3.26
Durable Markets			Newspapers	1.62	3.10
			Toys/games	4.87	2.77
Records/tapes	4.35	3.39	Beer	0.34	0.96
Cars	1.87	1.77	Tobacco products	0.92	0.64
Women's clothing	0.29	0.15	Wine	0.55	0.54
			Petrol	0.17	0.21

(Source: Advertising Association)

Similarly, international comparisons published in a US research magazine show quite wide variations, for large numbers of companies, between countries and between consumer and industrial goods advertisers.

Why should these differences occur? Obviously, they reflect some kind of general feeling by managements involved in the markets about the effectiveness of advertising and the need for advertising, as opposed to other forms of competition. Cosmetic and toiletry markets, for example, tend to have high A/S ratios, since they depend to a major extent on direct and often psychologically-based appeals to the consumer, and they are generally low-unit-value items. Electrical 'white goods'—fridges, washing machines, and the like—tend to have low A/S ratios because they carry high price tags, have high distribution and service costs, and are more effectively and actively sold by the retailer.

Within any market, though, there may well be forces leading to changes in the overall A/S ratio and that of individual brands. Intensive product innovation, as occurs in many toiletry markets, leads to heavy launch expenditures—and heavy spending by established brands to ward off the new competition. A rapidly growing market encourages the brands in it to advertise to maintain the growth and to gain a bigger share in it. Strong competition may encourage an increase in advertising as a defensive—or offensive—move.

It is, therefore, for any but an established and comfortable brand in a static market, a dangerous idea to set an appropriation solely on the basis of the company's own 'norm' for A/S ratios. The facts of the marketplace are liable, in most circumstances, to make this a highly risky procedure. The A/S ratio is, certainly, a useful indicator of the degree to which you are a heavy or light advertiser, and a convenient part of any cross-check on the structure of your overall marketing costs. That is, however, about as far as its value goes.

Watching the competition

In most markets you will have competitors: competitors whom you may fear, respect, or even despise. However, their presence is a fact of life, and their activities are, frequently, designed to make life difficult for you.

It is their advertising activity, combined with your own, which establishes the market's A/S ratio. It is, indeed, the fact that all the individual brands in the market probably have different A/S ratios, possibly from virtually zero to 15 or 20 per cent, that makes the market's A/S ratio, or your leading competitor's A/S ratio, a dangerous guide.

There is a further problem, too, in watching the competition. All your data—apart from carefully inflated press releases by your competitors about the size of their next campaign—are historical. You may know, reasonably precisely, that last year your leading competitors had an A/S ratio of 5 per cent. You still have no idea what they will do this year—though there may be a lot of clues around if you hunt carefully: have you looked at their expenditure, region by region, to see if they have been trying to pressure test?[*] If so, has it achieved anything? Because if it has, the odds are they will increase their spending this year to try to repeat their success. If they do, how are you going to reply?

Clearly, as soon as you start watching competition, you are liable to be

---

*Pressure test: a test of advertising expenditure weight in which spending in one or more regions is raised or lowered above the level of the rest of the country.

driven mad. Perhaps you should never have started—but personal computers can make the whole exercise a little easier.

The fact is, of course, that it is one thing to start off the year with a carefully planned budget, with everything neatly in its place and a satisfactory profit on the bottom line. It never actually works out that way, for all the obvious reasons—your strikes, suppliers' strikes, transport strikes, the weather, tax changes, the economy . . . and, indeed, competition.

In other words, an advertising plan, like any other business plan is—or should be—reasonably flexible and tactical. You have to plan with a tactical reserve and a willingness to adapt. Ideally, this should involve a readiness to spend more if necessary, and a reluctance to cut the budget if this can possibly be avoided. This is not just advertising agency wishful thinking: you can do long-term damage to your market position and profitability by cutting the advertising budget in a last-minute drive for short-term profit to satisfy the accountants—and it is only too easy to raid the advertising budget: it does not involve any of the company's physical resources at all.

In preparing this flexible budget, it makes a great deal of sense to take note of competitive action, as you know it from past experience and can anticipate it from that knowledge and any other clues you may have: rumours of new activity, changes of advertising agency, changes of management, etc. The behaviour of your competitors, and of leading companies in similar markets to your own, can provide a basic guideline as to the sort of spending levels that appear to be reasonable in relation to sales in your particular type of market. Collective wisdom of this kind might not be right, but it has a fair chance of being so, and it can at least provide a basis from which you can, yourself, experiment and develop.

Using the marketplace

As soon as you start watching competitive behaviour and, perhaps, setting your target A/S ratio according to your market's apparent norms, you are, whether you like it or not, using a 'model' of the market. A 'model' is, quite simply, a conceptual theory of how something whose workings are only imperfectly understood actually works. It is usually, but not necessarily or invariably, mathematical in character. We all use models all the time, usually without realizing it: these non-explicit models are usually called 'experience'. If we decide to align our A/S ratio with the market's we are, in effect, saying 'If we spend the same amount as our competitors, other things being equal we will not suffer'. Implicit in this is a model which says that equal amounts of advertising produce equal results in the market for equal levels of market share. Which *may* be true—sometimes.

From this very simple—and almost universally, intuitively, accepted—view of advertising follow the corollaries:

1. If I increase my advertising relative to the rest of the market I will increase my market share.
2. If I decrease my advertising . . ., my market share will decrease.

For reasons unknown to me, people in marketing find it far easier to accept the first corollary than the second.

Obviously, for all this to become more than sticking a finger in the air to see which way the wind blows, it helps to do some measuring, and to try to construct a rather clearer mathematical picture of what actually happens when advertising—or, indeed, other—expenditures change in the market-place. It would obviously be very helpful to know that an increase (say) in our share of our market's total advertising from P per cent to Q per cent would lead to an increase in our market share from X per cent to Y per cent. We could then feed the figures into the spreadsheet program on our personal computer to see if this was going to be a worthwhile exercise.

Unfortunately, although it is possible to get some way along this line with the aid of econometric market models (for a brief discussion of this very technical subject, see Chapter 9), it is in practice difficult to be very precise. Work by various researchers has shown reasonably clearly that if your share of advertising rises in a market you do, in fact, usually get an increase in market share, but the quantity of the increase depends very much on factors other than the change in share of advertising, and it will, therefore, vary markedly from brand to brand and from market to market. Similarly, the AC Nielsen Company, in a study of 25 extremely successful UK grocery brand leaders, established that all of them had higher-than-average A/S ratios for their markets; this reflected both scale economies and, apparently, a commitment to advertising over other forms of promotional activity.

The conclusions to be drawn from all this are, I would suggest: first, that if you wish to be, or to remain, a brand leader you should aim to keep your A/S ratio above your market's average (and, too, that there are grave dangers in being consistently below the average level); second, that if you want to change your position in the market you will probably need to increase (or decrease) your A/S ratio by a fairly significant amount—perhaps by 30–50 per cent (e.g., from 3 per cent to 4 per cent or 4.5 per cent) to achieve visible results. With luck, this latter level will be sufficient to increase your share of the market's advertising. 'With luck', because you must expect your competitors to react, and there is always the possible threat of a newcomer buying his way into the market with heavy spending.

This points up, of course, the uncertainty implicit in even very sophisticated model-based budget setting. Except in the very short term (perhaps two months at most), it is unlikely that you will be able successfully to predict competitive behaviour. Models are fine as interpretations of history, but limited (at best) as guides to the future. Effective forecasting of details of competitive market activity will always be virtually impossible, though techniques such as games theory can help. What improved and developed models can do, however, when allied to rapid intelligence gathering and powerful computers, is to make it possible—at a price in information gathering costs—to predict more quickly the effects of new competitive activity, and identify the best course of action to counter it.

No satisfactory answer

It is clear from this discussion that there is, in fact, no very easy, satisfactory answer to the question of how much to spend on advertising—even if, as I have done, you look at advertising more or less in isolation. If you include the other possible claimants to the marketing budget, and start to juggle with these, too, the problem is complicated considerably.

In practice, of course, the situation is usually made a bit simpler by the existence of a stream of past experience—you can at least use as a starting point 'What we spent last year plus an allowance for inflation'.

Then again, experience and the company's past practice give at least a basis for dividing the total available money between elements of the marketing mix. After that, you can start looking at the market's dynamics and competitive threats and opportunities. You must, too, consider the size of the task the advertising has to perform. You will, I hope, have objectives for the advertising (see Chapter 7): have you allowed sufficient money to achieve them?

In the last resort, the great majority of advertising budgets represent a compromise between an ideal sum and what the brand manager would like to spend, adjusted for the demands of the marketing director, the accountants, and the sales director. In many multi-brand companies, the last 10 per cent or so of the total marketing budget is often distributed on the basis of, in effect, rival bids by competing brand managers.

All this explains, perhaps, why so many agencies believe that they are getting a £300000 account and end up with a budget of £225000 if they are lucky, and why the figures for the size of accounts changing hands always appear to be inflated by reports in the trade press.

Lord Leverhulme said, notoriously, that he knew that half of his advertising expenditure was wasted, but he did not know which half. What he did not add was that he did not know how much would be wasted if he did halve his budgets—or double them.

Almost the only 'rule' that exists in this grey area is not to spend too little, because that is a total waste. But defining 'too little' is virtually impossible. There are, however, *some* guidelines, and I will come back to these in the chapters on media planning and individual media (Chapters 10–13).

3 Do I need an agency?

Agencies—and their clients

If you have decided to advertise, you are faced by the problem of how to go about it. Sooner or later, you will at least consider using an advertising agency.

Advertising agencies make up what is usually thought of as the advertising industry. They exist primarily to help industry to produce advertising and to place it in the appropriate media. There are, probably, over a thousand of them in the UK, but many are very small, and most of the more reputable ones belong to the industry's trade association, the Institute of Practitioners in Advertising, which has some 250 members.

Advertising agencies range in size from one or two people to over 500, and the largest—very few of them—handle advertising billings totalling over £100 million. Most are much smaller than this, and even in the 'top 300' agencies, the one-hundredth (in 1992) only handled billings of some £15 million. This means, of course, that few agencies have very big individual accounts of the kind that make news in the papers when they move agencies. For the majority, a typical client is likely to be spending perhaps £40 000–£50 000 or less, and many clients—most advertisers, in fact—are spending less than £15 000 on media advertising.

The reason for this is that the advertisers you notice all the time, Persil and Mars Bars, Ford and Abbey National, Tesco and Oxo, are the rare exceptions. Indeed the majority of advertisers are probably not advertising direct to the consumer at all. They are involved solely in selling and promoting their goods to commercial and industrial customers, in media which the general public rarely, if ever, sees.

As a result, while the agencies that are talked about are usually those which handle the big consumer goods accounts, there are actually far more agencies that are specialists in handling industrial advertising, and would never try to take on a consumer goods account. There are, indeed, not only agencies specialized in industrial, as opposed to consumer, advertising: there are agencies which aim to deal only with a limited range of industries; agencies specialized in direct response or direct mail advertising; agencies which do virtually no media advertising, but specialize in exhibitions, brochures and other sales literature; and so on.

What agencies do

The first advertising agencies were space brokers: they sold advertising space, on commission, for newspaper and magazine proprietors. Towards the end of the nineteenth century, some of these space brokers discovered that they could increase their business by helping the advertisers to whom they sold to create the advertisements with which to fill the space. From this, it was a simple and logical step for the agencies to become specialists in producing advertisements—a far more complex job than selling space, and one in which they could build their reputations without depending on their principal's paper. Their role as brokers for the papers remains, however, in the traditional method of agency payment (see page 27).

By now, advertising agencies exist to produce advertising material for their clients and to place it in appropriate media. This is their primary function. (Some small agencies, and many in less developed countries, still do little or nothing in the way of creative work, and act almost entirely as space brokers.) Beyond this, however, agencies can, and often do, provide a very wide variety of other services to support their clients' marketing and selling operations. At its most elaborate, this service can include what is, in effect, a full-blooded marketing consultancy service, providing detailed advice and assistance in business planning, together with the production of the whole range of supporting materials—advertising, sales literature, sales promotions, point-of-sale material, public relations services, etc.

Quite a small industrial agency will usually expect to do most of its business outside the sphere of media advertising: industrial advertising budgets are mostly small, and much of the activity involved concerns the production of sales literature (often very technical), the development of other aids for the client's salespeople, planning, designing and mounting exhibitions, and various public relations activities. What is more, a substantial part of the work often involves not just the home market, but similar activities overseas as well.

In order to do this, the agency has to employ experienced and specialist people with the appropriate skills to perform all the tasks involved. Obviously, in theory at least, the smaller the agency the less easy it will be for it to cover all these tasks. There are agencies run by one or two people, which, by judicious use of freelance help, can provide a very good service, by virtue of the experience and managing abilities of the proprietors.

This is, quite simply, because for every specialized function that can be found within an advertising agency (and a large agency may have 50 or 60), it is possible to find individuals or, indeed, companies which specialize in that function. As a result, the small agent, can, in practice, use a vast range of subcontractors. For example, a freelance team can be employed to create advertising material; a public relations consultant to plan and subsequently implement a PR programme; translators, typographers, exhibition designers. In any event, the small agent will almost certainly use a commercial studio to produce the finished artwork for the printer, and, certainly, he or she will use a commercial printer to produce any print material. Even in large agencies there are very few studios to be found producing finished artwork, and printing is a completely separate business.

Advertising agencies, from all this description, are a sort of clearing house for commercial communications of all kinds. But few agencies would recognize themselves as this. The heads of any agencies worth their salt will tell you that their job is to produce *ideas*. They may not put it like that. They will probably say their agencies are 'creative', or perhaps that they produce 'ideas that sell'.

Essentially, of course, they are right. Any successful agency depends for its success on its ingenuity in helping its clients—or, just occasionally, in convincing its clients that it *is* helping. To do this, it must be able to produce either effective new ways of talking about the client's products or more effective means of selling them, through clever use of the various available methods. Clearly, if the two can be combined, so much the better.

So, should you use an agency?

It is certainly not essential to have an agency in order to advertise. I do not know how many different people place an ad in a shop window or in the classified columns during a year: it certainly runs into hundreds of thousands, and very few of them use an agency. More to the point, there are large advertisers, spending hundreds of thousands of pounds, who do not use agencies, or who handle some of their advertising completely themselves. A spectacular recent example of a major advertiser setting up a 'house' agency is that of the UK Rover car company; in France, Chanel is a company that has always produced its often exciting and original advertising in-house.

There are, in practice, three ways of handling advertising. You can do it yourself, you can use an agency, or you can use a half-way house between the two. The last of these is something which a lot of advertisers have experimented with in recent years. It is a natural development from the existence of the various specialist sub-contracting companies described earlier. In effect, you can construct your own agency by buying the creative side of your advertising from a 'creative consultant' and having the ads placed in the media by a media shop. Media independents have flourished in the UK since the mid-seventies, to the extent that major full-service agencies have developed their own quasi-independents in response (the Saatchi group's Zenith subsidiary is the largest). Clients, too, in addition to using media independents, have taken to centralizing their media buying with one of their roster of agencies, in the interest of business efficiencies.

Media buying specialists originated in the USA, where they are an important market force, and by now—depending on definitions—probably control 40–45 per cent of UK display advertising. On the Continent, except in France, the home base of the massive Carat organization, they are somewhat less well developed, but there is a strong trend towards their use as multinational advertising campaigns become more common. There remains, however, a substantial difference between UK and French practice, since French media 'shops' tend to be media brokers—buying time or space in bulk and selling it on—as well as merely media planners and buyers. This *may* develop in the UK in the future, though the Independent Television Commission's public stance is against it, and there is no obvious enthusiasm for the idea among newspaper and magazine publishers.

It is a natural assumption, in most developed industrial countries, that a business that wishes to advertise should go to an advertising agency. Agencies are assumed to have the talents and the expertise appropriate to the job. This view of agencies is not necessarily well founded: like most professions, advertising has its ration of incompetents and charlatans. And it is certainly possible to advertise without an agency. It is probably more difficult, and, unless you have the appropriate experience, you are likely to make mistakes. The better you know the advertising business (in which case you are unlikely to be reading this book, except out of morbid curiosity), the more feasible it will be to do without an agency. On the other hand, you may simply feel too poor to take your business to an agency; or you may be confident that you can cope yourself. You may be right.

If we take our three basic alternatives, it is possible to draw up a list of advantages and disadvantages of each, as shown in Table 3.1, so that we can compare them—bearing in mind that the use of an agency is the accepted 'standard'.

As can be seen, there are points in favour of all three approaches, and the decision between them need not, necessarily, be a simple one. It is worth considering, then, what criteria might influence the decision. There are lots of possibilities, but some of the main ones can, again, be tabulated fairly simply as shown in Table 3.2.

A combination of adequate experience and a more or less complex task can point towards a 'specialist' solution rather than an agency. As a general rule, though, it would be unwise to set out on the 'specialist' route without extensive experience. It is difficult to handle well.

The cost and how you pay it
The final element in the decision may, however, be one of costs. In order to assess this, it is necessary to know how agencies are paid, and what the payment covers. As I said earlier (see page 25), agencies originally sold advertising space, on commission, and the method by which they are still paid in most countries in the world derives from this. Basically, the formal payment of the agency comes from the media owner, who pays a standard rate of commission to a recognized agency on the space (or time) which the agency buys from him or her to sell to its clients.

For major consumer media in most countries, this commission is 15 per cent of the space cost: for many trade publications, however, it may be 10 per cent or even 5 per cent and a few media may give 20 per cent. In practice, for simplicity's sake, most media accounts to agencies are rendered net of commission, and the agency then reclaims the commission in its bill to its clients.

Table 3.1   Advantages and disadvantages of the three ways of handling advertising

	Agency	Specialist services	Do it yourself
Advantages	All-round skills All-round experience Objective outsider's point of view of your business You can learn from others' mistakes They do the whole job for you Continuity of work contact	You can pick the real experts for each part of the job You can fill the gaps in your capabilities, without having to buy the complete service of the agency May be cheaper May be faster	Everything in your control Full understanding of your problems Learn as you go along (no embarrassment at lack of knowledge) May be faster Probably cheaper
Disadvantages	Lack of specific knowledge of your business (usually) Cannot devote all their time to you May do a poor job for a small client Probably expensive to use	Need careful control and coordination: this needs experience Require extra careful briefing—every time Difficult to get extra services in a hurry	Easy to make mistakes—no one available to cross-check Lack of required skills Lack of specialized know-how Limited view—no outside knowledge to provide a different viewpoint or stimulus

Table 3.2   Decision-making: should I do it myself?

Factors to consider	Questions to ask	Decision directions
1. Experience	Do I know about advertising?	If yes, do-it-yourself is a possibility
2. The task	Is it simple or complicated?	If simple, do-it-yourself is a possibility
	Am I sure *what* it is?	If 'no', you probably need an agency
3. Money	Would my account interest an agency?	Probably!
4. Confidence	Do I need a second opinion?	If 'yes', try an agency
5. Workload	Is there likely to be a mass of detail involved?	If 'yes', try an agency
6. People	Do I have people who can do it for me?	If 'no', try an agency or specialist

This means, in practice, that a 15 per cent commission on the gross space cost becomes 17.65 per cent on the net cost, and the agency bills its client 'net + 17.65 per cent'. (This is because, if the gross cost of a space is £100, and the medium removes the £15 of the agency commission, leaving £85, the agency has to bill its client £85 + 17.65 per cent to reach £100 in total and get the £15 due to it, £15 being 17.65 per cent of £85.)

In addition to the commission on media spending, usually the agency will also take a similar commission on most items involved in the production of advertising materials, and, where overseas advertising is involved, it may well take an additional 5 per cent to cover the costs of planning advertising overseas (the total 20 per cent may well be shared with an overseas agency which helps to prepare the ads for the media, and provides other advice—see Chapter 19).

In spite of the apparently generous commissions offered by the media, such generosity obviously depends, for its impact on the agency's finances, on the total sums involved. Fifteen per cent of the £250 cost of a quarter page in a trade magazine does not go far to pay anyone's wages. As a result, most agencies operate a system of fee charges alongside the commission system. The usual basis of this is an agreement between the client and the agency that the agency's total income from commission should not go below a certain figure—say £25 000—and that if it does, the client will bring the figure up to £25 000 with a fee. Conversely, an increasing number of really large advertisers, especially retailers, demand that agencies accept reduced commissions, because of the large income the agency earns on their account. In the past 10 years there has been considerably greater erosion of the commission system than previously, helped by the Office of Fair Trading's decision that the commission system was not enforceable, though the facts are—understandably— hard to come by. Figures collected by the IPA, the agency trade association, show that between 1983 and 1986 member agencies' income, as a proportion of billings, fell by some 8 per cent.

From the agencies' point of view, there is substantial pressure from their clients to reduce the levels of commission and fees, and the 1989–92 recession resulted in an intensification of this. At the same time, some of the press media started to question the whole basis of the commission system, or to attempt to reduce commission rates unilaterally. As the agencies brusquely pointed out, if you reduce commissions from 15 per cent to 10 per cent, you cut the agency's income by a third.

There are other alternatives, of course. A common one is that the client should pay entirely by fee, and in this case any commissions paid by the media to the agency are remitted to the client. Fees are based, usually, on the agency's workload, normally in relation to manhours worked on the account. (This can give rise to considerable dispute, even if the agency has an efficient time-keeping system: it is usual only to use time records as a cross-check to ensure that work is not totally out of line, and to work on a standard agreed monthly or quarterly fee.) Finally, as a sophistication of this, there is an increasing, but still small, trend towards various forms of payment by results, where the agency receives, for example, a basic fee plus additional payments if specific, agreed objectives are achieved.

These fee systems may apply either to the whole of the activity which an agency undertakes for a client, or to parts of it only. The latter arrangement is most likely where activity in addition to a fairly large media advertising budget is involved: for example, where the agency also does a pack design project, or organizes the client's sales conferences.

From all this, it is clear that the cost of using an agency depends very much on the scale and type of services which you require from it. If you are going to want merely media advertising, but are going to spend very little, you will, almost inevitably, be faced by a request for a fee—unless, of course, you can persuade the agency that you are going to be so successful next year that they should be prepared to lose money on your business this year.

On the other hand, if you are going to be involved in a variety of different forms of promotional activity, all of which would have to be bought in on a fee basis anyway, it is likely that going to an appropriate agency may actually reduce your costs because of the reduction in the time which you would spend in briefing different suppliers, and the elimination of at least some of the costs which would be incurred in reviewing and understanding the brief.

In evaluating the costs of all the various activities for which you may find yourself being charged fees, it is always worth while considering what it would cost to do it differently. If you were to do it yourself, there would be the cost of your own time, or the cost of additional staff—bearing in mind both the cost of finding them and the fact that they might well be underemployed most of the time. Usually, there will seem to be little advantage in doing it yourself, except at very low levels of overall expenditure, or for particularly specialized jobs where the likely time cost of briefing and checking on the agency would be quite excessive.

In all this, the possibility of buying a package of specialized services has been somewhat neglected. The major justification, in cost terms, for this method of working is that when you employ an agency you are, whether you like it or not, paying for your share of the *whole* agency, whether you use all its services or not. If, by contrast, you buy only individual specialist services, you pay solely for what you use. This argument has been weakened by the growing use of fee or commission-plus-fee systems by agencies, but is still attractive to certain large advertisers with limited demands from agencies. On top of this, you can place the element of quality: it can be argued that no advertising agency is good for everything, so that it makes sense to buy from a specialist, who is sure to be good at his or her speciality. This proposition *may* be true but, at least in the UK at present, the best creative people and most of the best media planners and buyers are still in the agencies.

One final point. The recent rush to reduce costs, leading to sharply lower commissions and fees, must, inevitably, risk damaging the ability of agencies (in whatever form) to provide the high standards you will, of course, be demanding. In any business it remains true that if you pay peanuts, you get—sooner or later, at least—monkeys.

Do you still need an agency?

After learning what it might cost, the thought of using an agency usually seems doubly intimidating. Advertising, and other forms of promotional communication, are expensive and uncertain tools of business.

It is possible, of course, not to advertise. But we have been through this in the first two chapters. Or you could do it yourself. But is that really what you are good at? Surely you are in business to make things, or sell things, or to make something happen. It is perfectly possible to start off by doing your own advertising if you have to. But if you have a business that you expect to grow, you are probably going to want—and need—to do a lot more advertising and you will need help. So it probably makes sense to start off on the right foot: rather than make *all* the mistakes in the book, it would probably be better to call in an experienced outsider, learn from his or her past mistakes, and expect to spend just a little bit more money on doing everything rather better than you would yourself.

Not only would you be giving yourself a better chance of making the most of the advertising funds that you have available, but you would also be learning another necessary set of lessons—how to handle an advertising agency.

All in all, therefore, if you are starting from scratch in using advertising, it is likely to be best to find a suitable agency and start learning. The only problem is how to find a suitable agency: and that is a problem for the next chapter.

4 The marriage business (how to find and love your agency)

Every year, nearly 500 advertising accounts, averaging nearly £200 000, move in or out of (and usually between) the major advertising agencies in the UK. This process is accompanied by headlines in *Campaign*, agonized and frantic activity in as many as a dozen agencies, endless pestering of the client's managers, a whole circus of meetings, briefings, burning of midnight oil and, often enough, several formal presentations of proposals by suitor agencies to the errant (nubile? eligible?) client.

How does this process occur? And how best should it occur? Given that the two (eventually) parties' aims are theoretically identical—to achieve the best possible advertising for the client's brand(s)—where do the means to this end diverge or converge? There are two different sides to the placing of an account with an agency, and both have their own problems.

The client's-eye view

There are plenty of ad agencies available. The IPA, the agencies' trade association, has over 250 members, including virtually all those of any significance in the market (there are one or two exceptions). There are as many agencies again outside the IPA, but they are mostly small—I say 'but', yet that may be just what you need, or think you need. Quite apart from agencies, there are the specialist consultancies discussed in Chapter 3.

But you, the client, want an agency. You start off, usually, knowing little about agencies. You may have got one already, but the fact that you are leaving it shows that you have, one way or another, drifted apart. The reasons for this are legion. Whatever is said is press releases to *Campaign*, the reasons for parting are more likely to be reasons of personality clashes or sheer inefficiency in running the account than failures of creative ideas. Of course, if you want to get rid of the agency, the simplest way to do it is to turn down *all* its creative ideas, regardless of merit, but that way you could actually be doing yourself damage. It is a curious, but not inexplicable, fact that very often the best work done by an agency for a client who sacks it is the last campaign that it runs. Anyway, if you already have an agency, at least you have an idea of what to expect, and experience of some things to try to avoid or achieve. If you have not, then you are very much in the dark, and one thing you need to do is to read the rest of this book (especially Chapter 5) in order to know what sort of animal you are hunting, and how it might behave when cornered.

You start off, then, with a need to advertise, a need to find someone to help, and at best a limited awareness of the agency world. You know—probably—that there are lots of agencies about; you have seen advertising (at least some) that you think may be rather good, and which you think looks like what you want for your brand; you probably believe, however, that your market and your product are unique in the problems and opportunities they offer, and that no one with less than 15 years in your business could begin to understand them. With luck, you have done some planning for the future of your business, and have ideas about which products you want to advertise, and how much you want to spend: possibly you have a very clear idea of what you are trying to do with your advertising.

All you need is an agency that will deliver the goods.

The agency's-eye view

The agency may well never have heard of you before it discovered—let us not go into how—that your account was 'on the move'. It very probably does not know anything about your market, though the chances are that there will be someone there who has at least a nodding acquaintance (enough to drop a few significant names) with it. They will not know you, or anyone who works for you—and they will feel uncomfortable about this, because there is little doubt that every agency in the world believes (rightly) it is in a 'people' business, and that building a suitably close relationship with its clients is a critical key to success.

The agency may have its doubts and hesitations about whether it wants your account (though it is not often an agency will turn down the prospect of a new client of a reasonable—in its terms—size). It will, however, have its own approach to trying to get your business if it wants it, and will try to tailor its relationship with you, as it develops, to favour this approach.

The analogy with marriage, or rather courtship, is a compelling one.

The client's role

The client is in the more or less happy position of calling the shots, making the rules, acting as referee and, ultimately—to change the metaphor—being both jury and judge. It is, in effect, the client's job to decide how he or she wants to find an agency—and it is up to the individual agencies who want the business to adapt, or else to talk the client into a new, more convenient set of requirements. It is, after all, going to be the client who will make the main running in the relationship with the agency eventually chosen, since he or she holds the purse strings: but a predisposition to listen to reasoned argument undoubtedly helps.

It is, then, up to the client to decide what criteria to use in selecting an agency; to draw up a list of agencies to see; to decide the way in which he or she is going to find out which agency best meets the chosen criteria; and, in general, to run the selection process.

It is then up to the client to work with the chosen agency in such a way as to enable it to produce the best possible work.

Criteria for choice

Agencies, as we have already seen, are a pretty numerous breed, and most of them seem to have satisfied clients. They must be doing something right—for somebody. Could they do it for you? And how do you try to judge?

I suggest that there is a quite small number of rather basic criteria which will help to separate the sheep from the goats and at least start to select the best sheep.

Size   It is difficult to be dogmatic about size, but there is undoubtedly a relationship of a sort between the size of an agency and the type of service it can or will give to a client of a given size. If you have a large account—say, over £1.5 million in the UK—you are *probably* too large for an agency billing less than £5–6 million: but you are quite big enough to be important to one of the top 20 agencies. If you have a small account—say £50 000—your business is likely to be of limited interest to anyone billing more than about £2–3 million, and even an agency of this size will probably ask for a fee for handling your account. If, however, you think your account will grow rapidly in size, it may be worth while going to an agency at the top end of this rather arbitrary sort of scale, since it may well be more capable of growing with your account.

Track record   Successful agencies (which mostly means growing agencies) are able to attract good people to their business: advertising is an industry in which success tends to breed success. If you have any ambition to grow—and I assume you will have—you are likely to look for a growing agency.

Growth, however, is not enough. The agency must have shown the ability to service, keep and do good work for successful and satisfied clients—not purely an ability to get new business.

Business ability   An unbusinesslike agency will usually be difficult to do business with. It is difficult, obviously, to assess the competence of the billing department on the basis of talking to the management (but there are ways round that). What is important, though, is that the agency should be capable of understanding your business and, ideally, complementing your own business expertise in a practical and helpful way. This applies both to its methods of planning its own business—advertising—and to the general business acumen and understanding of the senior people who might work on your account.

Compatibility   Are the people with whom you would work at the agency the sort of people with whom you would like to work? Obviously, this is very subjective: it is a bit like identifying candidates for a job, and subject to much the same uncertainties—but also to the same sort of rules: notably, I suggest, giving time for second thoughts and taking a second opinion. Remember, the agency will work not only with you, but also with your colleagues, subordinates and probably superiors. And you can always take up references. Talk to some of their existing clients. Ultimately, getting the 'chemistry' right is vital.

Creativity This is what all agencies claim to have, and is the most difficult thing to judge. The best guide to an agency's creativity is, for reasons I will explain later, the work it does for its existing clients—but this is especially difficult to judge, as you are very dependent on the agency for an explanation of why particular material is good. All you can do, really, is rely on your own judgement of whether the agency is capable of producing striking and distinguished advertising that you would be proud to have as your own, in fields not too far different from your own—if you are a steel stockholder, you cannot expect cosmetic advertising.

Relevant experience This is an area you can argue about. I do not personally believe it to be essential for an agency wishing to take on a cheese account to have personnel experienced in handling a cheese account: I do not even think it is essential that they should have food advertising experience. There is no doubt that such experience of your business can cut corners, but it can also imply more or less closed minds and a willingness to conform too closely to the so-called 'rules' of the market, when these 'rules' are purely arbitrary and baseless. In fact, the more I think about this one, the more I think it is a bit of a red herring, for two reasons. First of all, the relevant kind of experience: if you have worked in lots of markets, you can—in theory at least—adapt readily to new ones, and bring something new to them from your wider experience. Second, any agency of any size can nearly always dig up at least some relevant direct experience among its staff—even if it is only that the receptionist used to go out with your biggest competitor's leading salesperson.

There are perhaps two exceptions to my scepticism about 'relevant experience'. First, if the agency has recently lost the account of a major competitor: then, it may really know a lot. That is why, some years ago, Crown Paint moved into JWT, without any competitive selection process, within weeks of Berger moving out. The second exception is if the agency already handles a major competitor: but then the conventions of the industry tend to prevent the agency from handling your business too. The argument about conflicting accounts is an old one, and 'conflict' is open to numerous interpretations. In general, in my experience, conflict lies chiefly in the eyes of clients, but agencies are obsessed with it. It would, obviously, be difficult for a small agency to handle two directly competing brands, but what I can only describe as corporate possessiveness and hypersensitivity justifies the sort of policy that prevents an international agency which handles Gillette razor business in one country from handling Schick razor business in any other country—to quote a specific example. (Yes, I am sure it was written into the client–agency agreement at top level, but it still demonstrates an almost obsessional attitude which is all too common.)

The conflict argument has been exacerbated in recent years by the spate of large agency mergers and acquisitions started by Saatchi & Saatchi and WPP and enthusiastically followed by the major French agencies. These changing relationships tend to lead to conflicts. When Saatchi acquired Ted Bates, the eventual outcome was the movement of some $500 million worth of billings. The recent formation of the French agency Euro RSCG meant that the new group, as a whole, handled three major car marques—an automatic recipe for potential trouble.

The short list

As I have said, there are lots of agencies, and few clients know much about many of them. One of the major marketing tasks of most agencies is, quite simply, to become better known to more clients. Searching for Mr/Ms Right Agency among the 600 or so possible candidates is distinctly tough.

You can, however, start to eliminate on the basis of the first criterion—size. The difficulty is, of course, knowing what size an agency is, and whose accounts it handles. Actually, unless you are looking for very small agencies, it is not that difficult. Every year, *Campaign* publishes a list of the top 300 advertising agencies, which in 1992 went down to agencies billing only some £0.5 million: you can use this as an initial screening for size. As a cross-check, you can ask the IPA for a list of suitable agencies within a given size range. You can then look up each of the agencies in the 'Blue Book' (*Advertisers' Annual*), published each June, or the *BRAD* (British Rate and Data) *Agency and Client List*, which appears quarterly. From this, you can find out what sort of accounts each agency handles and whether they are, in fact, the sort of company you would like to keep. Furthermore, assuming you *do* know any of the accounts concerned, you will have an opinion on the quality of the agency's work on that account at least. And you can eliminate the agencies of your competitors.

But the chances are that you will still have a long list of possibilities—which are either possibilities because you know a certain amount about them or because you know nothing about them. For the latter, I suggest that the quickest way of eliminating a few more is to ring up (or write to) the managing directors of a couple of clients—ideally one major and one minor—for a brief comment on the agency. You might learn a lot.

Of course, you can start the other way: by thinking purely of agencies you and your colleagues know or know of, and building up an initial list. This at least has the merit of being based on some form of personal experience or recommendation. But it may mean you miss someone good simply through not knowing about them.

There is one added type of check you may want to run before starting to talk to agencies. There is an organization called the Advertising Agency Register which holds on file details and a 10-minute VCR film about over 100 agencies. For a small fee you can see just what each of a list of agencies has to say for itself, without needing to visit any of them. Similar data are available from Advertising Agency Assessments, and the bi-annual *Campaign Portfolio* is a useful data source. Again, this way you can eliminate some, confirm a few prejudices, and perhaps get a few surprises. (Alternatively, you could hand the entire process over to a consultant: there are one or two specialists in this field.)

Then, perhaps, it is time to start talking to agencies.

One final word, though, about lists. How large should they be? I believe that you are unlikely to gain anything from talking fairly tentatively to more than a dozen or so agencies, and that a serious selection exercise should rarely extend beyond four. So if you have more than four agencies on your list, you ought, in fairness both to yourself and to the agencies, to devise a quick, simple screening system designed to reduce the numbers on the basis of perhaps a letter and a single meeting.

By the time you start doing this, you will almost certainly have started being approached by other agencies—the news of an account on the move gets round the agency world very quickly and sooner or later it will appear in *Campaign*, unless you are very clever or very lucky. There is, I think, a very simple answer to the approaches you get. Ignore the first approach altogether, or brush it off. That way you get rid of the non-triers. Then take a very hard line indeed with the rest, and only begin to consider any which not only appear to meet your criteria but show extra qualities of ingenuity, persistence or style. You might find something you do not want to miss, but if you have been really thorough earlier, this will have reduced the risk.

Testing against the criteria
The classic way of choosing an agency is to give several agencies the same brief for your advertising, allow them time to consider it and to question you about it, set a date for a presentation, and leave them to get on with it. You make a choice on the quality of what they say and show you on the day.

The problem with this is that you are usually asking the competing agencies to put forward, after limited consultation with you, the sort of campaign proposals that would normally develop over a period of intense client–agency discussion taking a period more like months than weeks. It is rare for a creative proposal made at a presentation to be used in an actual campaign.

The problem, of course, is that every client wishes to see advertisements for his or her product, while not being very interested in ads for other clients' brands X or Y. He or she is interested—quite rightly—in Number One. It requires great restraint to resist the temptation to ask the competing agencies to have a go. The fact is that there is no possibility that the agencies will be able to give realistically of their best. The circumstances are all against it.

So what should you do?

I believe that if you have done your homework and pre-screening correctly, you will have a short list who are all capable of doing a good job for you creatively: they have shown that they can do it for others, and you believe them. What you want to be sure of is that they can understand your business and can work with you—and working with you includes, I would suggest, the ability to sell ideas to you.

What is needed, therefore, is a rather structured process that leads up, to be sure, to a presentation. You should set aside at least a day for each agency to visit your works, offices, stores or whatever, to meet both management and other personnel, and brief themselves thoroughly about your business and its problems and opportunities. You should encourage them—they should not need encouraging, but it is nice if you do it—to question anybody they like, either then or later. As part of this exercise, you should give them a brief—a specific brief, covering perhaps a small part of your business. This brief should involve developing an advertising plan for a particular situation: NOT the advertising, just the plan. Since no agency will resist the temptation to produce advertising ideas, you should probably specifically ban these, in no uncertain terms—and mean it. (If you then judge on the basis of ads, that is grossly unfair to those who follow your instructions, but it certainly happens, all too frequently. This is a tactical problem on which the agencies must exercise their ingenuity.)

Then you fix a date for presentations, and sit back and watch the results.

By doing this, you are able, I suggest, to judge your list of agencies against all the criteria. In the briefing and follow-up contact you can judge compatibility, business ability, experience, and enthusiasm. In the presentation itself you can see how these virtues interpret themselves in the direct context of your own business. You already know that the agency appears 'creative' from its work for others. The quality of its analysis of your problem should give at least a strong pointer to its ability to apply creativity successfully to yours.

Selection

During the whole selection process you ought, I suggest, to keep a running score for each agency on each criterion: ideally, a score computed not only by yourself, but by one or more colleagues. The greatest weight should, arguably, be given to scores on the final presentation, but the lead-up to it should not be ignored. You will learn plenty during this period.

There is, I suppose, one caveat. Any agency will try to turn its new business pitch to its best advantage. The people you meet and who present to you will be selected as far as possible to make the best impression. Any client wishes to be dealing from the start with the people who will work on his or her account. The two things are, clearly, somewhat incompatible, except in a very small agency. In practice, I think both sides have a point, but I suspect clients make less allowance than perhaps they should for the agency's division of labour: in a formal presentation they have to make the best possible impression, and the people who can do this may well not be the people who should work on the account. What is important, therefore, is that the client should *meet* the people who will work on the account, preferably during the briefing phase; but he or she should not automatically expect them to play all the major roles in the presentation.

The agency's role
If clients choose agencies, in the last resort agencies can do much to choose their clients. Any agency worth its salt has a more or less formal business plan, with targets for growth, targets for new business, and criteria for the sort of clients it wants to gain.

For the agency, new business is an essential part of its growth, and its success in getting new business is an important sign of its ability, as well as a valuable source of PR. As a result, agencies devote a very considerable amount of their time—especially management time—to the pursuit of new business. This is a fact of life which many clients find it hard, at first, to accept. Surely, the business of the agency is to look after its existing clients first, and to look for new ones in its spare time? In practice, that is usually, or should be, the effective balance of the agency's activity. New business getting is the task, essentially, of a small minority of the staff, for the greater part of the time. It is only when a really major prospect demands a full presentation that resources are diverted from the existing business to the potential future business: but if the right resources are not thus diverted, the agency runs the risk of collapsing for lack of nourishment.

A good agency is always on the lookout for new business, but it always carries a set of reservations and conditions in its mind. To the agency, clients are a mixed bag, not merely in terms of size and profit, but in terms of relationships and complexity. There is, even, an added dimension of prestige—is the client the sort of company I want to be seen with? As a result, just as clients draw up lists of criteria against which to assess agencies, so agencies tend to have criteria against which to assess possible new clients. The sort of questions an agency will wish to answer in respect of potential new clients are:

– Can we do a job for the client?
– Can we work with them: are our people compatible with theirs?
– Are we likely to produce the sort of work for this client that both they and we can be proud of?
– Is their business with us likely to grow?
– Can we make a profit?
– Are they financially sound?

If you think about it, some of these questions are quite tough to answer—indeed some you cannot really answer until the client and agency have started working together. But they do reflect the legitimate concerns of any serious-minded and progressive agency: in particular, the major concern of any agency management which is, or should be, money. It does nobody any good to produce award-winning ads at a loss. Any sane agency handles accounts on a very simple basis: that income should, at the least, exceed expenditure.

An agency's new business efforts tend to operate on several levels. First, trying to ensure that the agency is known to, and preferably in regular contact with, its major target clients. This involves the selection of a group of targets, and the pursuit of them by telephone, mail, or whatever other direct form of contact seems appropriate. Second, the active pursuit of live prospects which are revealed by the trade press (or any other source of information) as looking for a new agency: a client whose name appears in *Campaign* is sure of a busy time answering the 'phone, letters, faxes and personal calls. Third, the agency can hope for at least some approaches from potential clients who are looking for an agency: they may come by recommendation from mutual contacts or from clients; or because the client has seen and liked advertising done by the agency; or from a systematic search of the kind outlined above.

Once the agency has accepted the proposition that it should try to get business from a particular client, it is its job to decide how best to do it—against the background of the client's expressed intentions, which may be extremely vague ('we are just looking at a few agencies') or extremely specific ('here is a brief').

The agency's job is to structure its approach, within the limits of the client's expressed requirements, to achieve a sale—to demonstrate to the client its ability to provide the specific range and quality of services required, and to do this better than any competing agencies. (In the nature of this part of the game, the agency may well not know who the competition for the account is—and I am not sure it helps even if this is known.)

This is a process which involves, in microcosm, the whole business of planning an advertising campaign: gathering information, assessing the situation of the client, preparing objectives and strategy and, perhaps, creating campaign ideas to fulfil the strategy. As part of the process, the agency has to try, very fast, to learn as much as possible about the client company and its problems and, also, about the key people in the client organization.

The end product of this process will almost always be, one way or another, a presentation by the agency to the client. This can, in theory, be done in a wide variety of ways, from a more or less informal conversation in the managing director's office to a fully-produced song-and-dance act. Different agencies have different strengths, and the song-and-dance act is not everyone's cup of tea, but it can impress clients enormously. The decision as to how to present the agency to the client is very much a matter of the agency management's experience and assessment of the agency's strengths: and the agency's preferred approach has to be weighed up and positioned against the client's apparent preference.

I do not think there are any real rules for agency presentations, beyond the standard principles of selling. The major risk is that of boring clients by telling them what they already know better about their own markets—but if you do not show that you really understand the problems, you run the risk of being thought superficial.

For the agency, as for the client, there is both the temptation—and the compulsive need—for a creative presentation of advertising ideas: just as the client usually wants to see creative material for his or her business, so the agency likes to show how clever it is. But, just as there is the risk for the client of being decided by the flashy irrelevancy, so there is the risk for the agency of failing to do itself justice. Arguably, the better the agency is at planning its advertising, the less likely it is to show its best form in a 'creative' presentation, since it will normally do better after a longer and more thorough acquaintance with the client.

A full-scale pitch for a major account is, in any event, an expensive business for the agency. This does not stop agencies from competing when the rewards look high enough, but it is very easy to let the costs get out of hand. In consequence, few agencies in the UK are prepared to pitch against more than two or three others, and it is increasingly the practice to ask the client for at least a contribution towards the cost of the pitch. There is no question that a major pitch, involving four or five agencies, should provide a client with a significant amount of what is, in effect, free consultancy about his or her marketing and communication problems and opportunities. An agency can easily spend £25 000 in staff time alone, on a major pitch, and that is without the costs of finishing up artwork, experimental sound or music tracks for commercials, possibly producing an animatic film, and carrying out a limited programme of consumer research. If the client provides a really detailed briefing and a complex brief, costs can readily go up into six figures.

No wonder some agencies operate on a 'no fee, no pitch' basis, as far as possible; though among major agencies, I believe only Bogle Bartle Hegarty consistently refuse to make presentations that involve new creative work.

Tying the knot

The final stage in the agency selection process, once the decision has been made, is settling on the terms of business. Most agencies like to operate on the basis of a more or less standard contract or letter of terms, setting out the basis on which client and agency will do business. The Institute of Practitioners in Advertising (IPA) and the Incorporated Society of British Advertisers (ISBA) both publish specimen letters of terms as guides for agencies and clients, and it is worth studying these.

A typical letter of terms will specify:

- the range of services the agency will provide;
- the basis of payment for these, whether commission or fee;
- any system by which the agency is to be guaranteed a minimum income;
- contingencies under which additional fees may be due;
- the length of credit allowed to the client for different categories of bill;
- conditions relating to copyrights, confidentiality of client material and information, etc;

– conditions for terminating the agreement, in terms of length of notice.

Agency financial practices vary, but the tendency, certainly, is to bill at least part of the production costs on acceptance of estimates, and to allow a basic 30 days' credit on most bills, charging a surcharge for late payment. As a general principle, too, an efficient agency will aim to present detailed estimates, and argue about these, rather than haggling about bills. It is, at least, a reasonable basis on which to try to operate.

Increasingly, as agencies and clients move away from the old fixed-commission system towards a variety of fee managements, agencies are looking to spread their income more evenly over the years. This often runs counter to the patterns of business (75 per cent of fragrance or boxed chocolate advertising runs in November – December), but may be helpful to both sides' cash flow.

Managing the marriage

Running a client–agency relationship is, like a marriage, a matter of give and take. The best clients do their best to provide the agency with all the information they can, and to share their thinking with them. Their objective is to work *with* the agency. For this to happen, of course, the agency has to earn, and keep, the client's respect. Less satisfactory clients treat the agency as just another supplier, employed to produce a product to a specification, to be kept firmly in its place, and to be screwed down financially if possible. The idea of a constructive partnership, in which the agency can contribute something that the client lacks, is barely considered.

If you consider the amount of sheer hard work—on both sides—that goes into the business of finding and appointing an agency, it seems to me that it is very firmly in the interest of both parties to build a relationship that works. The investment in management time required to select an agency, and the length of time likely to be involved in the learning process before the agency both fully understands the client's market and knows how to work with the client's organization, dictate that agency changes are best made infrequently. Like marriage, agency relationships should not be entered into with divorce in mind, even though their expected life span may be rather shorter than the average marriage. It is, after all, quite possible for a client to be with an agency for 50 years or more, though this is pretty rare.

The ideal basis for a client–agency relationship is one of mutual respect. If this can be backed by the expectation of high standards of performance, and a cooperative effort to attain these high standards, the result should be good advertising. If it is not, it is important to have a system for reviewing the relationship to see what is going wrong. That is why an increasing number of clients and agencies have a system of regular reviews, not just of advertising plans and campaigns, but of the relationship and how it works: to assess gaps in performance (on both sides), and the strengths and weaknesses of the relationship. By doing this, it is possible to eliminate most of the small problems that can eventually lead to the breakdown of confidence and cooperation, and to ensure that both sides are contributing fully and effectively to the task of producing the best possible work on the account. Advertising is, above all, a cooperative effort.

Agency styles

A final consideration, which ties in with this need for cooperation, is that agencies' styles differ. As a client, you need to be clear what you want and what you are getting. Some agencies, especially those with a high 'creative' reputation, will virtually instruct you to buy their ads, and be extremely difficult about modifying them. Others will be a great deal more pliable, to the extent of giving you precisely what you ask for—even if they know in their hearts that it's no good.

It can be argued that the arrogance of the creative agencies is justified—but you need to be prepared to put up with it, and to insist on your right, as the client, to add in the essential details. Equally, too supine an agency does no one any favours, least of all its clients. For the great majority of clients, I believe the ideal is an agency that listens; works with its clients; uses its imagination to fulfil the brief; and then argues its corner without trying to bully. In the end, it is the client's money that pays the bills, but a good agency is entitled to have its views respected.

5 Meet the agency

It makes it much easier to understand how an advertisement appears in its appropriate medium, if you know how an agency works. An agency is not a sort of plate-glass fun-palace in which be-jeaned intellectuals dash off a few lapidary phrases in praise of Surf or Oxo between polishing the rhyme schemes of their latest book of sonnets or (more likely) the lyrics of the next chart-topper. Which is, perhaps, sad for the writers of television series, or even for those more serious people who think agencies are full of a breed of viciously frivolous vampires bent on sucking the blood of the poor innocent public.

An agency is a business, in many ways like any other. It is a service business, providing a very specific service to its clients. Like many service businesses it provides, in fact, a quite recognizable 'product'—advertisements. To do this, it is usually organized in a more or less formal way, with different departments covering the various specialities of the business. In an agency, indeed, you will find, in effect, most of the usual functions of a manufacturing business: management, the shop floor, sales, accounts, buying, and so on. It is not an analogy to be pushed too far, but the point should be clear by now. You ought to expect an agency to behave recognizably like a business: if it does not, it is reasonable to expect that it will be unbusinesslike in other respects. Conversely, it ought also to be recognizably an advertising business—not an insurance office or a bank or the civil service.

Recognizing this is perhaps less easy. The clues lie, probably, in an informality of style; in signs—at least—that someone has thought about the environment of the office; evidence of a lot of the agency's work around the place (if they have nothing to be proud of, they cannot be much use); an approach which is clearly geared to the idea of selling. If you are in an agency without someone trying to sell you something, even if it is only an old joke or a cup of coffee, within five minutes, you should be suspicious.

A double structure
Agency structures are something of great interest to agencies, but of less concern, generally, to their clients. After all, the clients' interest is merely in getting an effective job done for their money. How it is done is less important. However, it can be quite useful to know how it is supposed to work, because it may explain what is going on, sometimes . . . .

The important thing to remember about agencies is that they have two different ways of structuring themselves. One is the formal, departmental structure (see Figure 5.1) which recognizes the various specialisms within the business and leads to what may be thought of as an 'orthodox', function-based management structure. The second, which is far more important for the client, and a much more meaningful reflection of the way in which the agency operates from day to day, is the 'account group' system, used by the vast majority of agencies, whereby every client's account has a particular group of people, drawn from all the relevant departments of the agency, working on it.

In what follows, I want to look very briefly at the formal structure, and the various departments that may be found in it: and then in rather greater detail at the account group as it may operate on a single client's account, and how it may—with luck—interact effectively with the client's own operations.

Management

Agencies usually have rather large boards of directors. This is, for the most part, because clients like to feel that they are important enough 'to have a director working on my account'. The logic of this means that the majority of directors tend to be account executives—the people with the main responsibility for maintaining contact with the client (see page 46)—rather than heads of departments.

In any but the smallest agency, though, there will be directors in charge of the main functions—creative, media and finance—as well as those who are account executives. In the largest agencies there will probably be a small management group, drawn from among the 20 or more directors, which has the task of managing the agency, in the orthodox sense of management.

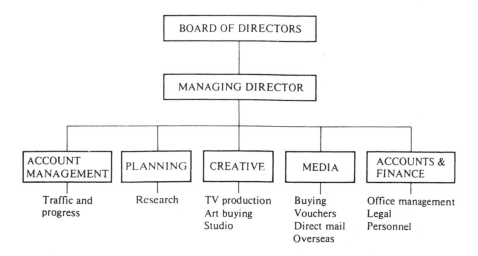

Figure 5.1   A standard agency structure: main functions and subsididary departments

Apart from those 'directors' who are actually directors of the company, the agency business has a disarming weakness for spawning hordes of other more or less high-flown titles—associate directors, senior associate directors (even!), creative directors, art directors, supervisors, chiefs, group heads, and so on. In a business which is actually rather short of bureaucratic levels or visible forms of promotion, this title-mongering is a useful way of signifying at least some form of status, both to one's fellows and, indeed, to clients. It may not always mean a great deal (though sometimes a title of this sort can be read as a genuine sign of worth), but it plays an essential part in reassuring people in a notoriously insecure and uncertain business.

The departments

Agency departments are a mixture of 'functional' departments—those concerned specifically with the business of handling accounts and making advertisements for them—and ancilliary and service departments. The dividing line is not a clear one, but the functional departments consist, basically, of account management, planning, creative, media, and progress/production/traffic.

Account management

Every account has in charge of it a manager, usually called an account director or account executive, whose job is to make sure both that the client's needs are met and that the agency makes a profit.

Within the department there will be, usually, a number of levels, with directors acting in a more or less supervisory role, executives doing the bulk of the detailed work, and, maybe, assistants or trainees helping the executives.

Creative

The typical agency creative department (which probably does not exist) includes both writers and artists. The writers can, usually, write. The artists do not have to be able to draw, though it helps: they do, however, have to be able to 'visualize'[*] a design or a film and be able to explain their ideas by words and rough pictures so that a specialized artist or photographer can produce the finished illustration. It is because of this essentially conceptual and guiding role that agency art people are usually called 'art directors'.

In the late fifties and early sixties, British agencies used to have a copy department and an art department, and then a separate TV department. As TV has become more important, and agency working methods have evolved, the most common arrangement is for agency creative people to work in 'teams'. The core of the team is usually a copywriter–art director pair, who normally work together on all their accounts. In larger agencies they may have one or more assistants: the assistants' tasks may include working out the minor details of a layout or storyboard, and providing paste-ups (see page 177) and other material for production once the basic idea is approved by

*Unfortunately, the word 'visualizer', which perfectly fits the job done, is often used in the agency business for a rather less important member of an art department.

the client. The creative team works in all media, but usually calls on the services of an agency TV producer to help to set up TV and cinema film production—and often radio, too.

In addition to the creation of ads, the creative group probably also, from time to time, does such things as pack design, devising promotions, and creating point-of-sale material. This is a field which involves rather different skills from those needed for advertising, and some agencies, my own for one, have a separate design department to handle this type of job.

The creative department is usually run by a creative director who is, ideally, a working director, performing primarily either a copy or an art function within a team, as well as setting standards and providing guidance and inspiration to the rest of the department. Occasionally, at the other extreme, he or she may be primarily an administrator. This latter type of arrangement, however, rarely seems to work as well.

Media

Media, too, has two sides to it: planning and buying. Usually the two functions are combined, though the largest agencies may split them. In particular, TV buying has come in recent years to be regarded as something of a separate skill—arguably to the detriment of the media operations of agencies as a whole. The media department works closely with the planning and creative departments to determine which media should be used for a particular campaign, and then negotiates with the media owners to obtain the best possible positions and prices.

Progress/production/traffic

Or, indeed, 'control'. Whatever you call it, this is the department that makes sure that everything actually happens, working in close liaison with the account executive. The range of the job varies from agency to agency, but basically it involves: progress chasing, making sure that jobs are taken through their various stages on time; production, making sure that jobs go to and from studios and publications in the appropriate form, and the appropriate sizes and shapes; and record-keeping, ensuring that a record is kept of what is going on on each account and every job done for that account.

Without a good traffic operation an agency flounders. It is an absolutely essential part of the nuts and bolts that hold the thing together—though the client rarely meets a traffic person except in a crisis.

Account planning/marketing/research

The majority of the larger agencies have a function called 'account planning', and here the planner is an essential part of the functional team. The planner's role is to use market research to develop the advertising strategy for the client's brand, and then to help evaluate the results of the advertising. As such, he or she has to work closely with the creative people and with media: in some agencies this includes the media planning, too.

In other agencies, this role is filled by the account executive, but then there may well be a research specialist who fulfils a service function, advising on market research and its interpretation, and perhaps doing some small-scale research personally.

Very few agencies now have their own market research department as such, and the only major agency group in the UK with significant research interests is WPP, which owns BMRB, Research International and Millward Brown, among others.

The 'service' departments are a mixed bag, one or two of which may claim 'functional' status.

Accounts

The one really essential service department for any agency is its accounts section. Without it, obviously, the agency has problems, and so do its clients. An efficient accounts set-up can not merely save the agency lots of money: it can improve relationships with its clients. And an inefficient billing system can so irritate a client as to lead to the eventual loss of the account by the agency.

Other departments

A large agency may have in its offices a large number of other departments: information and library, data processing, legal, personnel, art buying, contracts (with TV and radio actors, personalities, etc.), home economics, exhibitions, overseas, direct mail, merchandising and sales promotion, public relations, audio-visual production, secretaries, receptionists, telephonists, and purely 'logistic' departments such as mailing, messengers and office management.

In a smaller agency many of these tasks are carried out either by the managing director, the finance department or a general manager, with help where necessary from other members of other departments.

The agency account group

When you meet your agency account group, you may see very little of all this. Indeed, with a very small agency, you may see only one person—who may be both account executive and copywriter, and obtain most other necessary services from outside organizations.

If, however, you are using an agency capable of providing a reasonable service—even if it is not a 'full service agency'*—you are likely to meet, at one time or another, an account group, consisting of at least five or six people, who will be doing between them all the tasks involved in creating and placing your advertising. This group is comprised, and relates within itself, as shown in Figure 5.2.

(The planner is included with dotted lines only, because his or her function is often performed by the account executive.)

* 'Full service agency': An agency that offers a complete advertising service, in-house: account management, planning, media, creative and production and, probably, some additional services in print, package design, etc.

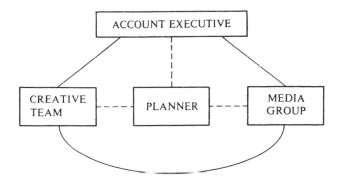

Figure 5.2 The nuclear account group

Just who are these people, and how do they relate to you and to the rest of the agency?

The account executive
This is the person with the suit—the one you will see most of and who will be present at nearly every meeting you have with the agency, the one whose job it is to look after your interests within the agency, and to look after the agency's interests in dealing with you. The account executive is ultimately responsible for planning your campaign and ensuring that the agency delivers the goods. In order to do this, he or she has to have considerable experience of the advertising business, and may well have spent some time working for a client company.

The account executive must be efficient and well-organized, and have the perspective and ability to see and appreciate business problems in depth.

On top of this, a degree of diplomacy is necessary for the job, as much of it is likely to be spent resolving various forms of disagreement between client and agency. Finally, an ability to motivate, and generate the enthusiasm for your product that will encourage the creative team to give of their best, is essential.

The account executive will, usually, take the chair in meetings at the agency, and will be responsible for producing the minutes of every meeting— these may be called 'call reports' or 'contact reports', and are usually designed solely to record decisions and list action to be performed by either the agency or the client. When the agency has produced specific proposals for your campaign—or anything else you may have asked for—the account executive will normally introduce them, and may present the entire pro- posals personally, without calling on other members of the group to cover their specialities.

Occasionally, if you are lucky, your account executive may take you to one of those much-talked-about business lunches, or at least buy you a drink.

Expect the agency too, at least to have discovered that you like ballet or horse racing, though you have no *right* to expect either to be bought tickets for these entertainments or to be accompanied to them by your account executive. It is polite, true, and it is the sort of thing a lot of clients like. It even, from time to time, causes them to change agencies. But it is hardly a rational basis for a business decision.

If your agency is large enough for your personal account executive to be below the level of director of the company, he or she will probably be reporting to a management supervisor (or some such title) who will be a board director. This sometimes invisible deity is usually meant to keep an eye on the working of the account, provide advice and experience if problems arise, and share a drink once or twice a year with your managing director or chairperson. If the account is well run, you should not need to see the management supervisor often, but, to be serious, a valuable contribution may well be made to your business through his or her wider experience—a senior agency account director has usually acquired a very passable working knowledge of more different businesses than most middle managers (at least) in the agency's client companies.

Your account executive may, too, have an assistant. This will usually be someone who has relatively little experience as an account executive (but may well have been in the agency for some time, as a progress controller or planner, for example). The assistant's task is to deputize, where necessary, for the account executive; to run meetings covering minor points of detail (often follow-up action for major meetings), to attend to detail within the agency; and, in general, to provide a lower level of contact between the client and the agency—on a par with your own assistants or subordinates.

As you will see from this description of the account executive role in your account group, the agency has to try to allow for different levels of contact with your own organization. With very large client companies—the Unilevers and Cadburys and General Foods—it is usually necessary to do this, because of the hierarchical structure of the client organization. It does, however, almost certainly increase the amount of time spent by the agency in working on a given account, without necessarily making the results any better, except perhaps in the very general sense of keeping the client organization happy. From the agency's point of view it is usually more satisfactory to keep the size of the account executive team as small as possible, giving full responsibility to one senior account manager who can provide a high quality of service at a level where it can be most effective—yours.

The creative team
Generally speaking they are the ones who do not wear suits—or look rather uncomfortable when they do. In a sense, this is an affectation, since it is not necessary to wear jeans, baseball boots, studded leather jackets and ear-rings to devise good advertisements, but good creative people are sufficiently rare and expensive for agency managers to be prepared to pander to most of their

their foibles. What is more, there is some evidence that clients expect it, too: if the creative people look too prosaic and orthodox, clients think that they will get prosaic and orthodox advertising, regardless of any evidence to the contrary.

You may not see a great deal of your creative team—many agencies take the quite reasonable view that the creative people should be busy making advertisements, not chatting up clients, and in one or two like Collett Dickinson & Pearce, the creative department holds itself superior and aloof and deals with clients only through its emissaries, the account executives. When you should definitely see them, though, is at the beginning, when you are briefing the agency on what you want, and the agency is learning about your business. It really is vitally important for the creative people to see your factory, try out your hotel or visit your shops or warehouses; to talk to the people who make or devise your product, whatever it is, as well as to those who sell it.

Personally, I believe that the creative group should also present its ideas for advertising to the client, and discuss them with him or her. I think that they are likely to give a better idea of what the finished advertisement will look like and can do a better job of communicating the necessary commitment to their way of presenting the product than can the account executive. And, certainly, it is important for the creative group to be present to discuss the client's reactions to their ideas, so as to understand why a particular point may need to be changed.

The creative group will usually, as we have seen, consist of a writer and an artist. Quite often the artist, whose job is to develop rough pictorial ideas to show how an advertisement would work, will not ever produce any very finished 'art' for you. Often, this is done almost in the form of a doodle (technically a 'scamp' or rough) which shows how the elements of the design of the ad will fit together, and may also give some idea of the character of the illustration. The writer, by contrast, is a finisher. When an idea starts, perhaps only a slogan or a headline will be produced, but in the end the writer is going to have to write all the words in the ad (though most clients tend to write a few themselves, sometimes over the agency's dead body).

Between them, the writer and artist, prodded by the account executive and guided, perhaps, by an account planner, have the task of producing the ideas to sell your product. How they do it is very much their problem, but as far as the client is concerned this is, in a sense, the agency's factory floor. The client is entitled to want a good product: if the agency has been well chosen, this should be obtained without the need to worry too much how it happens. (It may, occasionally be produced by a freelance team working outside the agency, and this may be another reason why you do not meet the creative group. Given the shortage of good creative talent, this is not that unusual, and if you find that your agency is using freelances, your immediate reaction should *not* be to fire them on the spot: give them credit for both knowing their own limitations and for buying good work from outside, always assuming that it is good; but press them to get a permanent team working on your account soon—it is not in your interest to lose continuity of creative work on your account.)

The account planner
In most agencies, the task of deciding what strategy should be followed in developing an advertising campaign is basically that of the account executive, working together with the creative group. Large agencies, however, usually have a specialist function, that of the account planner, to perform the major part of this task. The planner's job, narrowly defined, is to assemble all the available information about the client's product and its market, from the client's brief, from published information sources and from market research commissioned by the client, and occasionally, by the agency. This information is then analysed and translated into an advertising strategy, which provides the basis on which the creative team will work in devising the advertising.

The reasons why this type of job has arisen in agencies are complex, and reflect weaknesses both in existing agency staffing and structure and in clients' ability to brief their agencies in the right way. On the agency side, account executives rarely have the time or the depth of market research know-how and experience to make the most of the interpretation of market research. Some, certainly, are very good at it, but there is a clear tendency for much of their thinking to be rather superficial. *Vis-à-vis* the client, some agencies have found that clients' marketing management, especially at brand manager level, has a similarly limited ability to use and interpret market research and, in particular, to interpret it in a way which is appropriate for agencies' creative people to use. This has been exacerbated by a continuing tendency for clients to reduce the size of their marketing departments.

These two interlinked sets of factors suggested the need for the specialized account planning function which was pioneered by Boase Massimi Pollitt and J. Walter Thompson at the end of the sixties. An effective planner works very closely with the creative team on an account, and interprets the client's brief in terms of the consumer's present and intended perception of the product, to convey what is needed to the creative people. At the same time, it is the planner's job to identify gaps in the picture of the market provided by the client, and to suggest research to fill the important gaps. The planner is thus a sort of *agent provocateur* on behalf of the consumer, working on both agency and client.

The role and the value of account planning is widely debated in the industry. The 'fashion' phase of recent years seems to be over, and it is clear that planners have to justify their place in the agency by their value to the agency and its clients. A clear dichotomy is emerging, too, between the tightly defined research-oriented role of the BMP planner, and the 'advertising consultant' role typified by JWT. My personal view is that the latter direction represents the more promising future.

The media group

Most often, a particular account team will include just one media specialist, whose job is, first, to work with the rest of the account group, especially the creative team, to decide what type of media should be used—press, TV; colour or black and white; large or small spaces; etc. This is, in the jargon, the '*inter*-media decision'. It is a decision that has, in principle, to be taken early on, so that the creative group can concentrate their efforts on the right type of ads—though because some creative ideas work better in one medium than another, the initial decision may be left more or less open.

Then, once the ads have been developed, it is the media person's job to identify the specific places where they should appear, and to plan and cost a media schedule for the campaign. This is, specifically, the job of media planning.

Finally, once the client has agreed the schedule with the agency (which may well be done before the content of the ads is finally agreed), it is the media person's job to go out into the marketplace and buy the press space, the poster sites or the TV, radio or cinema spots. When this is done, there has to be negotiation, in order to get the best possible deal, in terms of the positions of the ads and the discounts or special prices that can be obtained. To do so, an intimate knowledge is needed, both of the prevailing media rates and the people with whom it is necessary to deal.

In addition to this purely functional role of planning and buying, a good media person has a more creative role, too, of suggesting to the rest of the account group new ways of using a medium, and of bringing to their attention any special opportunities that may exist. The sort of thing he or she might do, for example, is to suggest the use of a particular pattern of spaces across two or more pages of a magazine; the use of a particular daily newspaper in order to exploit the merchandising services it can provide in support of the advertising; an especially good offer by a TV station to new TV advertisers; a new publication giving especially favourable rates for its first few issues; and so on. The ability to suggest—and then buy—a two-and-three-quarter minute spot at midday on Sunday for the chairperson of a hotel group to give a message to all the hotel staff on every ITV station simultaneously is an important part of a media person's skills.

The rest of the agency

The people described in the previous section are possibly the only ones you, as a client, will meet at the agency, apart from the receptionist and your account executive's secretary.

As I have indicated on page 48, there are a lot of other things an agency can or might do for you, and lots of departments it could have to do it. As this is not a book on careers in advertising, the best thing I can do to give you an idea of the sort of people you might conceivably find in an agency is to refer you to the books by Norman Hart and Felicity Taylor (see page 232) which describe them all very comprehensively. All I ask is that you should bear in mind that in an agency with 25 or 30 people you are unlikely to find all the jobs described: indeed, you are quite likely not to find them all in an agency with 500 people, and there are precious few of those in Europe, and not many in the USA.

Plate 1 An emotional and evocative visual that positions the brand perfectly. Words are superfluous.

Plate 2 Tight targeting, precise media buying and humour make a small budget go further.

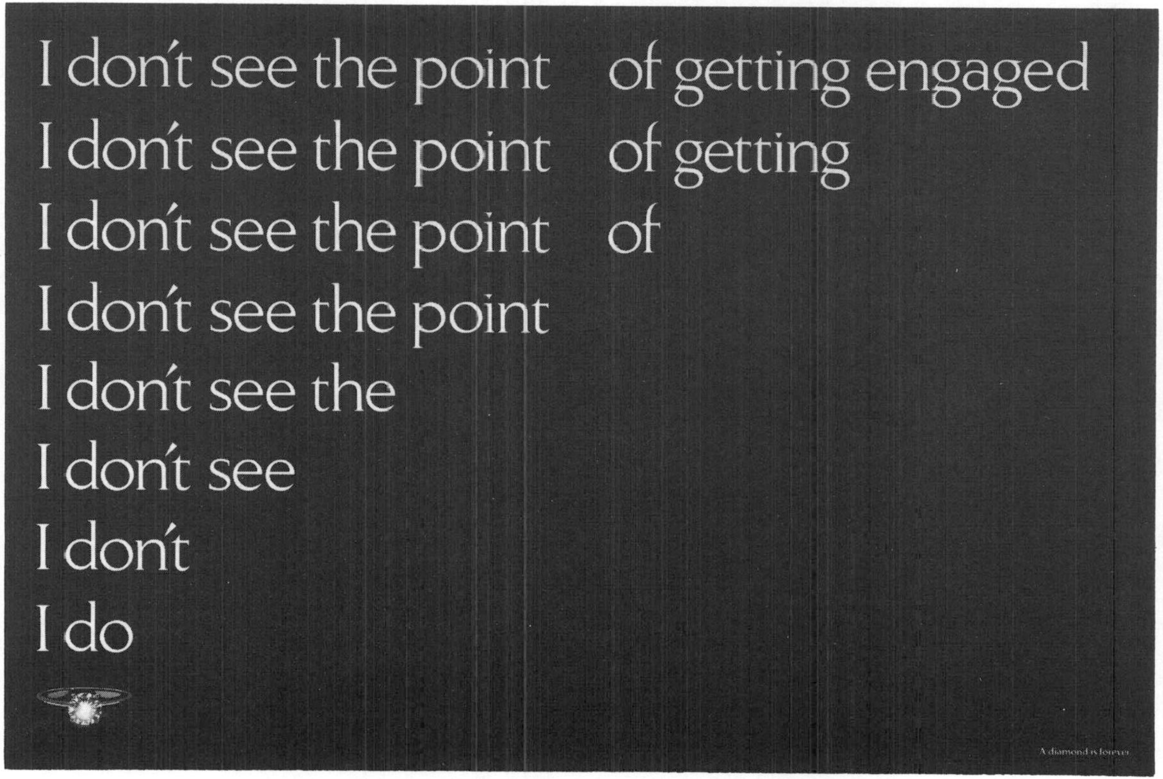

I don't see the point   of getting engaged
I don't see the point   of getting
I don't see the point   of
I don't see the point
I don't see the
I don't see
I don't
I do

A diamond is forever

Plate 3 A beautifully succinct argument presented with maximum style, minimum fuss.

When you've settled into a long motorway journey there's time to consider your surroundings. It's one of the times a Mercedes-Benz driver learns to appreciate how more than a century of automotive development has resulted in a driving environment that helps bring out the best in the man or woman behind the wheel. You're in a faultlessly constructed haven. The Mercedes-Benz 230E.

How to improve your performance

EVERYTHING YOU NEED TO KNOW – IN AN INSTANT

You scan the instruments as they tell their predictable tale: nothing untoward to report. Each of the thousands of precisely engineered components that make up this remarkable car is doing its job – actively or passively.

The miles roll effortlessly by. Mercedes' ergonomic specialists have tried to anticipate your every need.

The information you require is there at a glance. There is no electronic gimmickry. To operate any of the controls is finger-tip simple. The only background to your relaxed concentration is a subdued mechanical hum. Wind and road noise virtually absent.

PEACE OF BODY AND MIND

Here is a driving experience like no other. You feel the car's sensitivity through your fingertips, its considerate design shows in the relaxation of your shoulders and a general feeling of well-being. You're cocooned in a safety cell built by the inventors of the safety cell. The vault-like body is welded at more than 5000 points. The design of the body shell has been painstakingly developed to help the dissipation of energy in the event of an offset frontal collision. Little is left to chance.

NOW IT'S YOUR TURN

Alert but relaxed – you're in an ideal mood for the meeting ahead. And when you draw into the visitor's parking slot, the initiative remains firmly in your grasp. Because, when you step, refreshed, out of a 230E, you can be sure that the calibre of your transport has been duly noted. But the part its performance plays in your performance can remain your secret.

For more information, please contact your local dealer. Or call 081-554 5000, or write to Dept. 124/5, PO Box 151, London E15 2HF.

Engineered like no other car

Plate 4 Car ads often have long copy. But rarely with such relaxed, confident authority.

Plate 5 A brilliant campaign that launched a flood of pale imitations.

Plate 6 English eccentric meets Italian luxury. A stylish exercise in anticipation.

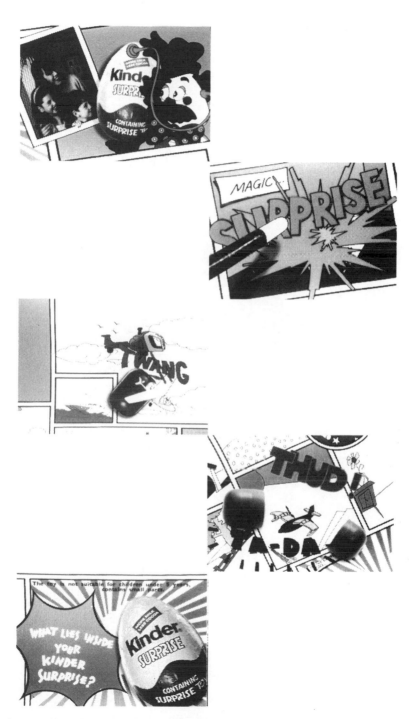

Plate 7 A totally different confectionery ad, successfully bridging the child-parent target.

Plate 8 At last, a sympathetic approach to the student target group.

Not all exchange rates fluctuate.

Plate 9 Small spaces add mileage in tune with the quirky TV campaign.

Plate 10 Lifestyle and cars, well mixed – and with no need for miles of copy.

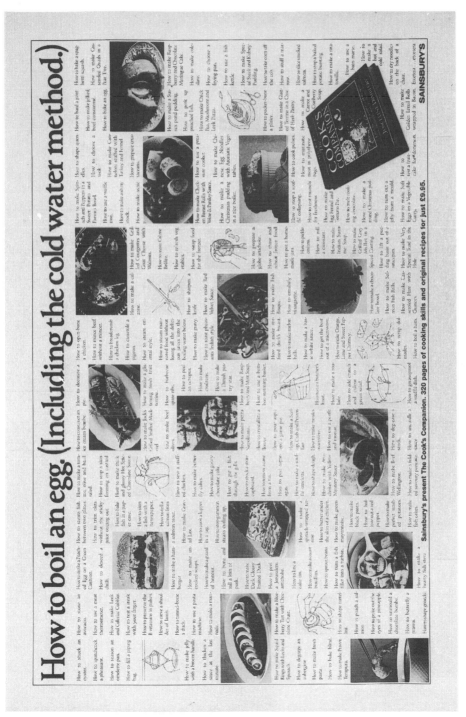

Plate 11 A grocery ad that doesn't go on about prices – and says a lot about the store.

Plate 12 Positioning the store (see page 75)

Plate 13 A typical financial direct-selling ad. Just look at all the extra 'nudge' points. Today, it would need more legal caveats.

Plate 14 Bringing ice cream into adulthood.

|There are times when you

can allow the

man in your

life to choose

your bra.|

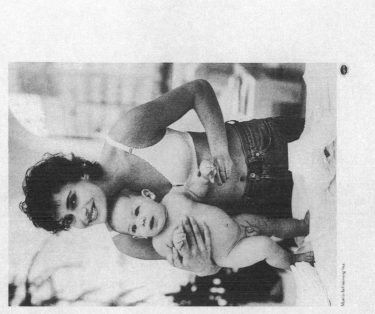

Triumph
INTERNATIONAL
The bra for the way you are.

Plate 15 Precise targeting – with unusual charm.

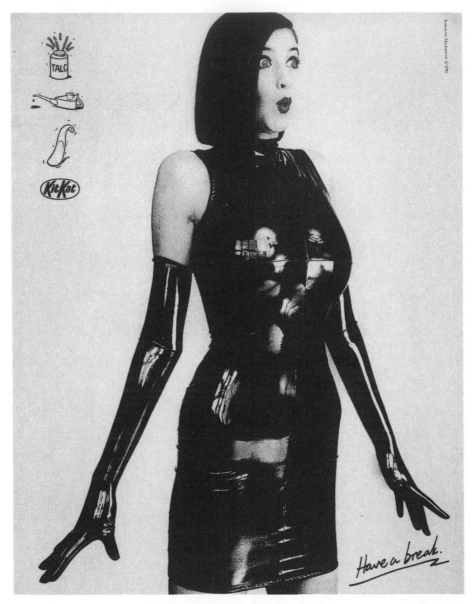

Plate 16 Wit and appropriateness in a specific setting. A small part of a clever campaign.

6 How advertising works

Advertising, of course, sells. Advertisements inform, persuade, remind, influence, change opinions; they even, perhaps, change emotions and attitudes. Advertising changes society; makes people buy things they do not want; enables multinational capitalistic monopolies to batten on the working classes.

Well, doesn't it?

The truth of the matter is that we do not know how—in any meaningful, scientific, experimentally demonstrable sense—advertising works. There are plenty of theories, and plenty of assumptions, many of which may have at least a part of the truth. But there is, certainly, no commonly accepted theory of how advertising works, and no sign of one evolving. Like much of what is, in effect, the study of psychology, advertising theory is stuck at a very basic level of sophistication.

Does it matter?

In a sense, perhaps it does not. In practice, advertisers go to advertising agencies, give them a brief, accept (after suitable argument) a recommendation on the content and media for the campaign, and advertise. If the product sells—because of or in spite of the advertising—all is well. If it does not sell—because of or in spite of the advertising—all is not well, and the campaign is changed or the agency is fired. This is, after all, the way of the world. Would an effective theory of how advertising works have helped?

Quite possibly, it would have made little difference. Clients are, in general, little concerned with advertising theory: they are concerned with results. If results do not occur, the marketing director, or, worse, the managing director, looks for a scapegoat, human nature being what it is. What is easier than to look at the most conspicuous item in the marketing budget and one which is largely the concern of an outside supplier, at that? It is a brave agency that will argue the toss in the circumstances, and a lucky one that will find a client ready to listen.

The fact is that unless you have a reasonable understanding of what advertising can and cannot achieve, you have absolutely no way of deciding what its role in a marketing programme is, what objectives should be set for it, and how to measure whether it has achieved those objectives.

Figure 6.1   'Black box' effect

Early theories

As little as 40 years or so ago, it often tended to be assumed that there was a nice simple relationship, a sort of 'black box' effect, that looked like Figure 6.1.

So long as you delivered enough advertising against the right consumers, the result could be measured in sales. This is, clearly, a pretty naive view, even of a direct response campaign. Something must be going on in the black box labelled 'consumer'.

A bit of thought indicated that, clearly, consumers, having minds, emotions, senses, and all the psychological paraphernalia that foul up our mental processes, would in some way 'process' the material coming to them in the form of advertisements. For this to happen at all, it was assumed, an ad would have to attract their attention. Once it had achieved this, if it was to go any further it would have to arouse their interest. For a sale to take place, however, would require more: a desire for the product. But everyone knew, even then, about unsatisfied or sublimated or postponed desires: the final step must be action. This, in essence, is the so-called AIDA model, from the initial letters of the steps in the process (Figure 6.2).

AIDA ruled the advertising world for a good many years, in the absence of anything better. It was still very difficult to see *how* the process might work, or to account for the fact that some ads worked, and some consumers took action, but others stubbornly did not; or that an apparently good campaign failed to achieve extra sales—for sales were still the only real measure of effectiveness.

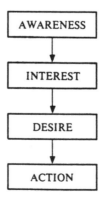

Figure 6.2   The AIDA model

Memory: a digression

There were, however, other measures of advertising. It could be assumed, in the absence of any evidence to the contrary, that if an ad had achieved, at the least, Awareness and Interest, it would be remembered. Therefore it should be possible to measure at least this part of the process by carrying out research into people's recall of ads. This is what people—many people, all over the world, but especially in the USA and the UK—proceeded to do.

The theory said, naturally, that the more of the ad that was remembered, the better it had succeeded in communicating. If you take that as a yardstick, it is a fairly short step to designing ads which say nothing much but which are extremely memorable. Conversely, an ad which is difficult to recall in detail, but (say) highly emotive and therefore, probably, rather effective, would score rather badly.

The fact is that memory is selective and fallible. It is also, very importantly, of two kinds: short term and long term; so that what is recalled in the short term (the classic example is a string of numbers) may fade rapidly from the memory, while other elements of the communication, which are not so easy to recall immediately, stay in the mind long afterwards. So there is liable to be a very different result according to whether a recall test is carried out within 24 hours, or a week, or three months, of an ad appearing: and 'pre-tests', based on showing an ad to consumers before it appears, and finding out what they remember of it within minutes, can be almost totally irrelevant—except as an indication of intelligibility.

There is, too, it has since appeared, a further problem. It does not seem to be necessary for an ad to be at all well remembered for it to have an effect. It was, indeed, at the height of recall testing that the great subliminal advertising scare arose. 'Subliminal' advertising, which was most publicly 'exposed' in Vance Packard's *The Hidden Persuaders*, is advertising that is supposed to work below the threshold of consciousness: a message flashed for a fraction of a second on a cinema screen was, it was alleged, able to increase sales of popcorn very significantly, even though no one in the audience could have taken it in—or, indeed, remembered it. The experiment on which this story was based has not been effectively repeated—but it sent a sufficient *frisson* through legislators and consumerists all over the world for subliminal advertising to have been solemnly banned in most countries where advertising is effectively controlled.

What no one seems to have noticed is that if subliminal advertising worked, recall measures were to a significant extent irrelevant. Subsequent research seems, in fact, to have shown a very weak relationship between recall (however measured, which is a technically very complex question in itself) and other measures of advertising effectiveness. It seems likely that a well-recalled ad is something of a bonus to a brand, but little more than that. Certainly, measuring recall gives no overall, consistent guide to a campaign's success. In spite of this, advertisers, agencies and researchers persist in pushing the interpretation of recall well beyond the limits of what it can tell them.

Some light is perhaps shed on the problem by the most recent psychological researches on memory, which have identified two rather different kinds of memory—'explicit' memory, which amounts to relatively detailed recall of a set of stimuli; and 'implicit' memory, which is distinctly short of detail, but enables people, in effect, to 'know I've seen it before somewhere'. There is no evidence that either type is more potent as a guide to subsequent action.

Attitudes

During the sixties, dissatisfaction with the AIDA model became widespread among agencies. The growing recognition that advertising was not the only thing that affected sales began to raise doubts as to whether sales measurement was an adequate guide to advertising's success or failure. But if sales were not to be measured, what was?

Clearly, advertising is a form of communication to the consumer about a product. But it is not just trying to get the recipient to learn the ad by rote: it is, surely, trying to give information—persuasive information—about the product, so that the consumer will prefer it to its competitors and buy it. Why do consumers buy one brand rather than another? Because they think it is better. In psychologists' terms, they have a favourable attitude towards it. Indeed, taking things a step further, you can break down an overall favourable attitude to a brand into a set of attitudes to different aspects of the brand.

To cut a long story short, the discovery of the sixties was that you can measure a range of attitudes to each of a group of competing brands, and get a clear, coherent pattern of differences between them: what is more, you can repeat the process at intervals, and monitor changes in these attitudes. The changes, too, can be clear and coherent. Now, if you set these changes against the objectives of the concurrent advertising campaigns for these brands, expressed in terms of changes of attitude, you find—if you are lucky—that the attitudes have, indeed, changed in the intended direction.

So, how does advertising work? By modifying attitudes to brands, of course!

Well, unfortunately there turned out to be flaws in this version of the story, too. It accounts rather inadequately for new products, where quite clearly a significant part of the task of advertising, and its main visible and measurable effect, is to spread awareness, knowledge and information about the new brand. It has proved extremely difficult, too, to find significant changes in attitudes in many markets except over a rather long period—which does not disprove the theory, but suggests either that advertising does not work very fast, which no one wishes to admit, or that attitudes are not the whole of the story. But perhaps worst of all, it has been clearly demonstrated that while a change in attitudes to a brand or product can precede a purchase of that brand, it can equally well *follow* the purchase: does attitude change influence a purchase, or does it merely result from it?—since people often feel the need to justify a purchase, especially a major purchase, after they have made it.

Back to the consumer

After this set-back, there were various attempts to rebuild the attitude theory, and it still has its uses. Certainly one of the things advertising *can* do is modify attitudes.

The latest step in theory building, however, has been to take the basic precept of marketing, that the consumer is the starting point, and see if that helped. If you consider how people—consumers—actually *use* advertising, as opposed to how advertisers hope, optimistically, to use people, it is quite clear that, to a given person at a given time, by no means all advertisements are equal. Some ads will be irrelevant: the viewer or reader is not in the target group, or has just made a purchase in that product group and does not want another just yet. Some ads will be about products which are most unlikely to be bought; some, even, may concern products or product fields in which the reader is actively looking for something to buy. Quite simply, the likelihood of a purchase in the product field is one key factor in the way a consumer might respond to an ad.

A second factor is the importance of the purchase. Over the years there have been a number of theoretical divisions of purchases into different groups, depending on the importance of the decision to buy. At its simplest, you can divide all purchases into 'day-to-day' and 'occasional', but it is more useful to make a more detailed breakdown, which relates both cost and frequency of purchase, and produces a scale, something like that shown in Table 6.1.

Table 6.1 Types of purchase

Type of purchase		Example
Day-to-day, convenience	'Trivial'	Baked beans, bread
Occasional convenience		Furniture polish
Minor luxury		Toilet water
Considered/small durable		Electrical 'brown goods'
Major durable, rare purchase	'Serious'	Freezer, car, house

It is a reasonable assumption—though little more than an assumption—that ads in the categories at the lower end of the scale as it appears on the page will be more closely studied, and more thoroughly and consciously used by purchasers, than those at the upper end of the scale. It is also likely that the ads for the more expensive and unusual products will be of greater general interest than those for the cheap day-to-day items: it is quite tempting to study in detail an ad for an expensive car, or browse through the 'houses for sale' columns, even if you aspire only as far as a second-hand Escort and have no intention of moving house within the next 10 years.

The logical consequence of this view of consumers' use of advertising is that there is a far greater chance of involving potential customers in the ads for more complex and expensive products. In one school of thinking, durables, pharmaceutical goods, insurance, etc., have been christened 'information-intensive' products, and there are agencies which set out to specialize in this type of product. A further consequence, which has certainly met with some interesting results, is that for certain types of advertising campaign it is possible actively to involve the public. This was done very effectively in the late seventies in campaigns by Whitbread, who ran a series of ads asking for public comments on a number of propositions about the law affecting pubs and licensing; and subsequently by the major banks, who ran a joint campaign partly designed to deter the threat of nationalization—a campaign which attracted many thousands of replies from the public. The GLC's campaign to prevent its abolition by the Conservative Government was also highly effective in generating public interest and comment. A very visible recent example is the campaign by the European Publishers Council in conjunction with the European Advertising Agencies Association, which is designed to bring to public attention proposals about advertising by the European commission which the EPC regards, with some justification, as potentially damaging to free speech and, even, free trade.

It is, perhaps, hardly surprising that these examples are all, in fact, from campaigns which were not directly *selling* anything. As far as I know, no one has used an ad which is actively involved in selling a product in quite this way. More usually, ads for these types of product can be found with extensive and detailed copy—but copy designed to sell as well as, sometimes, inform. (A common device, especially in trade advertising, is the 'how do you rate?' type of self-scored, multiple-choice questionnaire, but that is different.)

The corollary of the theory, of course, is that ads for the cheap, day-to-day, convenience type of product are of so little interest to anybody that they should carry a minimum of information, and that they will even then have great difficulty in achieving any very active response from customers. This may be true, and many advertisers of these categories of goods—which tend to account for the majority of advertisements appearing on TV and in major national newspapers and magazines—behave as if they believe it. It is difficult to find examples which assume the contrary, let alone to show that they can succeed.

This line of thinking, however, seems to me to miss at least one major point. If you consider the markets for most convenience goods, they are established markets, in which a large proportion of the buyers have tried most of the major brands available. A large proportion of the advertising in these markets, is, inevitably, in some sense, 'reminder' advertising—which, again, should not need much in the way of information, since it is preaching to the converted. But if the objective of the advertising for such a brand is, in fact, to talk to newcomers to the market (and there are always newcomers to any market), or to the unconverted, or to disloyal users of other brands, there is, obviously, a very clear, specific case for ads which carry quite a lot of information, presented in a suitably attractive way. As the research agency Millward Brown has pointed out, a lot of 'successful' advertising depends on the fact that it provides 'new' information. In most systems for pre-testing advertisements, 'news' has a quite disproportionate effect.

No single theory
To cut a still very shapeless and incoherent story short, this latest analysis has taken advertising well away, it seems to me, from any possibility of a single, coherent theory of how it can work. It will have different effects, on different people, in different markets, in different situations.

What is increasingly clear, however, is that the effects of advertising do not depend only on what the advertiser does. We are not in the sort of psychological laboratory where white-coated ad people administer a measured dose of pre-tested stimuli to pre-conditioned, salivating consumers. Certainly, advertising must involve a process of stimulation of responses from consumers— that bit of the adopted jargon of psychology is fair enough. What has to be recognized, though, is that to a large extent, consumers *select* the stimuli to which they will respond. It is up to the advertiser, by careful analysis of the precise situation in which the target consumers find themselves, to identify the appropriate stimulus, from among those available, to produce the right response among this particular target group.

The resulting success of this advertising may be due, in effect, to the following:

– The ad may produce an immediate decision to purchase.
– The ad may confirm a previous decision to purchase the product, and encourage the buyer to talk favourably to friends about it.
– The ad may alter or undermine an unfavourable attitude or group of attitudes to the brand (which may have been based on ignorance or emotion...).
–The ad may start a favourable train of thought which could lead to a purchase in a week's (or a year's) time.
– And so on.

Part of the process whereby these various results have been achieved may be conscious: but part may be virtually subconscious. It seems very likely that although there seems to be little in the idea of subliminal advertising, it is quite possible for a familiar ad for a familiar product to have at least some effect of reinforcing a favourable attitude without, to all intents and purposes, being consciously noted by the consumer at all. Certainly, psychological research shows that a single sight of a picture can produce clear *recognition* of the picture when it is seen again, even at intervals of months or more: 'implicit' memory in action.

What is clearly the case is that there is no simple, magic theory to explain what advertising does, and how it does it. In terms of an apparently satisfactory way of explaining what goes on we are far less confident than in the good old days of AIDA—but at least we know that AIDA was as inadequate as a theory as her operatic namesake was ill-starred in love.

Long term v. short term
One final area which requires some discussion is the question of whether

advertising has its effects in the short or long term. This is important at a theoretical level because mathematical analysis of advertising's apparent effects in the marketplace, as carried out by econometricians (see Chapter 9), has tended to suggest that the measurable effects of an individual burst of advertising decay very rapidly over quite a short (usually less than nine months) period.

It is rather difficult to reconcile this with the ability of major brands in heavily advertised markets to establish and maintain their reputations over many years. There is—for me—no doubt that the dominant brand leadership of brands such as Hovis, Persil, Brooke Bond, Cadburys in the UK, and Jello, Tide, Hershey in the USA is compounded both of the effects of their current advertising and of that accumulated over 20, 30 or 50 years. It is not easy to 'prove' this. But I can offer three pieces of rather different evidence which seem to me to be highly convincing.

The first, and most general, is the willingness of companies to pay over the odds when they acquire other companies. What appears in English balance sheets as 'goodwill' is, obviously, more than an attempt to capitalize just the accumulated effects of the advertising of companies acquired. (It is, in fact, an attempt to capitalize the total marketing effect.) Certainly, though, it demonstrates that the financial market, rightly or wrongly, is prepared to put a value, however crude, on the long-term effects of marketing activity.[*]

The second piece of evidence lies in the field of attitude change. I have already questioned the absolute relevance of attitude measures, but if they do measure some at least of the effect of advertising, some of the time, the general slowness of movement of these measures implies, at least, that such change occurs gradually as a result of the cumulative build-up of the message of the campaign. For it to do this, it must have some long-term effect.

The third type of evidence is considerably more anecdotal and tenuous. When a famous campaign is changed, it is still possible to carry out research on advertising recall for several years afterwards and find a substantial, sometimes even dominant, proportion of what is recalled being the old campaign. This happened, for example, when the chimps were dropped from Brooke Bond tea advertising; there is still significant 'recall' of such ancient slogans as 'Guinness is good for you' and 'Persil washes whiter'; people have by now quite out-dated 'favourites' from campaigns such as that for Heineken lager, and 'tick-a tick-a Timex' is still remembered after over 25 years. Individually, we probably all—even if we are not involved in advertising—have at least a small number of slogans or even whole ads which we remember readily, and sometimes even with affection, from a long time back. Some, like Toshiba's ''Ello tosh, gotta Toshiba?' have become part of the language for a time.

Now I have already criticized recall and memory as a guide to advertising effectiveness, so I am clearly vulnerable when I adduce this sort of thing as evidence for long-term effects of advertising. All I would claim is that given

*This aspect of financial accounting gained new prominence in the late eighties when some companies attempted to put a capital value on their brands, as a balance-sheet item in their accounts.

the existence of this phenomenon of extensive, very long-term memory of the campaigns of successful brands, the onus is on the mathematicians to *disprove* the existence of any long-term effect: the fact that they cannot find such an effect, with the somewhat rudimentary apparatus at their disposal, is not enough. Certainly, something is happening out there.

Conclusions

This brief chapter has been kept, deliberately, short and as untechnical as possible. The subject is one of great theoretical complexity, in which even the so-called experts find it easy not merely to disagree but to disagree about what questions to ask.

From the debate as it has developed so far, various things seem to me to be clear:

– Advertisements are used by people: it is very difficult for ads to use (=manipulate) people.
– Ads work in several different ways: these may be more or less intellectual or emotional: they may also be more or less conscious.
– In so far as advertisements 'sell' they generally do it more or less indirectly: rarely is an ad a direct (or the only) stimulus to purchase.
– A large part of all advertising is designed (deliberately or accidentally) as 'reminder' or 'reinforcement' advertising: it is not trying to *change* anything.
– It is likely to be more difficult to change attitudes or behaviour through advertising than to reinforce them.
– Consumers' use of ads is likely to differ according to their interest in the product field and the complexity and importance of a purchase in the product field.
– The effects of advertising, where these can be identified, are not necessarily short term. There is evidence for this both in the slowness of attitude change in response to advertising and in the long duration of memory of successful advertising.

The problem of how advertising works is largely a theoretical one, but its relevance to both agencies and advertisers lies in its importance for the assessment of the results of advertising campaigns. At the moment, the main results of work on the problem have rather negative implications:

1. Sales are clearly not due to advertising alone, and it is technically difficult to separate the effects of advertising from those of other marketing activity in order to provide an adequate measurement.
2. Memory is an inadequate guide to advertising effectiveness though, other things being equal, there seems to be quite a good *a priori* case in favour of memorability.
3. Attitude changes, too, are at best only part of the answer. They can be difficult to find, and may follow, rather than precede, a relevant purchase.

4. Clearly, if we are expecting our advertising to work in a particular way, against a particular sub-group of consumers, we should do our research in such a way that it will show up this sort of effect. This sounds obvious, but it is by no means what always happens!

We will return to the problems of campaign assessment in Chapter 9.

7 Planning advertisements

Advertisements do not usually spring fully formed into the mind of an agency's resident creative genius. Most advertisements, if they are any good, are the outcome of a process of careful, detailed and imaginative analysis, which leads to the formulation of an advertising strategy for the brand concerned. This strategy should be agreed in advance between agency and client, before any advertising ideas are put forward. If you are the client, you are, obviously, impatient to see some ideas. It is very tempting, as has been pointed out in the discussion on choosing an agency, to go for the ideas and ignore the reasons for them. This is a mistake. If the strategy is not soundly based, there is every risk that what seems on the surface a good idea is, in fact, misdirected and misconceived. It is, therefore, essential to develop an appropriate strategy for the advertising before starting to produce ideas.

Most large agencies have a special department usually called 'account planning', or simply 'planning', to develop the advertising strategy (see page 47). In the majority, however, this is the task of the account executive, whose job it is to take the client's brief, ask the appropriate questions, and translate the brief into clear objectives for the creative team to work to.

Objectives and strategies

At this stage, it is important to distinguish between a variety of different types of 'objective', or 'strategy', or 'intention', or 'role' for advertising. People in marketing have a tendency to use confused language and, in consequence, to set up requirements which, logically, cannot be met. In this chapter, I want to distinguish carefully between marketing (as a whole) and advertising, and between the various types of statement of intent.

Marketing

Marketing *objectives* are specific targets set in terms of sales, profit, share, distribution, consumer penetration, re-purchase, etc.

Marketing *strategy* is the statement of the means by which the objectives can be achieved. These means may (or may not) include advertising, as a major or minor element within the total marketing mix.

Advertising

The *role* of advertising within the marketing mix is the part it has to play in the marketing strategy. Because advertising is not the only element in the overall marketing mix (see page 5), advertising's role is almost certainly going to be to meet part only of the marketing strategy.* This may be anything from increasing brand awareness to improving specific aspects of the brand image.

Advertising *objectives* are more or less specific statements of what is to be achieved by advertising, in terms of (for example) increased awareness, or improved scores on certain attitude scales.

Advertising *strategy* is a statement of how the objectives are to be achieved, in terms of creative content and media deployment.

For the creative department of the agency, then, there are specific creative objectives, to be achieved through the fulfilment of creative strategy.

It is easy to labour this point, but I have seen far too many advertising briefs which put marketing objectives (like 'to increase our share of the market by 5 per cent') into the advertising objectives, or even the advertising strategy. This is misuse of language, and can be highly confusing.

Developing the strategy

The ultimate aim of the advertising planner is to develop an advertising strategy which provides the answers to two superficially straightforward questions:

– Who do we want to talk to?
– What do we want them to get out of our advertising?

In order to arrive at the answers, it is necessary to go through a more or less logical process of analysis, based on market research—whether published, or commissioned by the client, or (occasionally) commissioned by the agency—and on knowledge and experience.

What the planner needs to know can be set out in the form of a cycle of information and analysis—a cycle, because marketing and advertising are a continuous process, and knowledge gained from one advertising campaign can be used to develop its continuation. The cycle can look like that shown in Figure 7.1.

Different agencies use rather different versions of this, but they all look broadly similar.

The terms used in this version cover the following general areas:

The marketplace

The market in which our brand competes: trends in sales, consumption, distribution; the state of product development; the level of competitive advertising and promotional activity; patterns of consumption—are there heavy or light users of the products and who are they? etc.

---

*The obvious exception is direct mail or direct response. Even here, though, the marketing mix includes incentives, fulfilment, etc.

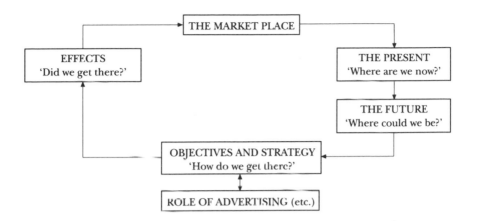

Figure 7.1 The planning cycle

The present
This sets out to describe the client's position within the marketplace: brand shares and trends in brand share; product advantages and disadvantages over competition—both in physical terms (laboratory test and blind consumer test) and in terms of consumer opinions and attitudes; planned and possible product improvements; recent marketing activity, in relation to that of competitors.

The future
This reflects, primarily, the client's objectives for the brand—what are the targets, in terms of sales, market share, consumer purchasing and usage? But to these targets needs to be added an analysis of what must be achieved in order to obtain them, in terms of both the behaviour and attitude of consumers: and of more functional matters such as (for example) greatly improved distribution—to put it in what is, from the agency's point of view, the most defensive way possible, it is too easy to blame the advertising when the sales force has failed to achieve the necessary levels of retail distribution to support the required sales.

The role of advertising
In practice, one should consider here *all* the different forms of communication of the product to the consumer, and allocate to each, and to sales activity, product development, market research, etc., their specific roles in meeting the objectives. For example, although most retail grocery advertising in the UK used to consist of lists of prices, and consumers tended to expect it to do so, it is unrealistic to expect advertising to do the major job of communicating large numbers of prices, especially promotional prices, when this can be done far better by window bills and in-store display: there are few shoppers who analyse every available grocery ad before deciding where to

shop. This fact was recognized in the early eighties, first by Sainsbury and then by Tesco: both chains ran distinguished—and successful—'image-building' campaigns alongside more limited, tactical price-list advertising.

Thus, it is possible to define the role of advertising for a product or brand as being (for example):

– to increase awareness of the brand and its characteristics;
– to encourage non-users to sample the product;
– to maintain the loyalty of existing buyers, and to encourage them to use more;
– to develop the belief among both users and, ideally, non-users that the brand is technically superior to competitors for reasons A, B or C;
– to inform consumers, especially lapsed users, that the product has been improved or reformulated;
– to generate requests for information;
and, even
– to encourage the retail trade to stock and display the product.

Advertising objectives and strategy
On the basis of this analysis, it is possible to develop specific objectives and creative and media strategies for the advertising. I will come back to this in a moment.

Effects
Presumably, the advertising will have some effect on the market. It is an essential element in the planning cycle to measure the effects of the advertising, as far as possible, together with those of other types of marketing activity, in order to take account of what has happened in the next phase of planning. This is discussed at length in Chapter 9.

Planning and advertising: objectives and strategy
Objectives
Once the role of the advertising has been defined, it becomes reasonably straightforward to set objectives for the advertising, which will usually be rather more specific interpretations of the role statement, including where possible specific targets, measurable by specific research. As I hope I have made clear already, the objectives have to be things which can actually be achieved by advertising—'to increase sales' is not an advertising objective, though it is something to which advertising can and should contribute.

The sort of objectives which are appropriate for advertising are objectives concerned with awareness and understanding of the brand, and with the attitudes and opinions people have about the brand. (There are, of course, one or two very obvious exceptions to this general statement. In direct response advertising, an increase in coupon replies, or sales, or the value of sales per coupon, is a valid objective: in retailers' advertising, an increase in customer numbers ('footfall') is equally valid.) Ideally, objectives should be quantified.

For an established and successful brand, the objectives might well be, to a large extent, 'maintenance' objectives: to keep a high level of awareness of the brand, ideally as one of the first two in its field spontaneously named by respondents to a regular survey (something often described in the US as 'share of mind'); to maintain a high level of belief in the brand's superiority over its main competitor on certain key attributes of the product type; to encourage people to offer the product to their visitors.

For a new or growing brand, the objectives will refer to the same sort of aspects of the market situation, but will be more concerned with increasing awareness, in developing a favourable view of the product, and persuading new buyers to try the product.

Strategy

Setting the objectives, then, is at least moderately straightforward, though it can be made more complex by the addition of sub-objectives relating to secondary groups of consumers, and there is always room for argument as to how much it is realistic to expect to achieve.

The difficult part—at least before creating the advertising itself—is to evolve a creative strategy to meet the objectives. This is a process which goes back to the two questions raised on page 66:

– Who do we want to talk to?
– What do we want them to get out of our ads?

Who do we want to talk to? If you are a sales person, one of the important parts of the job is to know as much as possible about the people you are selling to. The more you know about their fads and foibles, their strengths and weaknesses, the better you will be able to deploy your arguments to persuade them to buy. With advertising, it is exactly the same. The only problem is that instead of sitting across a desk from the one customer, you are talking to hundreds or thousands or even millions, in their homes or their cars or trains or buses.

All the same, you are not going to be talking to everyone out there. You are talking to the one in a hundred, or ten, or whatever, who might buy your product. And because it is just one in a hundred, that one is going to be *different* in one way or another, or he or she would not bother to buy. How do you spot this person? Well, if you consider that one in a hundred people in Britain means over half a million people, you are talking of a large group of people, who must have *something* in common to make them buy your product.

Is it possible to define what it is that they have in common? If it is, this will make it much easier for the creative people: if they cannot actually find a typical individual customer, they can at least get a reasonably good idea of whom they are trying to reach.

This is where the market research which is analysed in the first three parts of the planning cycle can help. If you think about people in very large numbers, you can divide them into groups in a variety of ways: age groups, different sexes, marital status, numbers of children, where they live, what they do, how much they earn, how many GCSEs they have, whether they own a car or a colour TV, the colour of their skin. . . the list is, in practice, endless, especially if you add in (say) readers of *Punch*, or buyers of Beecham's pills.

If I say to you that the typical buyer of your product is the wife of a coal miner, living in Yorkshire, with three children under ten, with a council flat, no car but a colour TV, you can start to deduce a lot about her way of life and, perhaps, her approach to the sort of product you have to sell. She is not likely to feel able to afford many luxuries, but she will want good, plain nourishing food and lots of it; she will welcome reasonably cheap ways of simplifying household chores; and every now and then she may want to splash out. By knowing more about her buying habits and the things she owns, we can fill in the picture. She is probably a price-conscious shopper (nearly everyone claims to be these days), but in her shopping this may be reflected in a reliance on branded goods bought at Asda, or private label from the Co-op. Possibly, we may know more still about her: that she has always voted Labour, believes in capital punishment, and thinks multinational firms are manipulating the world; likes reading romances, does the pools regularly, and watches *Coronation Street* every week . . . .

If we can build up this kind of detailed picture, it is much easier to begin to talk to our customers in the right kind of language, and the right tone of voice. But we do not often have that much to go on. Anyway, where do we get it from?

The sort of research that provides this kind of information can come from two or three sources. It may come from a published or syndicated source, like *Retail Business*[*] or *Mintel*,[†] or the *Target Group Index (TGI)*;[‡] or it may come from a survey you have carried out yourself. It is likely that, whichever it is, it will tell you about the buyers of your product and its competitors only in rather broad terms—those of the basic demographics: age, sex, social grade, area, presence of children. Possibly, too, in terms of readership of various papers and magazines and weight of TV viewing or commercial radio listening. Only if you have done a very elaborate and expensive piece of research will you have gone beyond this to the sort of detailed description outlined above.

Most of the data will be readily intelligible. The one that requires a little explanation is 'social grade'. The British are a peculiar people in having a class structure which is more complex and pervasive than that of any other western industrial country. The class structure affects people's attitudes and behaviour significantly, so that it is important for advertising to know which class is being aimed at. Unfortunately, it is not a simple concept, and is

*Published monthly by the Economist Intelligence Unit.
†Published monthly by Mintel Publications Ltd.
‡Published annually by the British Market Research Bureau Ltd.

difficult to research. So various market research interests have put together a classification for research purposes which the majority of research firms now use, which provides a kind of guide to people's status in the community and their likely spending behaviour. This sytem is based on occupation, and people interviewed in market research are usually classified by the occupation of the chief income-earner (the head) in their household.

The classifications, and their definitions, together with their approximate proportions in the UK population, are as follows:

2.9%	A	— —	Higher managerial, administrative and professional.
15.0%	B	— —	Intermediate managerial, administrative and professional.
24.2%	C1	— —	Supervisory or clerical and junior managerial, administrative and professional.
27.1%	C2	— —	Skilled manual.
17.5%	D	— —	Semi- and unskilled manual.
13.2%	E	— —	State pensioners, widows, casual or lowest grade workers.

(*Source:* JICNARS. *National Readership Survey 1991–2*)

Traditionally, the C2 and D groups were the so-called 'mass market', and they accounted for over 60 per cent of adults until the late seventies. A steady upward trend in the overall status of the population, due to changes in employment patterns and to increasing prosperity, has substantially altered the picture. The key large groups are now the C1s and C2s—who are often rather different in their attitudes and habits. In this sense, then, the 'mass markct' has partly disappeared.

The system is by no means an infallible guide to peoplc's spending habits or even attitudes, but the combined efforts of the market research world have failed, so far, to come up with anything better. One of the most promising directions, which has been pursued by some large advertising agencies, and which has been extensively talked about, is so-called 'lifestyle' research. This usually involves, for a start, a very extensive survey which asks several thousand people about their attitudes to a variety of aspects of how they run their lives and about their purchasing habits. From this survey it is possible, by means of complex statistical analyses, to divide people up into groups whose attitudes and purchasing habits appear to be broadly similar. It is then, of course, possible to describe the typical member of such a group.

The best known of these studies, internationally, is the now well established Values and Life Styles (VALS) approach pioneered by the Stamford Research Institute in California, and licensed to various European market research agencies (in the UK, Applied Futures Ltd); a number of others have been promoted by different interests from time to time, notably the Europe-wide RISC studies.

From the creative user's point of view, the problem with 'lifestyle' approaches is that they attempt to generalize, and by generalizing they lose the fine detail that distinguishes habits and attitudes in any individual market. A good example of a way round this is the use made by National Magazine Company, publishers of *Vogue* and *Esquire*, of the *TGI*'s lifestyle questions to construct cluster groups of both male and female populations on the basis of questions relevant to their readers' interests in fashion, style, shopping and so on. These clusters, which have been made readily available to agencies, provide a very useful 'shorthand' for analysing and describing relevant markets or brands covered by *TGI*, since the data provide a direct link between brand or product use and media use. Other magazine houses have used similar analyses. By way of illustration, the two cluster groupings, and their percentage of the adult populations are set out in Table 7.1:

Table 7.1   The National Magazine 'Clusters'. Percentages of the adult population 1990

Men	%	Women	%
Timid Traditionalists	21.8	Cosy and Comfortable	20.3
Brash with Cash	17.1	Harassed Housewife	19.6
Bullseye and Beerguts	13.2	Well Dressed but Not Obsessed	15.6
Business Class	11.3	Dash with Cash	14.7
Fastlane Free-stylers	10.0	Flamboyant Fortysomething	9.9
Man at his Best	8.5	Ritz with Glitz	8.8
One Foot in the Grave	5.8	Forever Frumpy	6.3
Beethoven and Books	5.8	Grannies but not Glamorous	5.3
	100		100

(*Source:* National Magazine Co./*TGI*)

The names given to the clusters are evocative and largely self-explanatory, but, to give a flavour of the material, here are short pen-portraits of two of them, from rather different parts of the socio-cultural scale:

Ritz with Glitz   Affluent, up-market, very fashionable: only the best will do. They are active shoppers and visibly social, using their social life to forward their careers. Meticulous about their appearance, their relaxation is active but not energetic. They holiday in exotic locations.

Bullseye and Beerguts   These are the elderly lager louts: men who have opted out, in favour of an easy life, an understanding job and regular drinking in the pub. Tabloid readers and armchair sports fans.

As can be seen, this sort of thing begins to provide a texture and context for thinking about a target group for a campaign, and helps to prevent the use of inappropriate stimuli. It is still necessary, of course, once you have decided your target consists of the 'Well Dressed but Not Obsessed', or 'Fastlane Free-stylers', to take into account how people like that perceive your product or brand. Cluster analysis is only a start. By way of illustration, Table 7.2 shows how it applies to some brands in the men's toiletry field.

Table 7.2 Aftershave usage by cluster – men = 1991: selected brands (Index: average = 100)

Cluster group	All after-shave	Aramis	Brut	Old Spice	Paco Rabanne
Timid Traditionalists	98	89	111	119	63
Brash with Cash	114	152	110	90	139
Bullseye and Beerguts	96	83	111	101	72
Business Class	102	94	112	113	111
Fastlane Free-stylers	120	123	74	67	234
Man at his Best	102	124	98	75	137
One Foot in the Grave	83	44	81	121	96
Beethoven and Books	70	30	71	79	57

(*Source: TGI Special Analysis*)

Lifestyle studies like these are usually the source of the acronyms such as 'yuppies', 'dinkies', 'glams', etc., that have been enthusiastically bandied about the media in recent years.

This type of analysis is helpful to agency creative people, but has practical limitations. *Ad hoc* lifestyle studies (as opposed to *TGI*-based approaches) cannot always be related, without further major research, to established data about media. It requires either a full repeat survey to identify the life stylegroups again if any follow-up research is to be done, or else the creation of a sort of shorthand classification for research and analysis; it seems that different products tend to be best looked at in terms of rather different life style groupings, so that, ideally, each requires its own major survey— which rather loses the point of the exercise—and researchers have had some difficulty in replicating the results. Conversely, of course, the *TGI*-based material described above can be justifiably regarded as inadequately precise from the creative planning point of view, even if it is extremely helpful for media planners.

Lifestyles are not, however, the only approach to segmenting consumers. During the last 10 years, there has been considerable interest in so-called geodemographic classifications, based on large-scale cluster analyses of Census data. There are now at least half a dozen of these available in the UK, the best known being the pioneer, CACI's ACORN (A Classification of Residential Neighbourhoods). ACORN divides the nation's households into 38 individual neighbourhood types, which—in turn—can make up 12 larger groups, ranging in size from 3 per cent to 18 per cent of UK households. This classification can be linked to postcodes, as a valuable tool for direct marketing, and to product-use surveys such as *TGI*, as an aid to advertising target-setting. ACORN's successors use similar techniques, but different detailed clusters. All these systems, inevitably, suffer from erosion of their database, since the

Census is only taken every 10 years, and populations are not static. There is no question, however, that geo-demographics has added a valuable new weapon to the marketing and advertising planner's analytic armoury.

Finally, a different and simpler approach, developed by Research Services Limited, is 'SAGACITY': this is a combination of occupational classifications and family life cycles, designed to reflect the different spending patterns of different types of family.

The whole area of classification is one which is regularly the subject of Market Research Society working parties, and from time to time provokes a rash of articles in the technical press, but at the time of writing there is little sign of any real breakthrough to a new and better system. Meanwhile, the most useful descriptions remain a combination of the 'traditional' social grades, *plus* the other demographics (age, sex, etc.) *plus* media exposure (which can be obtained for most products and many individual brands from the *Target Group Index*), *plus* any other relevant information about their behaviour in relation to the product concerned.

This means, then, that the sort of target group description the agency may want to develop for the advertising will be something like this (for a brand of ice cream):

– young adults, of both sexes, aged 18–30, but *not* exclusively the unattached 'post-teen' group;
– mass market: C1C2(D);
– with money to spare for small luxuries;
– may have tried our product or its direct competitor;
– used to eating ice cream in-hand, out of doors;
– convivial, with a sense of humour;
– ACORN group D.

Or, for a chain of hotels, for bargain weekends:

– adults, especially men, over 35, especially 45–60;
– AB, C1, well off;
– regular hotel users for business, at least occasionally for holidays;
– probably acquainted with at least some of our hotels;
– able to take a weekend away more or less on impulse;
– attracted by the idea of second holidays and 'getting away';
– ACORN groups I J.
– 'Man at his Best', the 'Business Class'

Obviously, to even arrive at this sort of description, it is necessary to have found out by one kind of research or another, and by the added use of imagination, a lot about the sort of customers the advertising is trying to attract.

The process can, of course, be elaborated, on the basis of a suitably detailed marketing strategy. If the strategy for Bovril Cubes is to gain sales at the expense of Oxo, the Bovril Cube target group will, inevitably, consist primarily of Oxo users. If Oxo needs, defensively, to fight off Bovril's attack,

Oxo's primary target group will be some or all of existing Oxo users: it will be a matter of agonizing argument and discussion to decide whether to go all out to keep regular, heavy Oxo users at all costs, or, instead, to concentrate on lighter—and therefore presumably more vulnerable—users.

What do they think about our product? The process of identifying and defining the target group, and the research required to do this, will usually have provided a lot of information, too, about how the consumer thinks about our brand. (If it has not, then we probably need to do some more research, to find out.)

The sort of picture that we need to have includes the answers to the following types of questions:

– What do people use the product for?
– How often do they use it?
– Where do they buy it? How often?
– Do they buy one brand only, or several?
– How do they judge between different brands? (Taste, colour, smell, size, price . . .?)
– What do they think is good about our brand?
– What is bad about it?
– And what about our competitors?
– Have they even heard of our brand?
– Is our brand actually any better than its competitors (a) on the basis of scientific tests? (b) when consumers try the products 'blind'—without knowing which brand is which? (c) when they do know the brand?

That is a fairly brief 'shopping list', but a reasonably comprehensive one. If you can answer all those questions, with a fair degree of confidence, about your product, you should have been able to decide what your brand's strengths and weaknesses in the marketplace are. From this, it is a short, though sometimes difficult, step to deciding whether to build on its strengths or counter its weaknesses. (This is part of the process of setting the objectives.) It is likely, in general, that advertising can build on the strengths, but that it may need improvements to the physical product to eliminate the weaknesses.

It may be necessary, however, to tackle a weakness. Allied-Maples, the present group title of what used to be Allied Carpets, built its reputation on aggressively-priced, high street carpet stores. In the mid eighties, the group started to expand into out-of-town superstores that sold a full range of furniture, bedding and furnishings, as well as carpets. This raised three different problems (or opportunities, as we say in marketing): overall, the quality of the stores was higher than expected by people used to Allied Carpets' promotional style; people were not fully aware of the extent of the offer—they did not associate Allied with furniture and beds; and, in a market where independent retailers are still the dominant factor, they had low expectations of

Allied's standards of personal service. As part of a programme to overcome these problems, Allied ran a series of ads in local papers, each of which highlighted a facet of the business. Three of these ads are shown in plate 12. This campaign has not yet been applied to all Allied's large stores, but where it has run, sales have increased and research shows a clear improvement in consumer perceptions.

In practice, it is likely that you will be trying both to re-emphasize or reinforce at least some of your strong points, *and* to reduce or eliminate at least some of your weak points. Probably, too, the way in which the eventual advertisement is perceived by the people to whom you are advertising will depend on their present or past experience of your product. In other words, different groups of people will get different things out of the same advertisement. Judging from reported research, the advertising campaign for Radion detergent, especially the launch commercials, ranked highly, among most consumers, as being offensive, brash, crude and unpleasant. But the brand quickly gained a significant share of the fiercely competitive market. Clearly, for those who found they actually did suffer from smelly clothes—evidently a lot of people—the ads struck an immediate and powerful chord.

A particularly good example is the TV campaign for Ariston—the one that goes 'On... and on... and on'. According to the agency (which may have its tongue firmly in its cheek) the technique of their commercials is based on research by the Japanese video game firm Nintendo, and the ads are designed to have an almost hypnotic effect. They even use Nintendo soundtrack music. Again, in research terms, this campaign is heartily disliked by many: but to some, it evidently sells.

What do we want them to get out of the advertising?   By now, we should know who we want to talk to, and what they think of our product. We also know that they may react in a slightly perverse way to our advertising. How, then, can we go about defining our strategy in the hope of getting them to react in the right way—the way we want them to?

Here, again, a definition is in order. The critical point about an advertising strategy is that it is a *guide* to making ads. It is not an advertisement. It is merely a statement about the desired results of the advertising, in terms of what the advertising is to communicate. You do, in practice, see a lot of advertisements which appear as if someone has written a strategy and then put it in the advertisement as it stood. Without a lot of luck, this is unlikely to work. Why not?

Quite simply, because people do not react 'logically' to ads. They attend to them erratically, remember them badly, perceive them selectively. If we send them that well-known telegram 'Send reinforcements. Am going to advance', they are unlikely to get anywhere near even 'Send three and fourpence. Am going to a dance'. They might—conceivably—end up with a picture of Doris Day singing *Ten cents a dance* from the film *Love Me or Leave Me*. (If, like me, they are old enough.)

If you think about how people perceive things—with any of their senses—and process them in their minds, you immediately realize that the human mind works to a very large extent by association, and by a more or less impenetrable system of mental shortcuts—just try playing word association games. Good advertising, it seems, is a means of second-guessing this process. If you see an ad which makes you really stop and take notice, someone has succeeded in getting through to you. When you find an ad incomprehensible, they have failed—probably.

If you then remember that the agency's creative people are—at least in theory—especially good at getting into other people's minds through a combination of words and pictures, it becomes a little clearer that while an advertising strategy may be a statement of intent about the communication of an idea to a target group, the *interpretation* of that strategy by the creative group may contain *none* of the words of the strategy (except things like 'the' and 'and'). Yet, if you show people the ad, they will tell you just the things that the strategy was looking for.

Then, given that the only way of being sure that your ad is communicating what your strategy says it should is to show the ad to people and ask what it tells them, it follows that the best way to write down the strategy is, as far as possible, in the language that consumers will use. Hence the rather long question that makes up the sub-title of this section.

So how do I write down my strategy?

Different agencies use different methods for actually setting down strategies, but an increasing proportion insist on using 'consumer language', expressed in terms of the intended or desired reactions or responses to the advertising. Probably the classic statement of this approach is that used by the J. Walter Thompson 'T-Plan', as described by Stephen King in *Developing New Brands*[*], where responses are divided into responses from the senses (what is perceived about the brand), from the reason (what is believed about the brand) and from the emotions (what is felt about the brand). A typical set of responses, for the recently launched Persil washing-up liquid, might be:

From the senses   Persil washing-up liquid. It cleans lots of dishes—really white. It's very easy to use.

From the reason   Persil washing-up liquid comes from the people who make Persil. It will get my dishes really clean, just as Persil does with my washing.

From the emotions   It's nice of the Persil people to come up with a washing-up liquid. I'm sure I can trust it—it'll be quite like an old friend.

The problem with this way of putting down the strategy is that the sense/reason/emotion division is difficult to handle in practice, and there is no clear guide to the balance required between the three categories. At the same

*Pitman, 1973.

time, there is continuous pressure from creative people for simplicity in the briefs they are given and the creative brief, clearly, needs to set out the strategy in a way that is intelligible to, and usable by, the creative team: if it isn't, it's useless.

For creatives, then, the strategy needs to be clear, brief, but also stimulating. It also needs to be backed up by simple guidelines, and supported by detailed product information: there is no question that the best and most effective advertising is based squarely in a complete understanding of the product.

In the last resort, when you are faced by a strategy, it is worth asking yourself whether you can imagine an ad based on it. If it is full of contradictions, or if it is too vague, this is very difficult. Even if you are not at all 'creative', it is worth applying the test.

Creative briefs

Many agencies have now arrived at a very similar format for creative briefs, which aims to condense and simplify the creative requirements into a single-page format—which may be supported, in turn, by a great deal of back-up information.

A typical creative brief, written to this type of format, is this one for Scholl:

CLIENT: Scholl   BRAND: Footcare (range) DATE: 17/9/90
TIME PLAN: Internal review   9/10/90
             Final revisions   15/10/90
             Present to client   22/10/90

CAMPAIGN REQUIREMENT

– A magazine campaign, primarily for women's magazines.
– Colour pages/half pages – but consider possibility of small-space b/w adaptations.
– Adaptable to communicate specific product benefits for several individual products.

TARGET AUDIENCE

Primary:
– Existing users of at least some footcare products, especially competitive brands.
Secondary:
– People who are relatively health-aware, and may become more sensitive to foot problems—actual or potential.
Primarily a female target, both as users and purchasers, but some conditions (athlete's foot, e.g., show a strong male bias—the campaign cannot be *too* female-oriented. Familiar with Scholl, but inclined to see the brand as very problem-specific, and also as a bit old-fashioned. Likely to neglect theirfeet— even when they know they have problems.

ADVERTISING TASK

To raise the profile of Scholl as the experts on footcare, with a range of products that can solve and treat every problem, and prevent further problems. To build on the Scholl heritage, but to make the brand up-to-date and caring, rather than purely curative.

BENEFITS

– Specific products cure/alleviate/prevent specific problems.
– Problem relief leads to positive good feelings for your whole body.
– Scholl alone has a complete range, to deal with all footcare problems.

POSITIONING

Only Scholl has the expertise to provide a comprehensive, effective, high-quality range of products to care for your feet and deal with all common footcare problems. Using Scholl footcare products will put new life into your feet.

PROPOSITION

If you use Scholl products, your whole body will come alive again.

SUPPORT

– The proven efficacy of individual Scholl products.
– The Scholl brand reputation ('Dr Scholl').
– The comprehensive Scholl footcare range.
– The importance of 'happy feet' to overall physical and mental well-being.

BRAND PERSONALITY

– Bright, modern.
– Friendly, caring.
– With a degree of humour.

GUIDELINES

The campaign needs to achieve a (difficult) balance between 'corporate' Scholl and selling individual products. There should be a common campaign feel and, probably, format, but individual ads should usually be focused on a single problem and its Scholl solution.

MANDATORY INCLUSIONS (LEGAL, ETC.)

– Clear, consistent Scholl branding.
– Specific medical claims must be supportable within the Code of Practice.

Two elements in this brief require a little further discussion and clarification.

Benefits These are basically of two kinds: those which are generic to the product category (clean clothes; a delicious, easy-to-cook meal; a safe place for your savings that gives a good rate of interest; fast, easy, reliable driving); and those which are specific to our product. These may be partly a superior performance on the generic benefits (quicker, more thorough, cheaper, safer…) and partly based in brand values such as status, security, fashionability, form, ostentation, reassurance. The task of strategy definition is to identify, precisely, the package of benefits that will do the best competitive job of presenting the brand to its target audience.

These benefits need, as far as possible, to be backed by supporting evidence—the ITVA (see page 126) will want it, even if no one else does!

Positioning   This is a definition of how the brand should best fit into its competitive market. It should be true to the brand (of course!), competitively powerful, and, as far as possible, unique. It is, in fact, what the brand stands for.

A good recent example is the TV launch campaign for First Direct (whatever you may think of an execution that can best be described as controversial).

The key *benefit* here is 24-hour banking, with no need to visit a branch—there aren't any.

The *positioning* is that of a modern, accessible, caring, and extremely good value banking service, that is quite different in character from the traditional high street banks.

In a market where the high street banks' advertising has for years been devoted to trying to humanize an essentially depressing sub-retail experience, the campaign was, to say the least, refreshingly different. It was targeted, obviously, at a minority with sufficient confidence and sophistication to buy into the concept, and it certainly succeeded, to a point.

The key response being sought was, presumably, 'Here's a really sensible way of running my finances: after all, I hardly ever go to the bank anyway. Let's find out more.'

A positioning statement has to be reformulated, in turn, into the brand proposition: a translation into something nearer consumers' language, around which the advertising must be developed. The proposition is not intended to be an advertising slogan or headline, but the clearest propositions are likely to come close to this.

A strategy set out in this format does not guarantee good advertising: that depends on the ability of the creative team, helped by the rest of agency account group, to produce a good idea; on the ability of agency and client to recognize it as such: and the team's combined ability to turn it into a real, working campaign. What the strategy *does* do, is to formalize and focus the analysis in a way that gives everybody concerned the essential basis for developing and judging good advertising—the two aspects that take up the next two chapters.

8 Creating ads

Creativity

I do not think anyone can tell you *how* to create an advertisement. It is possible to tell you—broadly—what ought to appear in an ad, except that you *can* leave out (for good reasons, of course) such apparently essential details as the name of the product or a picture of the pack. But ultimately, good ads are imaginative ideas. Having ideas is a pretty inscrutable process—rather well described in about 600 pages by Arthur Koestler in *The Act of Creation*—and is a very personal thing: different people who are good at it go about it in different ways. What *is* worth remembering, though, is that once you have got the idea, that is by no means the end of the story. The idea has to be made to work, commercially, in the right advertisement format—be it a large or small print ad, a poster, a TV or radio commercial. Ideally, it will need to be capable of working in all these media and of being extended. Ideas that can be developed beyond a single campaign into a campaign that will run for years are really worth their weight in gold.

Persil washed whiter, in one form or another, for at least 60 years, taking on new angles of development as a campaign as technical developments led to product improvements and new competitive situations. As the ITVA's rules on comparative whiteness claims in detergent ads have tightened, the (by now) several Persil products have not always been able to use this theme, but its development over such a long period was an astonishing piece of consistency by client management and virtuosity by the agency.

Corresponding to these divisions between idea and execution, and advertisement and long-running campaign, there are, in fact, two rather different types of creative skill involved. The more or less genuinely 'creative' skill of producing the initial idea has to be balanced with the development skill of making it work. The best agency creative people can do both, but much of an agency's creative department is likely to consist mainly, in practice, of 'developers' rather than 'creatives'. The problem, for the agency, is to recognize and exploit the distinction, without frustrating the desire of *all* the department to be allowed to have the original, creative ideas.

Ultimately creativity—defined as the ability to have ideas that sell—is what all agencies claim to be selling. Their problem is that they—and their clients—find it quite difficult to recognize, and almost impossible to turn on to order. Much of what passes for creativity is flashy or fashionable, or relies on advertising industry in-jokes.

So, are there any rules?

There is an American agency which, according to one of the trade papers, has the following statement about how it goes about making ads:

Rule 1. There are no rules.

Rule 2. There may be exceptions to rule 1.

Ultimately, I think all the 'rules' that exist are, in fact, not guides to making ads, but to deciding whether the ads might be any good. And judging ads, or deciding which are the good ones, either before or after they have been run, is the subject of the next chapter. However, because they are usually put forward as essentially rules for creating ads, it is probably best to discuss them in this chapter too. There are, also, a few more fundamental rules, of both language and design and sound, which certainly need to be considered as an ad is put together. While one cannot produce rules for having advertising ideas, some guidelines for, as it were, the physical construction of advertisements can be proposed—if only to be ignored. The problem is that the 'well-constructed' or 'textbook' ad is liable to be extremely boring unless it embodies a really good idea, and that it is possible for a skilled creative person to bend the 'rules' of construction in such a way as to make a moderately good idea look or sound much better.

First of all, then, some general 'rules' which may apply to ads in all media. Some, as you will see, I do not altogether agree with. After that, I will go on to talk briefly about individual media. Curiously, most of the rules seem to have been conceived for print media: there are few pieces of TV and radio 'folklore' of this kind.

General 'rules'

1. *Every ad should embody a clear, straightforward, proposition*

In other words, it should be offering the potential buyer at least one, possibly *only* one, clear reason for purchase. In its extreme form, this is an expression of the Unique Selling Proposition, or USP, which was developed as a philosophy by Rosser Reeves of Ted Bates in the USA. Very simply, the theory behind this is that any product has some characteristic which can be developed so as to make it unique in its class. Ideally, it is a major feature of this type of product, and one for which the advertised brand is actually superior: but it could be some general characteristic which, by getting in first and appropriating it to itself, the brand can make its own. Many of the best slogans—Colgate's 'Ring of confidence', 'Persil washes whiter', 'Oxo gives a meal man appeal', above all, perhaps, 'Guinness is good for you'—are simple statements of USPs.

The problem with USPs, it seems to me, is that while they can undoubtedly be very powerful and succinct statements, they are very limiting. Most brands, especially in fields other than the packaged goods for which the theory was developed, are potentially far more complex than the USP theory suggests, and a USP approach limits the opportunity for giving the brand a genuine personality. Similarly, a USP based on a physical characteristic is extremely vulnerable, in these days of increasingly strict advertising controls, to successful competitive product development, which would render the key claim untenable. As we have seen, in recent years Persil has found it increasingly difficult to sustain its traditional whiteness claim—which it was allowed to make 30 years ago whether it was true or not. (It usually was, in fact.)

The fact remains that it is undoubtedly important for an ad to have at its core a more or less straightforward main benefit that is being offered to the consumer. It is, however, a matter of judgement as to how explicitly and vigorously this is presented.

The physical benefit of Oxo is, I suppose, that it is a very easy and acceptable way of making gravy or flavouring stews and casseroles. Their highly successful current TV campaign, however, relies almost entirely on the relationships between the members of a distinctive, but quite ordinary, family in which individuals just happen to put Oxo into the meals they produce. The physical benefit is implicit in everything, but hardly explicit at all, and the benefit actually communicated is emotional.

2. *Say what you have to say in as few words as possible*
While this maxim applies especially to press, it can be extended to other media, too. At its best it leads to the best sort of poster—those for Guinness, Polo, Benson & Hedges—where hardly any words are needed. At its worst, it produces the sort of fractured English which has full stops in the middle of very terse sentences. Like this. All staccato. Ignoring grammar. And difficult to read. It seems to be assumed by many advertisers that this sort of thing makes it simpler for the (presumably illiterate) public to take in, but I have never seen any evidence whatever to prove that it is better than, or even as good as, writing in slightly more formal English.

The other side of the argument, that long copy is not only possible but often desirable, is most strongly put by David Ogilvy, founder of Ogilvy & Mather, and probably the greatest living English (Scottish, actually) ad man. His argument derives largely from direct response and direct mail advertising, where he is adamant that long copy, full of information, readably presented, is essential. I do not, myself, believe that it is impossible to write short direct response ads: there is no doubt, however, that there are plenty of highly successful very long ads in this field.

What is more questionable, however, is whether it is possible to extend the direct response approach indiscriminately. It seems to me that this is largely a reflection of the consumers' need for information.

Long copy can work, for example, for durables, especially cars, for financial services and products (you *need* both information and reassurance), and for slightly unfamiliar holiday products like Club Méditerranée. The process is taken to its limits by Epson's distinctive and witty campaign for computer printers. It is less easy to see it working for low-information products like, say, custard powder—though the popularity of recipes in food ads suggests at least one justification for longer copy even here. Interestingly, some of the relatively up-market brands of spirits—The Macallan, Glenmorangie—have been talking at length recently in their print ads.

For me, the length of copy is largely determined by the complexity of the message to be communicated—as well, of course, as by the limitations of space or time. In general, words should not be wasted: they should be used if they are needed. What is more, there is no harm in writing English. It is only fair to say, in conclusion, that the short versus long copy debate has gone on since at least the twenties.

3.   *There is no place for humour in advertising*

This was an *obiter dictum* of a great American copywriter, Claude Hopkins, and strongly supported by David Ogilvy. Hopkins went on to say that nobody buys from a clown. It is easy to see his point, especially on the basis of the USA direct response market in which he mainly worked: Americans, far more than Europeans, expect to be sold a product, in advertising as anywhere else. The only problem is that to make it a meaningful rule it would be necessary to find a way of drawing a line between humour (forbidden) and wit (encouraged).

The real problem, though, is that the basis of Hopkins's argument is demonstrably untrue. It is untrue in selling, where any visitor to a street market like London's Petticoat Lane will see humour being used to sell, very effectively. It is untrue, too, in advertising, where there are plenty of examples of successful use of humour. Hamlet cigars, Cadbury's Creme Eggs, Heineken, the telephone service, Persil liquid, Ferrero Rocher are all recent examples of successful, humorous advertising.

An article by David Stewart-Hunter of Saatchi[*] reviewed the available (limited) research, and discussed examples of both successful and unsuccessful humour, before arriving at the inevitable conclusion that you can't generalize about it. When it works, it works. Even, for example, for financial products, where the Leeds Permanent Building Society's long running TV series with George Cole as Arthur Daly is clearly effective.

The one real contra-indication to the use of humour is for campaigns which are to be used internationally. Except for very basic slapstick, humour travels uncertainly.

4.   *Give the consumer credit for some intelligence*

This is a 'rule' with which I do wholeheartedly agree. Granted you may be advertising to a sector of the market which does not have a university degree or even two GCSEs, you still have to recognize that few of them are illiterate morons. Many of them are likely to have a great deal more sharp, down-to-earth commonsense than you have. Research shows very clearly that people

Admap, May 1985, p. 268.

recognize when they are being spoken down to, and they resent it. If they resent it, they are not going to buy your product.

An extension of this is that people do not like being insulted. They like being flattered, or congratulated, or encouraged: they certainly do not like being put down. The assumption that they do not know how to run their house properly, or how to feed their families, or manage their money, is likely to lead to rejection. Nowadays, too, the suggestion that a woman's role consists entirely of slaving over the cooker, the kitchen sink and the washing is certain to irritate a significant number of people, though it is still a real enough situation for the majority of women.

5. *Be original*
To succeed, advertising has to attract attention. It can do this by using specifically attention-getting devices—enormous headlines in the press, rolls of drums, whistles or other unusual sounds on TV or radio, flashing lights on TV or cinema—but these are likely to be artificially imposed in the context of an ad.

It is far more desirable to develop a style of advertising that fits the brand and has a relevant built-in attention-getting effect—in other words *advertising* that is original and unusual, not just technical fireworks. The effects may be visual or verbal, in sound or music; they may be obtained by trick photography, by the use of Quantel computer trickery, or by clever selection of elements of sound or picture: Ariston's use of a Nintendo-style soundtrack to achieve an (allegedly) hypnotic effect, a rash of commercials using operatic arias, the use of music by Hamlet cigars, Rutger Hauer in the Guinness campaign, the talking animals in the Electricity commercials.

Certainly, originality is desirable. There are, however, two caveats. First, originality for its own sake is even worse than the unattached attention-getting device: it can actually detract from the product and the message of the ad. Secondly, with long-established products it may put off loyal users if you start messing about with 'their' brand and what they believe it to stand for. For brands like this, originality may lie in very small adjustments to an established formula.

Campaigns like Howell Henry's First Direct TV launch are widely criticized—I think rightly—for being so obsessed with being noticed that the message that is supposed to be communicated almost disappears.

Print advertising
The 'long copy' debate is basically a print debate, though it can apply to radio and, to an extent, TV. Other 'rules' are more specifically print rules.

1. *Put 'key' words in headlines*
Someone once worked out that there were about a dozen words which appeared more often than any other in ad headlines, and concluded— slightly illogically—that any ad would be better if it had one or more of them

in the headline. These are words like 'new', 'save', 'win', 'best', 'gain', 'buy', 'now', 'try'. Useful words, certainly, but surely not essential? By all means use them when they are needed or appropriate, but there is no call to construct a headline especially so as to include one or more of them.

2. *Put the promise in the headline*
(Or the 'proposition'.) This is good advice, but, again, not essential. If you have a strong proposition to put to the consumer, it certainly makes sense to draw attention to it as strongly as possible, and the headline *might* be the right place to do it. Equally, however, it might be perfectly reasonable to use a headline that encourages the reader to read on to find out what the proposition is. (Yes, readers can read: it is only a matter of getting them to want to.)

A special case where the promise—and, indeed, the price—usually does appear in the headline is in direct response advertising of the 'offer' type which is so prevalent in the Sunday colour supplements. You rarely see a direct response ad which does not put a clear offer—and the price—in its headline. It clearly works as a formula, and it is reasonable to assume that alternatives have been tested and found inferior.

3. *Keep the headline short*
(This applies, too, to copy on posters.) This makes good sense, as a headline is largely a device to put part of the message across and lure the reader into reading the rest. But long headlines can work perfectly well, if they are appropriate.

4. *Lay the ad out logically*
A good deal of research has been done to show how most people tend to scan advertisement pages in newspapers and magazines. In general, they tend to follow a more or less logical sequence, starting at the top with a headline (assuming it is there) and ending up in the bottom right-hand corner.

Once you have discovered this fact, it is rather easy to produce 'formula' ads. In the late sixties there was a joke among London agencies that all J. Walter Thompson press ads had a headline (sometimes, greatly daring, reversed out of the illustration), a squared-up half-tone illustration, a few lines of copy, and a pack shot in the bottom right-hand corner. Very logical, very simple, and ultimately very sterile: but easy to read and take in, if you wanted to.

It is, obviously, extremely easy to get stereotyped in layout: it is the art director's job to avoid this, without doing excessive damage to the way the reader will want to take in the ad. There is a tendency in much recent magazine advertising, especially for young adult target groups, to make layouts very busy and 'bitty'. This is in line with the editorial style of the magazines, and with design fashions, but it certainly doesn't make for easy reading. If, having read this, you pick up a magazine targeted at younger teenagers—for example, one of the pop music or video games magazines—the layout is so 'reader-unfriendly' that it seems clear that the criteria for 'correctness' in a layout need, at least, some re-evaluation for this target audience.

Perhaps all one can really say about layout, in this sense, is that you have to remember that in Europe and America we read from left to right and top to bottom, in that order. In Arabic, it is different, and in Chinese or Japanese different again. There is no real point in doing Chinese layouts for Western audiences. They will just get lost.

5. *Reversed out copy looks good*
Yes, it does: and that is why art directors love it—though it has only been fashionable for about 20 years. The only problem is that it can be terribly difficult to read—and you do want them to read the copy don't you?

There are, I suppose, two simple rules about reversing out. First, always do it out of a dark tone, preferably a uniform one. Second, never do it in type of less than about 10-point; and even this is really too small in newspapers.

6. *Double page spreads are best*
All art directors like to do colour double page spreads in magazines. They look super in the portfolio: far better than all those grotty 10 cm doubles that sold so many army surplus sleeping bags. So the temptation to use them, which can best be resisted by the media group, is great. The problems of using them are, too, quite large. It is notoriously difficult to design a DPS that really works as a whole without getting lost somewhere in the gutter between the two pages. The problem is, quite literally, how to bridge the gap and tie the whole thing together. It is very easy to lose half a letter of the headline, or a key element of the illustration, unless both typographer and art director are very careful; and it is very easy, too, to find you have produced two separate, incomplete pages of advertising with no real link between them.

7. *Only a full page will do*
Actually, very often, a full page is not the best size to use. This is, again, a media argument almost as much as a creative one, but there is a lot of evidence, mainly from direct response, that cost-effectiveness decreases over a certain size of ad. Certainly in broadsheet media like the *Daily Telegraph*, a 35 cm × 4 col space is likely to be every bit as good as the far more expensive full page, not least because it is set into news matter, rather than merely facing it.

Small spaces can certainly be made to work. They need strong headlines and very selective copy. They usually have to have small, drawn illustrations. There is very little room for waste or error. If anything, they need greater attention to detail.

8. *Photographs are better than illustrations: pictures are better than words*
We are told—usually by un-bought artists—that we live in an increasingly visual culture. Perhaps we do: I thought we had already had eyes for several

million years. What this is taken to mean is that people find it easier to interpret and take in pictures than words. This *may* be true, but I doubt if it is, just
so long as the words are right. Certainly, it is no justification in itself for rul-
ing out ads consisting entirely of words.

Photographs are, certainly, an idiom we are now all used to. They tend to
have a quality of immediacy and interest and they are, generally, believed.
But although techniques exist for playing elaborate tricks with the camera,
photography, as used in ads, is generally a very homogeneous medium. A
photograph is a photograph. So an illustration may offer far wider possibilities for the art director to achieve special effects and a distinctive style. It is
just a question of knowing when to use it: not, I would think, for food, or,
usually, cosmetics; but illustration appears to be more successful than photography for fashion, and it can clearly be used for most other types of
product.

Film

Most of the great advertising folklore is, as I have said, print-based. TV is a
post-war medium—and commercial TV is less than 40 years old in Europe—
while cinema advertising required the stimulus of TV to bring it alive.

In theory, film is the most powerful advertising medium, because it can
successfully integrate words and sounds and pictures to achieve its effect. It
follows, therefore, that the most successful film advertising is likely to be that
which best integrates audio and visual elements.

1. *Music is critical*

Not all commercials have music, but most do, even if it is only background
music bought from a library of such material.

In the early days of commercial TV, lots of ads were written as jingles—
composers such as Johnny Johnson in the UK made a fortune out of them—
and the best were sung by kids and ad people all over the country. Famous
voices sang them: who could forget Bing Crosby crooning 'We're going
well... you can be sure of Shell!'?

I *think* the use of music in commercials is getting subtler. Certainly, it is trying to create atmosphere rather than just a memorable sing-along tune.
Thanks to Bob Payton, formerly of JWT and now proprietor of a popular
restaurant chain, agency creative people are far more aware of the value of
music, in this pop-dominated world, in talking to specific generations.

Thus, ads targeted at 40-year-old housewives started to use hit tunes first
from the fifties and now the late sixties. With a revival in fifties and sixties pop
music, this has now gone further, to the use of hits of this period to sell to the
under 25s: the Levi's 501 commercials of the mid-eighties, with songs by Sam
Cooke and Percy Sledge, are now classic examples. Recently, too, there have
been a number of commercials using operatic arias, mostly by Puccini, and
this trend was endorsed by the 1990 World Cup's choice of *Nessun Dorma* as
its TV theme music. While this has coincided with a revival of interest in

opera among the 'chattering classes', I'm not at all sure that it means a lot to the average person, except, simply, as dramatic music.

Music, obviously, can make a mood, build familiarity and memory, make associations for a brand. I must confess, though, that constant use of 'The Four Seasons' by several different advertisers has undermined my enjoyment of Vivaldi considerably!

2. *Quick cuts are readily understood*
TV commercial production styles have developed rapidly, often in advance of film or TV programme techniques. In particular, the speed of cutting from one scene to another has accelerated considerably, so that commercials from the late fifties or early sixties now look incredibly slow. This technique has moved—to an extent—into TV programmes and film, and agency TV producers and creative groups tend to assume, automatically, that quick-cut films are understood and followed by everybody with complete ease. Since research into commercials consistently shows that a substantial proportion of viewers have difficulty with this type of commercial, this seems to be a mildly over-optimistic assumption.

The tendency has been heightened and intensified by the advent of techniques derived from pop videos—a language with which agency creative people are very familiar, but which can be opaque to anyone over about 25—and sophisticated computer graphics.

Much of the time, this does not matter, because the speed of cutting does nothing to obscure the storyline of the commercial, but occasionally it can lead to total confusion. It is, too, generally clear that younger audiences find it easier to follow quickly-moving commericals. It could, therefore, be the case that, in future, the TV audience will gradually catch up with the TV commercial producers' instincts. Certainly, recent suggestions from the USA that commercials are (in some sense) just as effective when they are abbreviated from 30 to 20 or even 10 seconds could be taken to confirm this. The evidence, however, is slim, and the logical conclusion—the two-second or five-second commercial—seems far away; while so-called 'subliminal' advertising, using flashes of picture or words lasting only fractions of a second, is not only totally unproven as a technique, but banned in most countries where advertising on film is available.

3. *Get the brand name in early—and often*
Alec Monk, formerly international advertising controller at Nestlé, refused to approve any commercial in which the brand name failed to appear in the first seven or eight seconds, and in which it was not repeated several times. The results appear, to me at least, very mechanical: the formula obstructs creativity excessively. There is, however, a fundamental truth embodied in this 'rule'. Too many commercials, especially those following the well-loved technique of building suspense before revealing the brand name, run the risk of losing their viewers long before the brand is identified. To spend

hundreds of thousands of pounds on remaining anonymous is gratuitous folly.

4.   *The consumer likes to identify with the commercial*

It is a reasonable assumption that people will find it easier to accept a product if it appears in a context into which they could fit themselves, being used by people whom they could—or would like to—resemble. Hence all those 'slice-of-life' commercials and cleaned-up kitchen sink dramas, so loved by the Procter & Gamble school of advertising. Hence, too, what Sam Rothenstein, then creative head of Masius, once called 'The wonderful world of telly ad-land, where 30-year-old mothers have two teenaged children' and every suburban semi has the space and furnishings of a Tudor manor house or a film star's Hollywood mansion.

Certainly, for household products, it makes sense to put them in a household setting. Once you have done that it makes sense, again, either to make the household as credible (average, ordinary, pleasant?) as possible or, for the sake of effect, as zany, improbable, and perhaps Addams-like as you can. It is, however, probably a considerable over-simplification to believe that simply by creating a familiar situation in which to demonstrate a product, you automatically win any Brownie points. It seems far more important to me to provide an effective and clear demonstration of those virtues of the product that you are trying to put across than to lose the proposition in the attempt to set up a credible context for it. This is particularly so in the UK where the social class implications of accent, furnishings and behaviour are so complex that it is rarely if ever possible to produce a domestic situation which is really widely acceptable, in the fullest sense of the word.

5.   *TV is ideal for demonstration*

Yes, of course it is. But this does not necessarily mean that a physical demonstration of the product in action is the only way to use TV for a demonstrable product—the Vauxhall Astra 'dog' commercial, in which the proud owner treats the car as a pet, and it reacts appropriately, is, in effect, a demonstration commercial, but the demonstration is done obliquely and with humour.

This illustrates, too, the other key point about demonstration: it does not have to be done every time by the sort of presenter you can find selling vegetable slicers in Selfridges' basement, as a straight, face-to-the-camera spiel.

In short, TV is great for demonstration. But demonstration is rarely enough both to sell a product and to establish a brand. To do this, you need to give the demonstration an extra, memorable, distinctive dimension that can separate your product from all the other demonstrations on TV.

6.   *TV is extremely expensive*

This is not just a media point, because producing commercials is a very expensive business. A 30-second UK-produced commercial can cost anything from £5000 to £300000+ to produce, and there is no guarantee that expensive commercials will be any better than cheaper ones.

There are, in practice, ways of cutting costs—up to a point—but it is difficult to produce a commercial you can be proud of for under around £60000—£70000 in the UK today (1992), and costs of over £150 000 are common. This means that, if you wish even to try the effects of TV in a small area, you have to be sufficiently confident to make a quite substantial investment. The most important consideration in controlling costs is to look for ideas that will be inexpensive to produce—not to try to produce a Ridley Scott Barclay's Bank epic on a shoestring.

During 1983–84 concern began to grow among both agencies and advertisers that production costs were getting out of hand. After an initiative by JWT, a committee was set up under former Treasury mandarin Sir Leon Pliatzky to examine production practices and to recommend action to control cost inflation. This committee reported in early 1987 and its recommendations are summarized in Chapter 11 (page 132).

7. *Cinema commercials must entertain*
A strong and consistent recent trend in cinema advertising by major advertisers—as opposed to local stores and restaurants—has been for films to be more or less entertainment, as well as commercial. Much of this has been done by alcohol advertisers, such as Bacardi and Gordons Gin, but there have been plenty of others. The greater flexibility of the 60-second format has encouraged the trend, and the fact that the cinema audience is known to be there expecting to be entertained is a powerful incentive to provide what it wants.

The point about ads as entertainment is, surely, that they are only any use if the entertainment embodies or springs from a commercial, selling message. The primary purpose must, always, be to sell the product.

Radio
In the UK, radio is still very much a poor relation in the advertising business. For many years, only Radio Luxembourg provided a commercial service, and this was clearly geared to a teenage audience. As a result, radio advertising is still underdeveloped and, perhaps, inferior in quality to that in the USA and other countries with a longer, stronger tradition. I say 'perhaps' because it is very difficult to put one's finger on the difference. Arguably, it lies in the fact that the very best American radio ads are genuinely original and imaginative, and these hardly exist in the UK. It is, also, true that the worst UK radio material is still very amateur, while the majority of US radio ads are, at least, professional. The notable exceptions to this are mostly found in work done by Mel Smith and Griff Rhys-Jones.

So, are there any rules for radio, specifically? I think, perhaps, only two:

1. *Remember it is not TV*
Some years ago Radio Luxembourg carried out a series of presentations to

agencies on the subject of 'visual transfer'—a term used in the USA for the more or less observable fact that most of the TV audience recognize TV commercials from their soundtracks, and that, therefore, using the TV soundtrack, or something close to it, on radio can greatly enhance the coverage and frequency of a TV campaign.

This is, obviously, one way of using radio. But not all radio campaigns are in support of TV, and all TV ads are designed for an additional sense: sight. Inevitably, the use of the soundtrack as a radio commercial involves some loss of effect, and it seems to me that in general a radio commercial is going to have a much better chance of achieving its desired effect if it is created from scratch. Certainly, it may be an adaptation of a TV or press campaign, but it should be specifically a radio treatment.

2.   *Radio means repetition*

Certainly, a radio campaign has to involve frequent spots, in order to build its coverage. This means that, at least for some listeners, a commercial will be heard many times—but these listeners will be few. However, given current UK time costs, it is unrealistic to believe that many listeners will hear a given commercial many times. It is, therefore, I suggest, a mistake to create radio commercials that are likely to need many hearings to achieve their effect. Certainly frequency will be higher than for any but the heaviest TV campaign, but it will hardly be dramatic.

Conclusions

I cannot tell you how to create an ad. A design school can, up to a point, teach you about layout. A competent English teacher may have taught you how to write. The good copywriters of the old school used to wander round council estates with tape-recorders talking to people in their homes to find out how they talked: market research, in the form of group discussions, now provides part of the same service. Really, though, learning to construct good ads is a question of looking at ads, analysing what makes them work, and learning by example: it is observation, experience and practice. It is also the ability to extract from outside advertising elements of music, or pictures, or language, that can bring new inspiration, and new steps forward, to the common currency of advertising.

Having the ideas is merely a matter of having ideas. Some people have lots. Some do not. Most imitate other people's good ideas, which is why so much advertising looks the same.

Having good advertising ideas depends, above all, on being steeped in knowledge of the product. The best ideas grow out of the product and are intimately linked with it. It is very difficult—though not impossible—to make good ads without this close relationship with the product.

The product, in itself, however, is not necessarily enough. To be effectively creative, you need a breadth and depth of visual and verbal references that can provide the raw material for the kind of mental associations that lead to really creative ideas. *Roget's Thesaurus* and a set of back copies of *Zoom* and *Creative Review* are not enough for this: creative people need, ideally, to have wide and varied interests, and a high level of curiosity about almost any subject under the sun.

One final point. Film advertising ideas are usually presented to clients in the form of a storyboard—eight or more drawn pictures pasted down on a board with the written commentary set out beneath. Tony Abraham, chairman of Lansdown Conquest, says, to my mind quite rightly, that if you can draw a commercial accurately on a storyboard, it is a poor commercial, because the film camera should be able to do things no pen or paintbrush can. Every medium has its own unique quality, and every ad should be uniquely tailored to its medium.

9 How to judge advertisements

Everyone is an expert on advertisements. They may know nothing about media selection, or how to produce a TV commercial, or what it costs to buy a 20 cm × 5 cols space in the *Finchley Advertiser*. But they do know a good ad when they see one.

Do not believe a word of it. Just pause to think, and you will realize that if you show the same ad to five different people there is a very fair chance that you will get five different judgements on its quality. There are two very good reasons for this. The first is that an advertisement is, at least in some sense, an artistic creation: people's judgements of art are virtually always subjective, and vary widely from person to person. I happen to like at least some pictures by Mondrian: you may respond to them by asking why anyone should get paid for drawing coloured squares. The other reason is that there are at least some rules for judging advertisements, but most of these are based firmly in the objectives which the ads are trying to achieve: if we do not know what the objectives are, any judgement we may make is without a real foundation.

There are, though, three or four fundamental criteria for judging advertisements which can be applied more or less universally. These are:

– Does the ad make me stop and look at it?
– Is there an original unusual idea in it?
– Does it work as a piece of design?
– Is it relevant to the product?
– Is it easy to understand?

These are all questions which can be asked—and answered—without knowledge of the purpose behind the advertisement. However, the critical questions are specific to the particular ad, and they are the ones that really matter. They are:

– Does this advertisement fit the strategy?
– Will it work?

It is only the answers to these questions that can really enable you to judge an ad, although it will certainly be good supporting evidence if the answers to the earlier questions are favourable. Basically, you can assess ads at two stages: before or after they have been run in the media—('pre-testing' and 'post-testing' are the trade terms).

Pre-testing advertisements and strategy

It has already been pointed out that one of the reasons for setting an advertising strategy is to assess the effectiveness of the advertisement. Advertising must be designed to communicate certain ideas to certain types of people. It does not matter if it communicates totally different ideas to other types of people. This is not relevant. So when the chairperson does not like it, or cannot understand it—or never sees your advertising—and your advertising is designed to appeal (say) to factory supervisors or teenagers, you can treat this judgement with the appropriate degree of (polite) contempt.

If you have set a strategy on the lines described in Chapter 7, the way to begin to judge whether you have a good advertisement is to go to your target group, or at least a few of them, and find out if the ad affects them in the way you intended.

This procedure is, I must admit, a limited one, and it is vulnerable to criticism. All the available methods of doing the job—within a reasonable cost—are artificial, in the sense that there is really no very feasible way of reproducing the circumstances in which people see the advertisements. People see advertisements out of the corner of their eye as they drive along a road or look through a newspaper or magazine; they catch a glimpse of half a TV commercial round their wives' or husbands' broad backsides as the biscuits are brought in during a commercial break. Even if they do as much as glance directly at an advertisement, they rarely stop and read it carefully, making notes as they do so.

But, in contrast, they may partly see the ad in this way a number of times during quite a short period. One of the main ways in which ads work is through this almost insidious process of being partially noticed many times; short of actual tests in the market (see below) there is no way of imitating this process.

What has to be done, then, to discover whether the advertisement is in line with the strategy, almost inevitably involves a form of cheating. The simplest way of getting an answer is to show the advertisement to a number of individuals selected from the target group, or to a group of them, and to get a discussion going about the ad. This needs to be done skilfully, and is usually done by trained researchers, who are adept at getting people to talk and at avoiding asking leading questions—because that is not merely cheating, it will lead to you deluding yourself: in this type of interview people are only too eager to tell you what they think you want to know.

From this kind of research, you can find out a great deal about your ad and your product. The sort of questions it can answer are, for example:

– Is the ad interesting?
– Is the ad intelligible?

– Is it liked or disliked? (It is not disastrous if it is disliked, but there need to be very strong compensating factors.)
– What does it tell them about the product? What will it taste or smell like? What will it cost? Is that good value?
– Do they believe this, or question it?
– Who do they think the product will appeal to? What sort of people will use it? In what circumstances?
– What sort of shops will sell the product?
– What kind of feelings do they get from the ad—cheerful, serious, sad, confident?...
– Might they try the product? Or try it again?

All these questions can help you decide whether the ad is right or whether it needs changing. This is, therefore, particularly helpful to the creative people who produce the ads, as they can get very detailed and constructive ideas about how to improve or modify the advertising.

This type of research can be done on a small scale. You need a minimum of two group discussions (but more are better, and essential if you have a complex target group), or 20-odd individual extended interviews. This research can be set up and carried out very quickly by a competent research agency, and will cost (1992 prices) some £1200 per group or £110–125 per individual interview. These British prices are somewhat lower than those to be found in Continental Europe or the USA, but have risen towards European levels in recent years.

Pre-testing advertising impact
What this sort of research will not have told you is anything about the advertising's ability to stand out and attract attention when it appears in the chosen media. This is something that you may feel a need to be sure of, and it is quite possible to devise tests which will give at least a good indication of the likely impact of the ad in these terms.

There is, however, a theoretical problem. It is perfectly true that an ad is useless if no one notices it. But it is by no means true that an ad which everyone notices is necessarily good—it may be noticed for reasons which are totally irrelevant to the strategy. And, furthermore, the ways in which people take in messages from ads are often almost subconscious. (This is not to say that you can deliberately reach people by advertising 'subliminally', merely that it is quite possible to get a message out of an ad without really being aware of it.)

In addition to the question of impact, the qualitative research so far described has the disadvantage—in many people's eyes—of not being on a large enough scale. Most managers are happier with numbers and measurements than qualitative judgements, and there is, certainly, some risk that a small-scale piece of research will turn out to have been done on a sample of people who are rather atypical of the desired target audience as a whole.

What you gain in depth of information you lose—to an extent—in reliability. Nonetheless, very considerable experience of using groups for this kind of research shows that they do tend to produce very consistent results, even where different researchers cover the same problem.

Nonetheless, to cover these two gaps in the knowledge provided by qualitative small-scale research, there are a number of techniques available to provide more quantified information about people's responses to advertising.

For *print* ads, these are all variations on the basic concept of a 'folder test'. In a folder test, a selection of about half a dozen advertisements, including the ad to be tested, is put in a file folder. This is given to the research respondents to look through. After they have had a reasonable length of time to browse, the folder is taken back and they are asked a series of questions about the ads. Typically, these questions will include the following:

– What products can you remember seeing ads for?
– Then (for each product remembered) what did the ad tell you about the product?
– Can you describe the illustration?
– What else can you remember about it?

In addition, a selection of specific questions about one or more of the products may be asked.

From this sort of questioning, it is possible to draw conclusions about the impact of the ad—was it the first or second mentioned by most people, or did no one mention it at all? Did they remember much detail about it, or merely that it was there? Did the things they told you about the ad or the product correspond at all to what you hoped they would get out of it? Did they describe your ad very well but ascribe it to a competitor's product?

Here, again, the situation is artificial, and the questioning some way removed from the real world. If you think about it, it is pretty unlikely that, if you yourself were reading a magazine, even if you looked quite hard at an ad, you could give a very detailed description of the ad even quite soon afterwards. What is more, because people's short-term and long-term memories operate rather differently, they may well remember something quite different three days later: and the chances are that in the real marketplace it is the longer memory that matters. Further, the *explicit* memory may then be more or less irrelevant. What is likely to matter most when someone is buying your product is a quite vague general impression that it is familiar and that they have heard good of it somewhere: not an explicit memory of an ad. So, although this type of research produces what may be comforting numbers, and can provide reassurance that, in some sense, your ads will be noticed, you need to be rather careful in interpreting the results.

The other available forms of pre-testing for print ads by means of survey research are all elaborations of the folder test—for example, an ad can be inserted into an actual magazine rather than a folder to provide something nearer to the real world. There are, too, a number of experimental ways of carrying out research into magazine ads. Typical of these is the use of hidden cameras linked to some form of eye-scan monitor so that a reader left in a waiting room with a magazine can be watched, to see how the magazine is read and which bits of a particular page or ad are most carefully looked at.

For *filmed* commercials, the standard type of quantified pre-test involves showing a group of commercials in a break in a short film show to which an appropriate sample of people are invited. After the film show a set of questions similiar to those used for the press folder test are asked. In addition, in some systems which have operated from time to time in the UK and elsewhere, there is a procedure whereby people are asked attitude questions about the product before the show and after it, and given the opportunity to select the test product (from a list) as a prize or gift. The testing system then provides measurements of changes in attitudes ('attitude shift') and the product choice ('preference shift') as a result of the film being shown. A further elaboration of this technique is the use by the respondents of computer-linked handsets that can be simply manipulated to show their response throughout the commercial: they can be asked simply to indicate an overall favourable or unfavourable response or to reflect some more specific description of the film—'exciting', 'funny', 'tasteful', etc. This technique *can* be used, also, as part of a smaller scale, group-based pre-test. The output is a set of charts showing how reactions fluctuate through the film. At present, the difficulty lies in understanding how this relates—if at all—to the advertisements' effectiveness in the marketplace.

In itself, the cinema-test technique is as good—or bad—as folder testing for press ads: it has the same clear limitations. What makes it both attractive to users and even more misleading is that the promoters of the technique tend to use a number of methods to produce 'norms' for, in particular, 'preference shift', but also for various attention measures. These 'norms' have been shown to have very little relevance to the commercial's subsequent marketplace performance, even if they are derived solely for the particular brand being advertised, and it is by no means clear what is actually being measured: it is certainly *not* the effectiveness of the commercial in the marketplace. Preference shift measures, too, are heavily influenced by the 'news' content of the advertisements, to the exclusion of other persuasive elements.

'Post-testing'

The obvious test for an advertisement is 'does it sell?' (or 'does it sell more?'). Unfortunately, it is very rarely that this question can be answered precisely. It is unusual, except in the special case of direct response or direct mail, for the advertising to be the only influence affecting sales. And even when it appears to be so, the level of sales is in itself a quite complex measure. It is easy, for example, to say that an advertising campaign failed to increase sales. But it may have succeeded magnificently in preventing sales from falling.

In any event, although a sales measurement is certainly the most desirable way of assessing advertising, it is not informative: it provides no clues as to how the advertising is achieving its success, or how it might be improved. To use advertising properly, it is important to find the answers to these questions.

Measuring sales effects

1. *Direct response*

The simplest way of testing an advertisement's sales effect is by using a direct response ad. In direct response, you can test different ads, different space sizes, different media—at least in theory. In practice, it is more difficult, because the effectiveness of advertisements falls off with frequency of exposure in a particular paper, so you have to be very careful that you are comparing like with like.

The one absolutely clear test is between two ads in identical positions in the same publication, on a 'split run' basis. Even with direct response, it is still not going to be clear, without a long series of tests, *why* the winning ad is best.

2. *Area tests*

It is usual to test an advertising campaign against another campaign, if possible, since this at least gives a reliable standard of measurement. Unfortunately, this is not as easy as it sounds. In principle, it is quite straightforward. You select an area of the country in which you run different advertising from the advertising you run in the rest of the country. You then compare your sales performance in the two areas—usually in terms of the percentage change on the previous years—and you have a measure of which campaign is the more successful. The problems are of two kinds. First, it can be very difficult to find media in which to separate off an area like this: it can be done readily in TV, cinema, poster or local newspapers, but is more difficult in national newspapers or magazines.* Second, the market environment can differ sharply from one area to another, for example, in terms of consumer attitudes to the product, or the competitive situation, or your own sales force's ability. It is important to be sure that your results are not distorted by such factors.

In the UK, and in most European countries, it is difficult to overcome these problems. In the USA, where there is a wide choice of local markets, it is much easier, and experience there has shown that much more reliable results, for all forms of market testing, can be obtained by using a number of markets simultaneously, rather than just a single test.

3. *Other considerations*

In any event, it is unwise to try to measure the sales results of advertising in isolation from other market factors. In particular, the activity of competitors is important. If you are spending less of your market's total advertising

---

*Local and regional advertising in national magazines and newspapers has become more widely available and, at the same time, less expensive.

money than you have market share, and a major competitor is spending significantly more, it is highly probable that you will fail to gain sales. This is not the fault of the advertising content. It is the fault of your budgeting.

Similarly, if you are spending money on advertising and your competitors spend nothing but cut their prices substantially, you are likely to suffer. Again, the advertising is not to blame.

Other measurements

A number of other types of assessment can be made of advertising in the market-place.

1. *Impact measures*

These correspond closely to the 'folder test' type of pre-test. Gallup (in the UK) and Starch (in the USA) used to run so-called 'reading and noting' surveys regularly, in which readers of a magazine are taken through the last issue and questioned about every page—whether they looked at it at all; read some of it; read all of it; etc. This is also applied to all advertisements. The results are presented as a series of measures: 'page traffic' (the percentage of people looking at that page), 'noting' (percentage seeing the ad), 'reading', etc.

The corresponding TV measure, very widely used in the USA but little in the UK, is a telephone survey of the '24-hour recall' type. People are rung up, asked if they watched a particular TV programme yesterday, and questioned about their recall of the commercials that appeared in it.

A rather more general type of assessment, in the same area, is the awareness survey. Here, after a campaign has been running for some time, a sample survey is used, in which questions are asked about the brands in the market in question:

– What brands of (soup, etc.) have you heard of?
– What others?
– Have you heard of any others on this list?
– What brands have you seen advertised lately?

and so on, to establish what media the ads were in, what they said, and similar questions. This type of survey provides a good guide to a build-up of recognition of a product, and some measure of what the advertising is achieving.

2. *Strategy measures*

The most useful—if expensive—measure of the effect of advertising, however, is the measurement of changes in people's attitudes to the product. This can provide a good indication of what the advertisement is achieving in terms of communication—what people are getting out of it.

The technique is simple. Before any advertising is run, you have a 'benchmark' survey, in which questions cover key attitudes to the product. Some time—probably three to six months—after the advertising starts, a second survey repeats these questions, and changes are plotted. After a series of such surveys, developments begin to show, and changes in the emphasis of the advertising can be planned.

A currently popular but expensive variant of this technique is the continuous tracking study. This technique, particularly associated with the Millward Brown research agency, involves a continuous survey with the results accumulated on a rolling four or eight-week basis, so as to relate changes in awareness and attitudes very precisely to changes in your own and competitive brands' advertising activity.

Millward Brown use their own proprietary system of analysis—a form of mathematical modelling—to translate the data for each individual brand into a so-called 'awareness index'; and many of their clients have fallen into the tempting habit of using this single number as a measure of the effectiveness of a commercial or campaign, rather than taking the trouble to make a more detailed study of the data underlying the index. There is now a sometimes acrimonious debate in progress in the market research journals, in which the various participants are questioning, on the one hand, the methodology by which the index is calculated and, on the other, its meaning in relation to the advertising. This argument will run for some years.

3. *Econometrics*

Econometrics is the science of mathematical analysis of economic phenomena. As applied to advertising, it can, in theory, be used to separate out from a product's sales the effects of different aspects of marketing activity, so as to assess the contribution of advertising. Great claims are made for the technique, by the few people who are selling services of this kind.

Econometrics relies on statistical analysis, chiefly of a kind called multiple regression, which is designed to establish correlations (and—hopefully—the causal sequence) between sales and advertising, price changes, promotions, competitive activity, etc. . . . Once this can be done, the 'model' of the market so created can be manipulated in order to try to assess the likely effect of different levels of advertising expenditure or different patterns of spending—heavy bursts or lighter-weight 'drip' patterns for example—on sales.

Fairly unsophisticated versions of this type of procedure are not new, and there is at least one commercial service in the USA, the Hendry Corporation, which has marketed a budget-setting system based on this type of analysis for many years. In the past 20 years, however, there has been considerably more activity and publicity for econometrics in the UK, leading to often vigorous debate in specialist magazines such as *Admap*. This debate has been, for the most part, concerned with the degree to which the (undoubtedly) rather crude models used by econometricians can be used for fine tuning of one aspect of the marketing budget, on the basis of figures which critics regard as of dubious significance.

To my mind, the major contribution of econometrics to our understanding of advertising so far has been to establish the relatively marginal effect of advertising expenditure level changes in comparison with price changes:

typically, price movements relative to competition seem to account for as much as 70–80 per cent of the changes in brand shares in a market. (This should not discourage us from advertising. Cutting prices is a *very* expensive pastime.)

The best demonstration of the present scope of econometric analysis in advertising is provided by the biennial IPA Advertising Effectiveness Awards competition and the winning case histories published by the IPA under the series title *Advertising Works*. As will be seen from the six volumes produced so far and—no doubt—their successors, many (not all) of the winning entrants use econometrics to establish that advertising is responsible for a specific sales effect (or part of it). This is fine and dandy, as far as it goes. To those of us working at this particular neurotic coal-face, it is very cheering to know that (at least in a number of prize-winning cases) advertising *does* work. Indeed, some of the cases show that different amounts of advertising 'work' differently.

The problem, it seems to me, is to go much beyond this. Yes, I can reassure management that it is worth spending money on advertising, because I can demonstrate, with good numbers, that it produces results. Perhaps, I can then proceed to manipulate these numbers, and use the findings to put forward more precise proposals as to the level of budget, or the way in which the budget should be deployed—in different media, over different periods of time, etc. I am still, however, none the wiser as to *how* and *why* my advertising works. I am still confined, for the most part, to knowing that if I throw advertising money at the market, sales will be higher than if I do not. (Just occasionally I may be able to say with reasonable confidence that a particular advertisement or campaign is quantifiably better at generating sales than another. The Beecham Group's AMTES experiments tend to show, indeed, that qualitative differences between advertisements or campaigns are likely to be *far* more important than quite large differences in advertising weight.)

What is needed is a means to link the essentially mechanistic—though technically quite tricky—process of econometric analysis to other information from the marketplace about responses to advertising. To my knowledge, only one major attempt to do this has been published in the UK. This is work done by the market research agency Millward Brown in conjunction with Leo Burnett and Cadburys. Millward Brown are pioneers and—to an extent— specialists in tracking studies (see above); and they have linked information on awareness from these studies to a model of advertising decay rates based on the Adstock concept, developed by Simon Broadbent of Leo Burnett, to develop a model that attempts to link advertising expenditures and awareness to market share. This is, obviously, a fairly limited model in its own right: further, the published reports seem to me to include sufficient logical uncertainties, and the model to require so much manipulation to deal with each individual case, to raise considerable doubts about its real value. The attempt, however, must be applauded as a genuine effort to go beyond the sterile and largely one-dimensional business of finding mathematical relationships between sales and advertising.

There is, obviously, quite a lot of work being done in the relatively straightforward field of identifying advertising's effect on sales through econometric methods, though it is still largely confined to about half-a-dozen large agencies and a similarly limited group of client companies. Its value is still constrained by the wide gap that exists between most econometricians and most managers, whether in client companies or the agencies. Econometricians are not, in my experience, very good at translating their findings into terms readily understood by those without at least A-level mathematics and statistics: those who are running their own consultancies also have an understandable reluctance to go into the full details of their equations and the modifications that may be required to fit equation and data more closely together.

So far, therefore, the findings have tended to be of more obvious value to the accountant than to those responsible for planning advertising. Econometrics appears to help in determining budgets, and in the deployment of media expenditure—but when an econometrician tells me I should adopt a 'drip' pattern on TV rather than a 'burst' pattern (see page 115), I want to know *why*. And the answer to my question, to be useful, should not be 'because my calculations show that this is so, and it will save your client £X to do it', but, 'because the way your market works is thus; and your advertising— or at least the campaign you are running—affects it so'. We are nowhere near that yet.

One further caveat. We all now have personal computers, of increasing power and sophistication, on our desks, and there are already proprietary do-it-yourself econometrics and expert system kits available on the market. In the present state of the art, the temptation to use these without—at the very least—first having had some academic training in econometric techniques should be resisted. There are lies, damned lies, and statistics, but there are no lies more damned than those created by statisticians who don't know what they're about.

In the first edition of this book, I wrote that the use of econometrics in advertising was roughly at the stage before the square edges of the first wheel were rounded off. Some 12 years later, we are still, I believe, trying to get our mind round the concept of the axle.

So, could you judge?

Certainly, it is not as easy as it looks. The techniques exist to answer some questions, but not all. No one can *predict* the sales success of an ad, and it is often difficult to measure the success even afterwards. What you *can* do, though, is use research to improve your advertising, by understanding how people react to it. That alone is a very valuable exercise.

10 Media: where the ideas can be seen

A wealth of choice

Every advertisement has to appear in some advertising medium or other, even if it is only a roadside sign or a newsagent's window. The range of media available in a sophisticated industrial society is very wide, both in terms of different types of medium—print, film, indoor, outdoor—and in terms of individual media of each type. In the UK, there are 12 national daily newspapers and 11 national Sundays, and hundreds of local papers; 15 commercial TV stations (but at present only one national network, using two channels), over 80 local radio stations and two semi-national; there are about 2000 consumer magazines, which can be divided into a number of different categories by audience and interest group, and over 4000 trade and technical magazines; around 1650 cinema screens, mainly in two large national chains, carry advertising; there are numerous poster sites, ranging from 'supersites' down to 'Adshel' bus shelters, not to mention illuminated signs, bus sides and cards inside buses and London underground carriages; then there are theatre brochures and sports programmes, football grounds, racecourses and other sporting venues; at least two firms operate 'truck posters', and you can put ads in or on taxis; not to mention direct mail, and electronic media such as Prestel. There is even an enterprising individual who has put ads on cows grazing beside the London to Brighton railway line, while sandwich-boards and street criers are perhaps the oldest media of all. Then there are balloons, 'blimps', milk bottles, lorry sides... and so on.

Within all these media, too, there are choices to be made: choices of size, of position, of timing, frequency and duration of appearance; choices between colour and monochrome. No wonder specialist media departments and even media buying businesses have had to be established, and a vast body of research into every aspect of media has been undertaken. On the face of it, it is a business ripe for computerization, and, indeed, a great deal of work is done with computers to analyse media research data and make the construction of media schedules more effective. There are few definitive answers, so that the skill, experience, judgement and negotiating skill of the media people remain vital ingredients in a successful advertising campaign. In this chapter, I want to set out, as far as possible, the key elements in planning a media schedule. Inevitably, this will involve looking from time to time at individual media, as each has its own characteristics, requirements, and available research resources. However, as far as possible, I aim to keep discussion of the peculiarities of the main media to the more specialized chapters which follow, and to confine the discussion in this chapter to reasonably broad principles.

Where do you start?
Usually, in practice, you start with a budget. As we have seen (Chapter 2), it is not the ideal way to start, but it is a fact of life, and the size of the budget does, to a significant extent, serve to set limits on the opportunities open to the media planner. £50 000 does not go very far in TV, except on one or two small regional stations; it is quite difficult, as the cigarette companies find, to spend £1 million plus on a brand without using TV at all: if you only have a few hundred pounds to spend there are few press media in which you can consider full pages or even moderately large sizes. Even with a substantial sum, the money available can buy you very different amounts of contact with the public: in conventional media analysis terms of coverage of adults and opportunities to see (OTS) an ad, £300000 could buy you, nationally, in early 1992, the 'campaigns' in the main media which are shown in Table 10.1.

Table 10.1   What £300000 can buy: adults, national, end-1991

	(1) Coverage %	(2) Average OTS	Index of coverage and frequency (1×2)
National Sundays	66	2.4	158
National dailies	62	2.6	161
TV	60	2.5	150
General women's magazines	58	3.0	174
Posters	46	13.9	639
Radio	36	3.5	126
Cinema	14	1.8	25

(Source: Lansdown Conquest)
Note: This table is highly misleading – see pages 108–109.

Money, then, is a limiting factor. The other limiting factor is the creative one. Decisions about which (broad) media to recommend are basically joint decisions between the creative and media groups in the agency—albeit with, usually, a strong voice from both client and account executive. Certainly, if the creative team has strong views on which medium to use, and can justify this by demonstrating a really effective approach using that medium, it can help to cut a lot of corners.

The inter-media decision
The first decision that has to be taken, then, is which medium—or combination of media—to use. In taking this decision, there are eight main factors to be taken into account:

– the money available;
– the creative group's preference and past experience;
– the client's preference and past experience;
– the target audience;
– the type of product;
– the activity of competitors;
– the likely reactions of the retail trade;
– the apparent relative effectiveness of the available candidate media.

Each of these factors can, and usually does, act as a limiting factor, so that when each has been taken into account the major decision may be reasonably clear, even if not conclusive. This will, however, still leave open the possibilities of using 'fringe' media to fill in gaps in the campaign or, indeed, of making an imaginative use of an alternative medium which would otherwise be discarded.

1.   *Money*
This has been briefly discussed already. It is probably fair to say that you cannot really hope to run an adequate national TV campaign in the UK for less than about £750000; or a national poster campaign for less than £250000. Beyond these very broad constraints, however, there is almost limitless flexibility: you can do almost anything on a small-scale, trial, or regional basis.

2.   *Creative preference*
Again, there is no real need to comment—except that it is the media planner's job both to discourage the creative group from trying to produce massive, spectacular ads when the budget is minimal, and to keep them aware of new ideas and ways of using the media. It is the media department of the agency that is constantly exposed to the approaches of media salespeople, who may well be offering interesting new ideas—occasionally. The sort of examples that have appeared in recent years include, in a variety of media, the following:

– the use by Trusthouse Forte of L-shaped and U-shaped ads in national newspapers as a means of increasing the impact of their line-drawn hotel 'street' campaign;
– the use of a series of different posters on electrically-changed poster sites to tell a story;
– the spectacular supersite poster: a car stuck to a poster site by Araldite adhesive;
– topping and tailing TV commercial breaks;
– the use of posters in and around agricultural markets to target farmers;

– series of posters on LRT escalators;
– large-scale 'teaser' campaigns on TV.

3. *The client's preference*

The client, whose money it is, has the final say. If a particular medium is wanted, the agency has to listen. The client is right very often, but sometimes can be demonstrably wrong—there is not enough money to do a proper job, or the medium reaches the wrong target audience. Then it is the agency's job to argue—rationally, I hope: there are plenty of facts available about media audiences.

Most brands, in fact, come to an agency with a history of past advertising, perhaps in a variety of media. From this, it may be possible to determine clearly which media work best for the brand, and this, obviously, must influence any new plans. (Though you have to remember that an 'unsuccessful' medium may just have been misused in previous attempts.)

4. *The target audience*

The target audience is, of course, a primary consideration. If you are advertising to teenage girls, you do not use *Woman's Weekly* (which has the oldest readership of the four big weeklies) or buy TV spots during *News at Ten*. However, decisions are rarely as simple as that. A housewife audience can be reached (for example) through TV, daily or Sunday newspapers, women's weekly or monthly magazines, radio, local newspapers, posters. . . .

5. *Type of product*

The type of product can often dictate, to an extent, the media to be used. The context of the particular medium, and the atmosphere it can create, can affect responses to the advertising. Some media refuse, or are legally not allowed, to carry ads for certain products. A newspaper, because it is a 'news' medium, may seem appropriate for a sale or a new product's launch, where a magazine might not. Most grocery store advertising in the UK appears on Wednesday or Thursday, in advance of the major grocery shopping days of Friday and Saturday, but for groups of smaller, local grocers, like Mace, which have a through-the-week shopping pattern, advertising on Monday or Tuesday, or even on Sunday, makes sense.

Family products tend to be advertised, if possible, on TV; women's products in women's magazines. There are still few general men's magazines in the UK, though male readers dominate specialist sectors like motoring and sports magazines, so it can be difficult to get wide coverage of an exclusive male audience, should you want to, without putting your ad into a rather specialized editorial context.

6. *Competitive activity*

There are, basically, two philosophies about competitors' media selection: to compete in the same media, because 'we must be seen to compete' or because it is the only really possible medium or (even) because 'they must know something'; or to try to avoid the competition and to 'dominate' a reasonable alternative medium.

(This idea of media 'domination' is an important one which you will certainly meet again. Like most advertising jargon it is a slight misnomer, since it almost always means, at most, that your advertising is the main advertising at that time, in that medium, for that product category. It *can* be taken to extremes, as when Woolworths took every ad in the *Daily Mirror,* or Fisons every ad in *The Times.*)

7. *The retail trade*

The reactions of the retail trade are hardly vital to the success of the advertising—if the salesforce is competent. However, the promise of TV advertising can still be a potent influence, and certain of the daily newspapers and TV contractors can provide a merchandising service which can be quite effective in stimulating some sectors of the retail trade—notably the confectioner/ newsagent/tobacconist group. On a rather higher level, one or two monthly magazines such as *Vogue* and *Good Housekeeping* can do a good merchandising job in department stores.

8. *Relative effectiveness*

This is, really the $64000 question, and the one where the evidence is least helpful. The reason for this is quite simple. As has been made clear in Chapters 6 and 9, no one is really agreed as to how advertising works; or how, and by what research means, to demonstrate that it *has* worked. It is, therefore, extremely difficult, *a priori*, to demonstrate that a single medium is successful, let alone that one medium is superior to another. No one has devised a research method, short of market trials, that can compare different media— and even such tests have their pitfalls.

That said, it is more or less generally accepted that TV is the most powerful medium available, being capable of building awareness and understanding of a product's advertising more broadly and faster than other media. This, however, presupposes that there is enough money available to do a proper job on TV. Beyond this there is little agreement, and the women's weekly magazines, for example, have argued strongly in recent years that their particular editorial qualities and high coverage of a female audience make them a superior medium even to TV for many products in, particularly, food and toiletry fields.

The fact is, as we shall see, that different media do tend to be rather better for different things—you cannot get a lot of information into a 30-second TV commercial, for example.

The technical problem facing the media planner is, in fact, rather more dramatic. Media costs are usually assessed in terms of 'cost per thousand': the number of pence (or pounds) it takes to reach an audience of 1000 (adults, housewives, men under 45 or whatever) with a given ad or campaign. The trouble is that what is measured differs from medium to medium, and, therefore, cost measurements differ almost completely between, say, TV and posters in what they are costs of. In TV, the cost is based on TV Ratings (TVRs),[*] which are the percentage of households in which the TV is turned on to ITV at the time the ad is run; in press, the cost is per thousand readers (or, occasionally, circulation) of the given publication; in cinema, it is based on audience sizes; in posters, on people passing the poster and, therefore, able to see it. Comparing these different measures is an advanced case of adding apples to oranges to cows—which makes the table on page 105 a highly misleading and dangerous animal.

One medium or several?

The objective of media planning is to ensure that a reasonably large proportion of the target audience (this is called 'coverage') sees the advertising a sufficient number of times (this is called 'frequency'). Obviously, it is a matter of judgement just what coverage, and what frequency to aim at—especially when you remember that the type of 'reach' being measured differs from medium to medium.

Common sense says that it is unlikely that one exposure to an ad will have any effect. Research by London Weekend Television, however, has shown that light ITV viewers, who can be expected to see a given commercial very few times, are just as likely to recognize it as those who should have seen it several times. While this is not measuring the effectiveness of the advertising, merely memory of it, it is possibly indicative. Research on visual memory, moreover, shows that recognition of pictures, after one quite short exposure, is normally very high over quite a long period. It is generally accepted—but only as a rule of thumb—that an average of two-and-a-half to three OTS (opportunities to see) is a fairly minimal level for a burst of TV advertising. (This is equivalent to some 200 TVRs, for a coverage of 70 per cent and, therefore, an OTS frequency of 2.9, since OTS is equal to TVRs divided by coverage.) It is only fair to say, though, that work by some econometricians (see page 103) has suggested that optimum rates of TV advertising require far less frequency than this, at least for well-established brands.

For press campaigns, which at least appear to be cheaper, a rather higher frequency of contact is usually aimed at: five, six or more OTS.

The need to use more than one medium, though, arises more usually from considerations of coverage, or from the nature of the campaign. It may be, to take the latter first, that a TV commercial needs to be supported by a rather more informative press campaign. Or that the campaign has two objectives: an information and persuasion job, to be done in TV or press, and a reminder job which may best be done in posters.

As far as coverage is concerned, this comes out of the definition of the target group and the media available to reach it. There is a continuous debate in media circles, for example, about how to reach light ITV viewers, who tend

[*]In the USA, Gross Rating Points (GRPs).

to be concentrated among better-off, and to an extent younger, people. If your target audience includes a substantial proportion of light viewers, but your campaign is on TV, you may need to supplement TV with suitable press or perhaps cinema advertising to reach this group. Similarly, while your prime audience may be, in demographic terms, the cinema audience, the size of the audience and the frequency of cinema-going are sufficiently low for you almost certainly to need to supplement a cinema campaign with selected press, probably magazine, media.

Which leads, inevitably, to the question: what is a desirable level of coverage, and how should this relate to frequency? Assuming a reasonable sum of money is available, I believe that, in general, coverage is the first priority, but that it is reasonable to start preferring frequency once coverage tops about 65 per cent of a 'difficult' target audience or 75–80 per cent of an 'easy' one. (Men under 30 are 'difficult', C2 housewives aged 25–50 are 'easy', for example.) It is, however, very much a matter of judgement how far it is desirable to pursue coverage at all costs. Clearly a public service campaign must, within reason, aim for virtually complete coverage. Few commercial campaigns can justify aiming far above 85 per cent unless, of course, they define their target audience as (say) 'readers of *Vogue*'.

The intra-medium decision

Intra-medium decisions—where to put the ads within a chosen medium or media group—allow for a rather different form of judgement, and have available rather more coherent research standards. The decisions involved are of three kinds:

– the choice of publication or radio/TV station;
– the choice of size or length of spot;
– the precise choice of position in the medium.

1.   *Choice of individual medium*

This type of choice depends chiefly on the cost effectiveness of the individual medium against the target audience or, in the case of TV and radio, the relative importance to the brand's objectives of different regions of the country.

Data from readership surveys make it possible to measure cost per thousand readers for most major publications, not merely against the adult population as a whole but against sub-groups of the population. This can most readily be done with the aid of a computer, and if your agency does not have the facilities, several of the media owners and one or two computer bureaux have suitable programs available on a fee basis. Usually, the media planner attributes importance weightings to different demographic groups in the population, and the computer is asked to rank media or groups of media against them in order of cost per thousand. The process can be extended to provide different ways of achieving specific targets of coverage and frequency against a given group of people. A typical cost-ranking might look like those in Tables 10.2 and 10.3.

On the basis of this type of analysis, the planner can then apply his or her judgement—of the suitability of individual publications for the product, and of the type of deal that it might be possible to negotiate—to select the final mix of publications. The cost-ranking is a guide to scheduling, not a tablet of stone.

Table 10.2   A cost-ranking for all women aged 18–35

Publication	Cost page Colour £	Cover '000s	Cover %	Cost per '000	CPT rank
TOTAL AUDIENCE		11 990	100		
Woman's Own	25 400	2 374	19.8	1 070	14
Bella	16 500	2 313	19.3	713	1
Take A Break	15 000	1 800	15.0	833	4
Best	18 900	1 676	14.0	1 128	15
Woman	20 500	1 661	13.8	1 234	21
Prima	15 225	1 538	12.8	990	11
Cosmopolitan	12 520	1 316	11.0	951	8
Me Magazine	18 200	1 152	9.6	1 580	27
Chat	9 500	1 015	8.5	936	6
Good Housekeeping	11 840	945	7.9	1 253	22
Essentials	8 900	938	7.8	949	7
Family Circle	10 750	934	7.8	1 151	17
Woman's Weekly	14 300	794	6.6	1 801	31
She	7 010	776	6.5	903	5
Just Seventeen	8 150	705	5.9	1 156	18
Woman & Home	9 000	613	5.1	1 468	26
'19'	4 855	595	5.0	816	3
Looks	5 775	590	4.9	979	9
Hello	5 670	578	4.8	981	10
Woman's Realm	9 200	556	4.6	1 655	28
More	5 520	549	4.6	1 005	12
Elle	6 500	509	4.2	1 277	24
Marie Claire	5 850	464	3.9	1 261	23
My Weekly	4 710	458	3.8	1 028	13
Options	5 250	435	3.6	1 207	20
Company	6 680	401	3.3	1 666	29
New Woman	5 600	395	3.3	1 418	25
Mizz	4 100	358	3.0	1 145	16
Living Magazine	5 595	333	2.8	1 680	30
People's Friend	3 800	317	2.6	1 199	19
Woman's Journal	5 385	281	2.3	1 916	32
Annabel	2 260	281	2.3	804	2

(*Source:* Lansdown Conquest: JICNARS Special Analysis)

Table 10.3   A cost-ranking on a specialized target group

	Adults spending £200 + on DIY	Coverage	Cost/000 (page)	Rank order (of 47 publications) – coverage
Adults spending £200+	5686	100		
Do It Yourself	207	3.6	12.8	36
Sunday	1623	28.5	18.5	2
Homes & Gardens	305	5.4	19.9	24
News of the World	1803	31.7	20.0	1
Ideal Home	342	6.0	21.0	23
Practical Householder	120	2.1	22.4	44
House & Garden	267	4.7	22.7	26
You	777	13.7	23.0	13
Sun	1334	23.5	24.4	3
Sunday Mirror Magazine	1012	17.8	24.7	10
Radio Times	559	9.8	26.9	15
Mirror/Mail Magazine	1237	21.8	27.1	5
Sunday Times Magazine	557	9.8	28.7	16
Country Homes & Interiors	100	1.8	30.2	46
Today	223	3.9	30.2	33
Sunday Sport	231	4.1	30.3	31
Sunday People	866	15.2	31.5	11
Daily Mirror	1036	18.2	31.7	9
TV Times	447	7.9	32.2	21
Sunday Mail Magazine	260	4.6	32.7	28
Sunday Mirror	1105	19.4	32.8	7
House Beautiful	137	2.4	33.5	43
Mirror/Record	1230	21.6	34.7	6
People/Mail	1059	18.6	36.0	8
Sunday Mirror/Mail	1307	23.0	36.0	4
Country Living	116	2.0	38.3	45
Daily Star	391	6.9	38.6	22
Observer Magazine	266	4.7	39.1	27
Sunday Post	260	4.6	41.2	29
Sunday Express Magazine	494	8.7	45.4	18

(*Source:* Lansdown Conquest, based on *TGI Special Analysis.*)

As far as TV areas are concerned, the question is, basically, one of market-ing priorities and objectives. Does the client wish to support strengths or bolster weaknesses? The problem is complicated by the fact that costs per thousand vary sharply by station, and it is especially expensive to advertise in the large London area. There is a long-running debate as to whether money for a national campaign should be allocated according to the proportions of a national rate card, or on an 'equal-impact' basis. The latter appears to make more logical sense, but concentrates funds excessively into London. An added complication which increases in importance from time to time, is the tendency for both ITV contractors and media buyers to negotiate 'share deals', in which the advertiser obtains a discount for giving a particular contractor a disproportionate share of the TV budget.

2. *Size and length*

Here, obviously, creative considerations are important, but in press, particularly, there may be considerable flexibility. What the planner has to do (always within the budget) is balance the benefits offered by the medium's rate card structure against the increased effectiveness that a larger size of ad may offer. In general, rate cards are constructed so that the larger the space or the longer the commercial, the lower the cost per column centimetre or per second. However, if a double page spread (DPS) is 75 per cent more expensive than a single page, or a 40-second TV spot is 33 per cent more expensive than a 30-second spot, is the resulting ad going to be 75 per cent or 33 per cent more effective?

The fact is that there are, as so often, no clear rules. There is, buried in some agencies' archives, material—usually based either on reading and noting research (see page 100) or on direct response returns—which shows rather clearly that over a certain size—somewhere around 35 cm×6 cols in a broadsheet newspaper—diminishing returns begin to set in. Indeed, I am not absolutely sure that it has not been proved that in terms of pure cost-effectiveness a space such as a 1 cm double is the best you can buy—the only trouble is that you need an awful lot of them. Similarly, *a priori* one would expect the same effect in TV, possibly over about 30 seconds. There is, furthermore, at least some limited evidence to suggest that most commercials do not need to be as long as they are in order to communicate at least the more fundamental elements of their message.

In practice, all the major media have certain 'standard' sizes which are far more popular—and thus easier to buy—than others. There is limited choice for the national advertiser in cinema—60 seconds is more or less standard, though 30-second spots are used; in magazines full pages, DPSs, halves and quarters; in newspapers full pages, and, depending on whether the paper is broadsheet or tabloid, 35 cm × 6, 25 cm × 4, 15 cm × 2 are very widely used sizes: on TV, 30-second spots dominate, with 20-second and 10-second spots becoming more popular; in posters, 4-sheets are still most common.

The press media are, of course, potentially most flexible, and a receptive editorial attitude can offer media buyers and their creative groups plenty of scope for imagination. *Company* magazine has actually run competitions for the most unusual and creative space bought in the magazine. The possibilities of series of ads, teasers, inserts, fold-overs, unusual shapes, stick-on coupons, are—at least in theory—endless.

3. *Position*

Different positions in different media attract different sizes of audience, in different moods. On TV, you can get ratings for every minute of every programme (but it is always history: you have to guess whether history will repeat itself). In the press, occasional reading and noting surveys show the relative importance of different parts of the editorial matter, but these data are much less systematically available. Posters are now graded according to the OSCAR[*] system, which covers over 90 per cent of roadside posters. For cinemas, you have to guess at the popularity of a given programme: it is, however, possible to buy PG or 15 or 18 only and, now, individual films, while you can also buy an Audience Delivery Plan, guaranteeing a number of admissions.

In most media there are premiums charged by the owners for 'fixing' ads in particular positions, and individual positions carry premium prices: TV is divided into peak, pre-peak, off-peak, etc., time, and into as many as seven categories by some stations, quite apart from special 'packages'; magazines charge extra for the covers, for certain key editorial spots, sometimes for righthand pages; and so on. If you want to 'fix' every ad in a campaign, you can pay 20 per cent or more over the basic rate-card cost, especially if you fix in premium positions. This is an extravagant way to behave, though it *may* be justified: no one knows for sure.

Usually, a media planner will aim to buy a mixture of different positions. Some peak-time or prime editorial to ensure coverage, plus off-peak or special time packages such as guaranteed TVRs or run-of-paper space to build frequency. The buyer's ideal position is to buy at run-of-week or run-of-paper rates, but to have sufficient 'pull' either through the size of the budget or the closeness of the relationship with the media sales agent concerned to achieve good times and positions regardless.

Schedule building

As the media planner works through the available choices, a media schedule begins to evolve. This is the formal listing of what ads are to appear and where. Schedules are handy reference points, ways of showing clients what they are getting for their money, and the bases on which the media people actually go out to buy time and space.

Schedules are generally constructed over a year, which is usually the client's short-term planning cycle, but may be for a single seasonal burst. The first consideration is the timing of the campaign during the year. This is, normally, a marketing decision to be taken in conjunction with the client, based on the seasonality of sales of the product and of competitive activity. Normally, clients will want to support strong seasonal sales, but if, as sometimes happens, market seasonality has been created by promotional activity, it may make sense to try to even out the cycle by advertising in the low season. If there is no major seasonal consideration, it will usually make sense to advertise at periods when the advertising market is normally 'soft'—January/

*See page 161.

February and July/August—since it is then possible to buy good positions and spots at more favourable rates.

The seasonality of advertising is the first consideration, either because the budget is too small to spread over a full year, or because even a very large budget could be weighted towards certain times of year. Assuming a budget which does not allow for year-round spending, the next major consideration is how to divide it up. The fundamental alternatives are to advertise in bursts of, perhaps, three weeks at a time, or on a more spread-out, 'drip' basis. Most agency people prefer to use bursts, with the idea of concentrating expenditure in such a way that the target audience will become more thoroughly aware of the advertising and may, even, come to remember a lot of the detail. Conversely, some econometricians have argued that it is more cost effective to use a 'drip' system, advertising more or less continuously over a long period at a very low weight. It would be much easier to begin to resolve this argument if we knew more about how advertising works, and if we could be much more sophisticated than we are about how to relate target audiences and purchasing patterns to advertising. As it is, all that can really be said is that the collective wisdom, such as it is, of the agency business favours bursts in most circumstances. There may, however, be a better case for 'drip' advertising for very long-established, regularly purchased brands. Certainly for the launch of a new brand, or of a new campaign for an old brand, there can be little doubt that an initial burst pattern offers the best chance of building awareness among the target audience.

The burst problem is, of course, particularly acute for brands using TV, where three weeks of national advertising at 100 TVRs per week can cost £600000, and three weeks is a very short time. With press media, it is possible to spread the same money over a much longer period, especially if monthly magazines are used, since monthlies accumulate their readership of as many as 10 or 11 readers per copy over quite a long period. Similarly, poster campaigns usually last at least a month, and frequently three.

It is, of course, possible to schedule a campaign in a series of bursts through the year, if the cash is available, and major bursts can be interspersed with minor ones—or the gap between TV bursts can be filled by using print media in the intervals.

A further consideration that needs to be taken into account is the use of advertising to the retail trade. Usually, this needs to be scheduled in advance of the main consumer advertising to inform the trade of what is going to happen.

Once these broad principles have been decided, the media planner can then begin to put the schedule together. For TV, he or she will have to analyse the scheduled programmes both of ITV and BBC to determine which ITV programmes appear to be good buys, and which will be poor ones, in relation to the rate card. Usually, as has already been pointed out, a mixture of peak and other time will be bought against a target level of TVRs. In the press, he or she will be selecting the publications and the sizes of ads to go in them; the days of the week on which the ads are required to appear; the positions particularly wanted. For reference, these are put into a media visual, which, at the planning stage, will look something like the schedules in Figures 10.1 and 10.2.

These two schedules are, in a way, extreme cases. The first covers only five weeks, for a specific product, and involves very specific sizes and dates. The second is a multi-media, schematic plan for a large advertiser, in which bursts of advertising have been blocked in as a basis for more precise, detailed planning at a later date.

At the planning stage, TV campaigns are usually indicated purely by a timespan and a TVR target. This can be disconcerting for clients who want to know how many spots they are getting. If you think about it, this is a naive question, since it would be possible (in theory) to construct a TV schedule to get 100 TVRs by using 100 spots which each achieved one TVR or by using four spots each of which achieved 25 TVRs. You cannot judge a TV campaign's weight by the number of crosses on a visual. (The same, actually, is true of a press campaign, but there is no reason to simplify, since the appearance of an ad in a particular paper at a particular time is determined, whereas the actual TV buying pattern needs to be left flexible.)

Once the basic schedule has been drawn up and discussed and agreed with the client, and the budget committed, the media buyer goes out and buys the campaign. In fact, options or at least verbal commitments will have been obtained already for some special buys which are wanted, but nothing will have been the subject of a formal order to any of the media before this. As the campaign is bought, the buyer will be negotiating with the individual media to achieve special deals, either on price or position in the media—or, indeed, both. As the orders are made out to confirm the buyer's telephone conversations with the media salespeople, copies are passed to the agency's traffic controllers to ensure that the control system is able to get the required material to the media on time. Most larger agencies now use one or other of several available computer systems to aid the whole planning and scheduling process, to print out orders, and to pass details to their traffic controllers.

Evaluation

As well as planning and buying the schedule, it is the job of the media people to check that everything has appeared as it should, to negotiate redress where the media are in error, and to assess, retrospectively, what has been achieved—this is, of course, essential for TV, where the medium is bought, as it were, sight unseen, and it is the media department's job to guess the ratings of the slots they buy into: if they guess right, they will achieve better ratings, and a better cost per thousand, than originally planned, and assuming the advertising does the job it is meant to, the clients' sales should achieve at least a very small extra boost.

For TV, the BARB service (see page 134) provides detailed ratings for every TV station for every programme and commercial break. From this, the

LANSDOWNEURO

LANSDOWNEURO LIMITED, ABBEY HOUSE, 215–229 BAKER STREET, LONDON NW1 6YA
071-486 7111 TELEX: 8952286 FAX: 071-486 5310

PROPOSED

Client: XXXXXXX   Date: 5 February 1992
Product: Foreign policy
Period: March/April

PUBLICATION	Space size	Rate £	No.	Total Cost £	March 16	23	30	April 6	13
NATIONAL									
Financial Times	21 cms × 3 cols	7100.00	2	14200.00		23	30		15
The Times	21 cms × 3 cols	3000.00	3	9000.00	17			8	
Evening Standard	20 cms × 3 cols	2910.00	3	8730.00	18		2	10	
Independent	20 cms × 3 cols	1700.00	3	5100.00		27	1	9	
Ind. on Sunday	20 cms × 3 cols	1700.00	3	5100.00	22	25	5	12	
Daily Telegraph	28 cms × 4 cols	6720.00	3	20160.00				7	
Sunday Telegraph	21 cms × 3 cols	4393.00	3	13179.00		29	5	12	
Sunday Times	7 cms × 8 cols	10531.00	1	10531.00		Date to be confirmed			
		TOTALS		**86000.00**					
REGIONAL									
Man. Eve. News	20 cms × 3 cols	1696.50	3	5089.50	19	26	2		
Aberdeen P & J	20 cms × 3 cols	744.00	2	1488.00	18	25			
Glasgow Herald	20 cms × 3 cols	1134.00	2	2268.00	19	26			
Birmingham Post	20 cms × 3 cols	393.00	3	1179.00	19	26	2		
Scotsman	20 cms × 3 cols	825.60	3	2476.80	18	25	31		
		TOTALS		**12501.30**					
TOTAL				**98501.30**					

Figure 10.1   A short-term press schedule, at planning stage

LANSDOWNEURO

LANSDOWNEURO LIMITED, ABBEY HOUSE, 215–229 BAKER STREET, LONDON NW1 6YA
071-486 7111 TELEX: 8952286 FAX: 071-486 5310

Client: XXXX
Product: XXXX
Period: 1991/1992

Date: 4 April 1991

NATIONAL

W/C MONDAY	MAY	JUN	JUL	AUG	SEP	OCT	NOV	DEC	JAN	FEB	MAR	APR	SCHEDULE SUMMARY TOTAL (NETT)
(ADDED VALUE TV)						30" X X	112 TVR						*(248.9K)
TELEVISION NETWORK	10" 125 TVR X		10" 625 TVR X X X X	10"	100 TVR X	20"/10" X X X X	790 TVR X		30"/10" 350 TVR X X X X X		100 TVR X	125 TVR X	2567.72
LOCAL – DPS MONO PAGES	X			X	X	X			X	X			174.80
5 COLS		X		X	X		X				X	X	624.28
2 X HALF PAGES				X			X						304.00
NATIONAL MONO PAGES	X		X X X	X	X	X	X X X X		X X		X	X	654.18
5 COLS	X	X X	X X X	X	X	X X	X X		X	X X	X	X	550.68
(ADDED VALUE – PAGES)						X *							*(71.25)
INSERTS/LEAFLETS								X	X				40.00
LOCAL STORE MARKETING													179.40
DIRECTORIES													100.00
ASBOF & PROD.													50.00
TOTAL CLIENT COST													5245.06

Figure 10.2 A complex multi-media visual, at the planning stage

media people can extract the ratings achieved each time a commercial appears—and a close eye can be kept on what competitors are doing.

In press, the media group should obtain voucher copies of all magazines, and examine copies of all newspapers, in which their ads appear. It is necessary to check not merely that the ad has appeared, but that it is in the right place, and that it has been properly reproduced—the quality of printing can vary markedly, and this may well be the fault of the publication: in this case, some redress is due. A further area for the media group to check is the loss of circulation due to strikes or other problems: during the continuing difficulties that beset Fleet Street in the early eighties it became standard practice for papers affected to provide a rebate for lost circulation.

Posters are far more difficult to monitor: in the past, agencies used to have their own teams of inspectors, but this is no longer done, and the only real check on the presence and condition of posters is a regular service run for the past 10 years by the Poster Advertising Bureau, which reports on the level of damage to posters, as a stimulus to the contractors to take care of their sites.

For the advertiser who is concerned as to whether he or she is getting a good deal from an agency or media specialist, companies such as Media Audits provide a service that compares the buying performance of different advertisers and their agencies in similar markets and media. Recently, too, a number of advertisers have started to ask for 'second opinions' on media planning and costs, usually by using a competitive agency's media department to 'shadow buy' the identical campaign.

Conclusion

Media is a complex, quite technical part of advertising which requires its own blend of skills. It requires an analytical and reasonably numerate mind to develop cost-effective plans; it requires a rapport with the creative group to achieve the best match of material and medium; it requires aggressive negotiating skills in order to achieve the best possible positions and discounts, so as to make the maximum use of the client's money; and it requires a great attention to detail.

It is a field that is full of mythology, but also of research; but the research tends to be compartmentalized between individual media, so that it is difficult to find meaningful material covering a combination of media in any very useful way. To be sure, surveys of readership ask some (very basic) questions about ITV viewing or ILR (commercial radio) listening, but this is really only paying lip-service to the existence of the inter-media problem. Since individual media are competing with one another this is, perhaps, hardly surprising; but where much of the research is done under the auspices of joint committees representing agencies, advertisers, and media it is slightly frustrating that so little seems to have been achieved.

11 Television

The structure of commercial TV in Britain

As an electronic medium using the airwaves, TV has necessarily been subject to governmental and inter-governmental controls on the frequencies that may be used and the coverage allowed to each transmitter. This means that airspace had to be rationed and licensed, and pirate TV is not a very viable possibility. In spite of the limitations imposed by TV's greed for bandwidth, the past 15 years have seen considerable developments in the shape of the TV business and in the number of channels available to viewers with the right equipment. Also, because of the licensing system, which restricts access to the medium to a quite small number of programme contractors, the government in the UK finds it necessary, from time to time, to mount a new competition for the existing licenses. (This system has, however, been effectively out-flanked by satellite – see below.) As a medium, therefore, TV is subject to a variety of pressures—commercial, political and technological—that have the potential to generate considerable changes; and because TV is such a powerful medium, these pressures ensure that it changes almost as much as other media that are less constrained by technological strait-jackets. The UK pattern is paralleled by the experience of most of Continental Europe, even though the actual systems may vary, and have different historical roots.

The basic structure of commercial TV in the UK has remained set since its introduction in 1956. Fourteen contractors, under the control of what is now the Independent Television Commission (ITC) are responsible for programming and for advertising sales for the original ITV Channel, ITV1. Apart from small areas of overlap, there is no direct competition between contractors in any region except London, where the franchise is split between weekday and weekend (Friday evening to Sunday evening) contractors.

During the eighties, three significant developments occurred. In 1983, TV-AM was launched, as a national morning programme on air from 6.30 am to 9.30 am, broadcasting on ITV Channel 1. In November 1982, Channel 4, also a national service, was launched, in competition with the second BBC channel, BBC2. Unlike TV-AM, which had its own advertising sales force, time on Channel 4 was sold regionally by the ITV1 contractors, and in the morning by TV-AM*. Finally, the late eighties saw the launch of satellite TV services, initially by Sky and then by the ill-fated BSB, which was taken over by Sky to

*Channel 4 became responsible for its own sales in January 1993.

form BSkyB when BSB succumbed to financial difficulties less than two years after going on air, in late 1990. BSkyB – as it is now – took advantage of relatively low cost communications satellite technology to open up a service that the regulators (national or pan-European) had failed to anticipate.

In addition to ITV1, Channel 4 and BSkyB, there are also cable TV services which can, in theory, provide a very wide range of continental channels, as well as the full range of UK-originated and UK satellite services. Cable has been slow to develop, as the necessary infrastructure has to be installed, and the British do not—mostly—live in the large apartment blocks that most readily lend themselves to cable. Only 2.5 per cent of homes – 25 per cent of those 'passed' by a cable service – had cable installed by mid-1992, compared with 11 per cent penetration for orthodox satellite TV.

Further considerations affect the future of TV advertising in the UK. First, there is a steady background pressure, from a variety of quarters, to finance some or all of the BBC's television services through advertising. It seems unlikely that there is sufficient demand for commercial time for advertising to take over completely from the TV licence system that finances the BBC: at £77 per household (1991–2 cost), the licence brings in approaching £1500 million, compared with total TV advertising expenditure in 1991 of £1974 million.

 The second key factor is the audience fragmentation implicit in the growing number of TV channels available, allied to the spread of video recorders. With over 60 per cent of households owning a VCR and virtually 50 per cent with at least two TV sets; with 11 channels available via BSkyB's Astra satellite, and over 10 per cent household penetration; and video film rentals running at over 500 million per year; the use made of a fairly stable total screen time per viewer is becoming progressively more diffuse. This fragmentation will be further increased if and when a proposed new national commercial Channel 5 is added to the available terrestrial TV services: this is due to happen by 1995, but there are doubts about its viability, and the precise format will remain unclear until a contractor is appointed, after a non-decision by the government in late 1992.

Finally, technical developments in TV broadcasting and receiving equipment mean that it is rapidly becoming inevitable that, for a time at least, most TV stations will be broadcasting in two formats, to take account of the new so-called high density TV (HDTV)—always assuming that standards for the system can be agreed.

The 1991 'auction'
The apparently set commercial format of ITV in the UK was rudely upset during 1991 by a novel—and pretty ill-thought-out—scheme dreamed up by the government to distribute new licences for ITV1.

A brilliantly opaque bidding system, requiring a combination of cash tenders and programming prospectuses, diverted the managements of established and would-be contractors for the best part of 18 months, leading—eventually—to a re-allocation of licences in November 1991, to take effect from January 1993. This exercise was perhaps most illuminating in the way in which it showed up the nerve (or lack of it) of the existing contractors' managements; and the results demonstrated the inherent impossibility of combining apparently objective cash criteria with inevitably subjective judgements of quality.

In the event, four contractors—Thames (London weekday), TVS (Southern), TSW (South West) and TV-AM—lost their franchises. Two brave (or extremely well-informed) firms, Central and Scottish TV, put in minimal bids, but turned out to be unopposed. Nearly everyone (except the winners) was unhappy.

The result of the process is that the map of ITV regions in the UK (Figure 11.1) has not changed, but we will have to get used to calling TSW and TVS by different names (Westcountry and Meridian, respectively), and TV-AM becomes GMTV. Thames is replaced by Carlton. More important is the possibility, after 1994, that one contractor may bid to take over another, and outside investors have the chance to buy into the contractor companies, opening the door to possible foreign ownership of some of the network.

It seems unlikely, however, that the basic geography of the network will change, since a whole range of marketing data and infrastructure—market research panels, sales force organizations, etc.—are based on the regions. As can be seen from the map, the regions vary considerably in physical size and—even more—in population and relative wealth. This is amply illustrated by Table 11.1, which shows the basic statistics for each station, including the 30-second average cost per thousand for 1991, which suggests that a customer in London is judged, by the market at least, to be more than three times as valuable as a customer in Ulster or Border regions. (In terms of spending power, this is, of course, hardly logical—but the laws of supply and demand do not always produce common-sense effects).

The basis of commercials on TV

TV time in the UK is primarily sold on a 'spot' basis, but forms of sponsorship, familiar in the United States, are beginning to become available. A proportion of ITV programmes on both ITV1 and Channel 4 are available for sponsoring, and BSkyB is even more active in supporting its sponsors than current ITV practice allows.

Commercials are shown in 'breaks' of about two minutes which occur at roughly 20-minute intervals during programmes: they are not bunched into blocks of 10 minutes or more, as occurs in some continental countries.

When commercial TV was introduced in 1956, time was sold in units of 7, 15, 30, 45 and 60 seconds. Since about 1982, however, time has been 'decimalized', and the standard units are now 10, 20, 30, 40 and 60 seconds. Although 30 seconds, traditionally the most popular format, still accounts for the largest single share of commercial airtime, 20-second commercials are increasingly popular, and there has been a general tendency over the years

Figure 11.1   Simplified ITV arca map, ignoring overlaps

Table 11.1   The TV regions

Region	Contractor (1992) (New 1993 contractors in brackets)	% of net ITV homes 1992	30-sec peak spot 1991		% of network ITV1 cost	30-sec equivalent cost/000 adults 1991	
			ITV1	CH4		ITV1	CH4
London	Thames (Carlton)		52000	26000	26.9	6.53	6.51
	LWT	19.4	25000	10000	(12.9)	6.94	6.92
South*	TVS (Meridian)	9.4	21160	12600	11.0	5.83	5.69
E. Anglia	Anglia TV	7.1	14000	8000	7.3	4.78	4.56
S. West	TSW (Westcountry)	2.9	4500	1800	2.3	4.36	3.12
Wales & West	HTV	7.9	13000	1350	6.7	3.50	2.11
Midlands	Central TV	15.8	25000	13000	12.9	4.07	2.44
N. West	Granada TV	11.3	20000	9000	10.4	3.44	2.94
Yorkshire	Yorkshire TV	9.8	18000	9000	9.3	3.42	2.77
N. East	Tyne Tees TV	5.1	7200	3000	3.7	2.50	1.64
C. Scotland	Scottish TV	6.1	10000	4500	5.2	3.37	1.99
NE Scotland	Grampian TV	2.1	4000	2000	2.1	2.45	1.53
Border	Border TV	1.1	1200	1200	0.6	2.25	1.40
Ulster	TV	2.1	3000	2000	1.6	2.47	1.66
		100	193060+	93450+	100	4.30	3.56
(TV-AM – National (GMTV))		100	– 8400 –		100	– 4.11–	

*Inc. Channel Islands
+Ex London Weekend
(*Sources:* BRAD, Company Rate Cards, BARB, Young & Rubicam)

for the average commercial to get shorter. This is both a natural response to cost pressures and a reflection of research findings that encourage the belief that shorter commercials (up to a point) are more cost-effective—in spite of pricing structures that make shorter commercials more expensive in terms of cost per second.

In addition to simply buying shorter spots, a growing number of advertisers are experimenting with how they use short spots. 'Topping and tailing' a commercial break is an increasingly popular practice.

How TV time is sold

TV time on ITV1 is marketed by the individual regional contractors through their own sales forces and marketing teams, who maintain close contact with agencies and major advertisers.

Some years ago, TVS absorbed Channel TV, covering the Channel Islands, as this small market proved not to be viable on its own. More recently, TV contractors have begun to emulate radio stations in establishing joint sales operations. STV and HTV, for example, have a joint sales company called TVMM, LWT and TVS cooperate through Laser, Yorkshire and Tyne-Tees in MAS, while Anglia, Border and Central are sold by TSMS. A more significant change has been the separation of sales of ITV1 and Channel 4: Channel 4 has been responsible for its own sales from January 1993, and this has introduced the first genuinely competitive element into national commercial TV.

The TV contractors publish their rate cards, usually twice a year, but sometimes more often. These rate cards can be quite complex. They start by dividing the day into a number of segments, which may be described by name—'peak', 'pre-peak', 'post-peak', 'daytime', etc.,—or, more frequently, simply by numbers. Each segment then has a basic cost rate for a standard spot, in each of the time lengths allowed. Costs are related to a standard 30-second rate with shorter commercials carrying a 'weighting', so that a 20-second spot costs 80 per cent of a 30-second spot.

Beyond these basic costs, most stations offer a number of 'packages' such as run-of-week, or based on numbers of TVRs, where they may run your commercial at any time they like, as many times as they like, so long as your eventual cumulative audience reaches an agreed figure. These packages are cheaper than the basic time cost, since they take away the advertiser's control over when the ad is to appear. Correspondingly, there are added costs for fixing spots at particular times. In addition, some stations may, according to the state of the market, either offer extra 'support' spots to buyers of sufficient peak time; or insist on buyers taking unpopular 'support' spots as well as the peak spots they want.

Going beyond these general 'offers' most stations offer special rates to genuinely local advertisers and for brands being advertised on TV for the first time. They also provide special rates for test market launches, and these rates may be supplemented by a (limited) programme of marketing assistance—mailings to retailers, subsidized market research facilities and so on. However, the restrictions imposed on these special rates tend to limit their usefulness for many advertisers.

The rate card is not, in practice, fixed. There is usually a formal system of discounts, for advertisers spending over a certain level with the station, and perhaps even for early booking, and whenever a station has time to sell which it fears it might fail to dispose of it is possible for the buyer to negotiate on the price. This is one reason why TV buyers may wish to keep part of their budgets flexible beyond the time when they might usually prefer to commit themselves—they may, of course, find that they cannot buy the time they want, but this is a risk they may be willing to take in order to get a better price.

With TV, especially in the major areas and London in particular, a very heavily sold market, the contractors have in good years been less willing to deal. Some have been accused—rightly or wrongly—of preferring not to sell all their available time rather than to reduce their price, and most areas now follow a practice which can only really work in a seller's market—'pre-emption'. This curious misuse of language means that if you book a spot at anything less than the top rate, some time in advance, the station can re-sell it, at a higher rate, to anyone who wants it, at any time before the cancellation date. I have heard several attempts to justify this method of doing business but none which succeeds in avoiding the suspicion that this is a highly opportunistic—though by now, after several years, established—version of having your cake and eating it.

TV time is bought well in advance, and is subject to a standard cancellation date—of eight weeks—beyond which the advertiser and agency cannot back out of the commitment to advertise (though in practice an agency may, in an emergency, transfer the time to another client or a different brand).

How a TV commercial is produced

The script

As we have seen, the decision to use TV is a joint one between (in particular) the creative and media groups in the agency, a decision which then has to be endorsed by the client.

The first stage in the process will involve the production of a script, and perhaps a storyboard, for discussion between agency and client. At this stage, the discussion is limited to the ideas, the words of the script and a general idea of what the visual will look like. The agency probably has not discussed the commercial with a production company, though they may well know which company they would like to use, and have a reasonable idea of the likely cost.

Once the basic script has been agreed, the next task for the agency is to develop it into a finalized pre-production script. Before this can be done, agency and client may agree to do some research to assess the likely consumer reaction to the commercial and to iron out any problems (see Chapter 9).

For this exercise, a script plus storyboard may be sufficient, but it may be found more desirable to produce an 'animatic'. This is a sort of 'semi-film', made by shooting the pictures of a specially drawn storyboard with a rostrum camera, which makes it possible to produce an almost moving picture with varying lengths of focus, to which can be added a recorded soundtrack. The whole can be made to look quite convincingly like a commercial. Indeed, from time to time animatics do, in fact, get used for actual transmission— apparently without any drastic ill effects.

ITVA clearance

Before they can be transmitted, all TV commercials have to be approved by the Independent Television Association, ITVA. This is to check that they do not infringe either the Television Act, which places some special restrictions on TV advertising, or the ITC Code of Advertising Practice (see Chapter 16). In addition, the ITVA has some criteria of its own, being stricter than either the Act or the Code in its judgement of the admissibility of some statements of apparent fact or of 'knocking' copy. In certain product fields, their standards of proof or competitive claims are extremely high—'whiteness' claims in detergent ads are a particularly strict example.

Because of the risk of rejection by the ITVA, the vast majority of commercials are first shown to them at script stage, and the discussion and negotiation that goes on in the majority of cases takes place on scripts alone. Since the ITVA can, however, approve a script and then reject a film on the grounds that it does not conform to the script (or the letter of the script), the agency and the production house have to be very careful how they interpret the outcome of discussions with the ITVA.

Persuading the ITVA to see the agency's point of view on a controversial film is not impossible: it is, by general consent, a very reasonable body. It does like scientific proof, where possible, of product claims, but will also accept the findings of consumer research where this is relevant. You can, too, win a straight argument with them if you have a sound case. For the industry, it is probably fair to describe the ITVA as a sort of benevolent despot, though it can be (and is) criticized for being excessively cautious in its judgements.

Production
Once the script has been agreed, the agency selects the production company to produce the film. This will be done on the basis of past experience of the company, its skill at producing the type of film which is planned, observation of its work for other agencies, and, to an extent, its cost quotation.

The first thing the production company and the agency have to do together is to plan the production and produce an estimate of the production costs. These will include everything involved in making the film— studios, actors, music, props, costs of finding and getting to locations, processing and editing, production of bulk prints for the TV stations. To this, the agency adds its estimates of the repeat fees for the artists involved, and its commission. The resulting estimate will look something like that shown in simplified form in Figure 11.2. It is increasingly common practice for clients to request tenders to produce a commercial from more than one production company—usually three—as part of the necessary process of controlling costs. Producing the estimate involves, already, a number of decisions and a lot of work by both the agency producer and the production company. Decisions have to be taken on the types of film technique to be used; locations; casting; music; sets; and any special requirements.

Out of the substantial number of TV production companies available, some can be found who specialize in any of a number of areas, either of product type or of technique. If you think of the variety of commercials you see on TV, there are many different things you can do in commercials: animation; live action, used in perhaps the majority of commercials; puppetry; mixed live action and animation; computer graphics and picture modification; a variety of special effects. Similarly, there is now available a fundamental choice between shooting on film or video. Video is—generally—cheaper, and sometimes quicker, though the end results are likely to be less polished. It is, therefore, more suitable for cheaper, straightforward commercials, while film may be preferable when quality, style and mood are important.

Some films have to be shot on location: you cannot create a moving 'face' out of several thousand people for a British Airways commercial in any other way. However, others, with apparently convincing exotic locations, can be wholly shot in the studio, with the aid of sophisticated scenery effects, often

LANSDOWNEURO

LANSDOWNEURO LIMITED, ABBEY HOUSE, 215–229 BAKER STREET, LONDON NW1 6YA. 071-486 7111 TELEX: 8952286 FAX: 071-486 5310

LANSDOWNEURO TV/CINEMA/RADIO ESTIMATE

Date:	21-6-91	Job No: 4715
Client:	XXXX	Production Co: Camet
Product:	XXXX	Director: PQRS
Title:	"FARGER"	

Basis for Estimate: 1 x 30", 2 x 10" commercials, 3 days location

AGENCY PRODUCTION ELEMENTS		
Preproduction Costs		
Music	5500.00	
Artwork		
Stills Photography		
Stock Footage		
Props		
Cast	5410.00	
Artiste N.H.I.	566.00	
Legal Fees		
Insurance		
P.R.		
Video Post Production	3000.00	
Hotel and Air Fares		
Incidental Expenses	1000.00	
Recording Studio		
Contingency		
Production Company Costs	157892.00	see page 4
Other Production Costs	15476.00	
Production Total (NET)	173368.00	
Agency Commission @ 17.65%	30599.00	
Production Total (GROSS)		203967.45
Playout Cost (GROSS)	see page 5	
Usage Fees Total (GROSS)	see page 6	
Grand Total (EX VAT)		

Signatures for approval and go ahead to production

AGENCYTV   AGENCY ACCOUNT HANDLING   COMPANY/BRAND/GROUP

Summary of estimated production company costs

	MARK UP RATES	25.00%	25.00%	25.00%	NIL	NIL	NIL
A	Preproduction	600					
B	Recce	2260	200				
C	Casting And Cast	2205					
D	Production Salaries			13500			
E	Unit Salaries	17927					
F	Electrical Unit	14688					
G	Camera Department	9035					
H	Art Department	21677					
I	Studio						
J	Location Costs	22120	4350				
K	Stock Negative and Processing	7100					
L	Editing, Optical & Film Finish	10225					
M	Editing, Optical & Video Finish						
N	Insurance	3146					
O	Sundries						
P	Animation Production						
Q	Video Shoot						
E	Sub-total	110963	4550	13500			
	Mark up	27441	1138				
	Amount						
	Sub-total	138704	5688	13500			
	TOTAL	157892					

PRODUCTION ESTIMATE
Weather Day 0

Figure 11.2   Extracts from a TV production estimate (*Source*: Lansdown Conquest)

using a moving matte technique to achieve verisimilitude. Photographing food, especially in close-up, involves very controlled and precise technique—and the constant services of an expert home economist to ensure the availability of the products involved, in exactly the right state. Most products—and even people—require special techniques to ensure that they look right on the TV screen. In the USA, some tricks have been banned by consumerist pressures for 'truth in advertising' but mostly these are not prevalent in the UK.

Casting

Just as there are production companies and cameramen specializing in different techniques and styles and product fields, so you can get actors and models who specialize in specific areas. Very often a film involving a close-up of hands will have used a special 'hand model' in place of the actor appearing in the rest of the commercial. Similarly, there are a number of actors who specialize in doing the commentary or 'voice over' on commercials: some of them can do a variety of voices and accents very convincingly, but others become extremely recognizable and, in effect, boringly over-exposed.

The choice of actors and voices is, obviously, a critical part of making a commercial. There are few rules about this. Clearly, the creators of the script start with a reasonably clear idea of the sort of people they want, and they should be able to describe them fairly accurately. The problems arise quickly, though, when the cast are, as so often, essentially stereotypes. It is one thing to find a group of 'typical teenagers' but the 'average family' can be extraordinarily difficult to put together. It may involve the agency's casting team (which may be a specialist in a large agency, but is usually the creative group head and the TV producer in a small one) in seemingly endless poring over directories of actors, and actually seeing a large number of them before a decision can be made.

Perhaps the most difficult decision, where it might be appropriate, is to use the face (or the voice) of a celebrity or, in particular, a TV, radio or film personality. Sometimes a commercial is deliberately written round a particular character, because he or she seems an absolute 'natural' for the product, but there is always the danger of a personality taking over a brand completely. This has not prevented a number of very successful examples in recent years: Fry and Laurie for the Alliance and Leicester Building Society, Hale and Pace for Clorets, and—more surprisingly—Dudley Moore for Tesco are just a few examples, while Maureen Lipman's 'Beattie' character practically became British Telecom for several years.

A further consideration in casting is cost. Celebrities, of course, cost money. But even 'unknown' actors can become expensive over time. A new contract between Equity and the IPA came into force during 1979 which meant that 'repeat' fees—the fees paid to an artist for each showing of a commercial—were increased fourfold, so that repeat fees for one actor for a fairly heavily used commercial could reach £20 000 a year.

The change caused agencies to re-think their attitude to TV commercials, and led to an increase in animation and product-based films using trick photography. It has also produced an increase in films shot overseas, with foreign casts. Finally, the possibility exists of 'buying out' an actor's repeat fees for a single payment—something Equity frowns on but can hardly prevent.

This contract was revised in January 1992. The main change concerned repeat fees which are now based on the audience, measured in TVRs, for each commercial, rather than on the number of times it is shown.

Locations

Selecting locations is another time-consuming and difficult process that can spend or save a great deal of money, given the number of people involved and costs of travel, hotels, refreshments and all the other incidentals. The fashion for exotic locations thrived during the early sixties, but has diminished as economic realism and improvements in studio techniques have respectively discouraged the wilder flights of fancy and provided generally acceptable substitutes. It requires a lot of hard talking to go abroad to film these days: the main justification is for filming out of season—this is sometimes essential, but can often be avoided by good planning. It can be quite difficult, however, to arrange to film next year's ice cream commercial this August, in order to be sure of sunshine and leaves on the trees, because decisions on products to be advertised might not be taken until the end of the current season.

Obviously the main justification for location shooting is for outdoor work, but, given the costs of set-building, it is often realistic to film indoor material in a 'real' house—it is a moot point how 'lived-in' it ought to look: studio sets do tend to *look* like studio sets, but real houses are often too run-down to provide the slightly artificial air of super-tidiness which many commercials strive for and which at least some consumers seem to respond to. Irrelevant details, like a full wastepaperbasket or a cobweb on a beam, *can* distract attention from the message of a commercial, and research exists to prove it.

Filming

The main thing which strikes any inexperienced observer on a commercial shoot is the large number of people and the small amount that seems to happen. The number of people is, to an extent, a function of union rules, but some of them have real jobs to do. As far as making the film succeed is concerned, there are really only three who matter, apart from any actors. They are the director, who comes from the production company, is in charge of the whole operation, and is the real expert; the lighting cameraman, whose job is highly skilled and is exactly what it sounds like, and whose expertise will totally influence the visual texture of the film; and the agency's producer (or creative group head) whose job is to ensure that the director fully covers the brief, and to make any awkward decisions that may be needed. (Also, from time to time, there may be the client, whose job it is, in general, to keep quiet and watch his or her money being spent. If this seems a brutal judgement, it is a realistic one.)

The sound track

The sound track of a commercial is usually recorded separately from filming, though some words may be recorded during filming in order to achieve lip-sync. The track will consist, typically, of a combination of words, music and sound effects (which appear in scripts as 'SFX').

Music, as discussed elsewhere (page 88), can be a mjaor factor in the appeal and success of a film, and the choice of music can be exceedingly difficult. From a production point of view, it can either be obtained ready-made from a music 'library', or be specially recorded—whether it is music composed for the commercial or an existing piece. Obviously, a special recording offers the opportunity of achieving precisely the right effect, but is considerably more expensive, even in these days of synthesizers, than library material. It is easy, too, to waste money unless you have either a musician or a music expert in the agency team.

Judging from my agency's research, music is becoming an increasingly sensitive issue among consumers: they are very quick to criticize uninspired music selections as inappropriate or boring, and in some categories (perfume, for example) the wrong music can kill a commercial stone dead.

Sound effects, too, are usually library material, or produced by one of a small group of specialists who know precisely how to reproduce, for example, the sound of a caterpillar dancing in a bowl of bird seed.

Words in commercials come in two forms: 'live' or 'voice over'. 'Live' voices are the voices of characters as they appear in the commercial—though they may, in fact, be recorded separately. A 'voice over' is the 'commentator' or other disembodied voice that tells you what is going on—or, usually, to go out and buy the product being advertised. Recording voices is, basically, a simple matter of work in a studio. The critical problem, of course, with TV commercials is that of time. The time taken by each set of words has to be very exactly calculated, and a large part of the skill of a voice-over expert lies in the ability to fit a set of words into a precise length of time while still getting the required clarity and intonation.

Clarity, it should go without saying, is virtually obligatory in commercial sound tracks—something too many producers of jingles appear to forget.

The results

One day's—or two days'— filming will produce a great deal of film footage. This first becomes available, as soon as it has been developed, usually the next morning, as 'rushes'—the uncut record of all the filming. That is why you have someone with a clapperboard at the start of each take: to make it possible to find everything in the whole length of film.

The next stage is to cut precisely to the right length and to link it up with the sound track. At first, the two parts of the film are simply run in parallel, not fully joined, in a form known as a 'double-head'. At this stage, it is still possible to change either part independently without reprocessing. Once this has been discussed and agreed by the client, the film goes back to the laboratory to be married to its sound track and to have its 'opticals' added and 'grading' of the print carried out. Opticals are all the special effects used to change scenes in films. The simplest way of changing scenes is, simply, to cut: but this is often rather drastic, and risks breaking up the flow of the film. Hence, there are a battery of effects—'fades', 'wipes', 'dissolves', and variations on them—designed to enable the film-maker to take the viewer through the film in the right emotional and psychological frame of mind. Grading is the technical process of ensuring that the colour tones of each sequence in the film go accurately together to produce the desired effect. Sometimes different sequences may need quite marked adjustment using filters and other devices to achieve the right harmonious effect.

The development of sophisticated computer techniques has added a whole new dimension to this 'post-production' stage of commercial-making. It is now possible to add or remove elements, and modify whole sections of the commercial, by means of computer systems such as 'Paintbox'—a system that contributed greatly to Peter Greenaway's feature film *Prospero's Books*—or 'Harry'.

The result of this processing is a 'married print'—the final master version of the commercial. (It is possible, but not essential, to have the intermediate stage of a double-head with opticals.) Assuming that this meets the client's approval, all that is now needed is to clear the finished version with the ITVA (see page 126) and order and dispatch the bulk prints to the TV stations. Although there are only 15 contractors, they have between them 50-odd transmitters, each of which needs two copies of the commercial (at least), so allowing for your own copies and back-up stock, you will need 115 or so bulks for a national campaign.

Costs . . .

Production costs, for all aspects of the advertising business, have become an increasingly major issue in recent years. Statistics collected by the Advertising Association show that the cost of TV production has risen even faster in recent years than that of TV airtime. As a result, TV production has become an issue both for agencies and advertisers.

The Pliatzky Committee (see page 91) spent some months examining the problem without arriving at any very clear diagnosis of the causes of rising production costs. What it did, however, was to recommend a series of procedures,[*] and to set out suggested working timetables, designed to enable agencies and production companies to control their costs more effectively. How far, if at all, this has succeeded in slowing cost inflation has yet to be seen.

At the end of 1992 it is probably a reasonable generalization that the

*Procedures for the Production of TV Commercials, IPA/AFVPA/ISBA, London, 1987.

average 30-second commercial, including the cost of bulk prints, but not of repeat fees (see page 129), would cost some £65 000–£70 000 to make. It is not difficult, however, to exceed this, for good—or bad—reasons.

... And quality

Arguably, the best reason for exceeding this fairly meaningless average cost is quality. It is frequently argued by agencies that the 'production values' are critical to the success of the commercial. This usually means, in essence, the combination of quality of photography, sets, editing, opticals and—in general—attention to detail.

I think it is important here to be absolutely clear about 'quality' as it is, certainly, a vital characteristic of most advertising: it is, above all, the agency's creative department's job to achieve a level of quality appropriate to its work. 'Quality', of course, has two meanings in relation to creative work: the quality of the idea, and the quality of its execution. The quality of the idea, surely, is the paramount consideration: what is then needed is—at least—a sufficiently good execution to communicate the idea effectively. Some very good ideas can be quite cheap to produce.

It can be argued—I think reasonably—that the better the idea, the more justified are attempts to execute it to perfection. Commercials are often produced which depend principally on being pretty for their effect, in the absence of an idea. This is, really, a cop-out, and can be an expensive one. Ultimately, arguments about quality are usually arguments about how far it is necessary to go to achieve the communication objectives. In many cases, I do not believe that the return from spending an extra £5000 or £10 000 on producing a commercial—rather than on showing it—can easily be justified. Sometimes it can: I have seen it happen, and it is usually with the better commercials.

I am not arguing for shoddy commercials. What I am arguing in favour of is simple, cheap solutions, where this is possible. I know my colleagues in the creative department do not agree. Sometimes, they are right. The difficulty, as so often in advertising, is to know when. This is a matter of experience—there is no substitute for it.

It is fair to say, however, that consumers, especially younger consumers in the UK, are sharp-eyed and critical of shoddy commercials. In particular, they respond badly—at least in research—to dubbed foreign-made films. Whether this actually has an adverse effect on sales is unproven.

Following the Pliatzky Committee's report, the ISBA published a very practical guide for its members, describing the process of making a commercial and detailing much of what is involved.[*]

Timing

From the original brief to air-date, making a commercial is a lengthy process. As a general rule of thumb, you need to allow something over three months, and that leaves little room for any consumer research to pre-test the concept

*The ISBA Guide to Television Commercials Production, ISBA, London, 1988.

or the commercial. It is, however, perfectly possible to write a commercial on Monday, shoot it on Tuesday, do the post-production on Wednesday and have it on air on Thursday: for large retail clients, at sale time, this is not that uncommon!

TV research

Research into TV commercials divides into two main fields: research into audiences and audience characteristics, and research into commercials' effectiveness.

Audience research can be divided into three different areas. The most frequently visible research is into the size and composition of the audience for specific programmes and commercial breaks, as a guide to the planner in selecting spot times and in evaluating what the schedule has achieved; there is also research into the viewing patterns of the TV audience, to provide the basic data from which cumulative audiences and viewing frequencies can be calculated; and research into audience behaviour and attention—when the research says that they are watching your commercial, what are they actually doing?

Head counting

The basic head-counting audience research used by agencies is that done by BARB (Broadcast Advertising Research Board), a joint body combining advertisers, agencies, the ITV contractors and the BBC. BARB's product has recently been upgraded to take account of the changing marketplace and the increasing use of computers by agency media departments. The system is now geared to be accessed on-line, typically through a specialist systems house, such as Donovan Data Services (DDS), and the thick weekly two-volume printed reports familiar to all TV buyers and planners for many years are no more. The 'new' BARB collects data from 4435 households, in an increased nationally representative sample set up and administered by RSMB and AGB Research. Each house has a sophisticated meter attached to its TV set, which records exactly what is being played (or played back on video). In addition, separate handsets ('peoplemeters') are used to record who is watching. These meters provide minute-by-minute data on viewing—or at least on what is being played on every set that is switched on. But although they add information as to who is present, they still don't tell the computers what everybody is doing. Work by Peter Collett, an Oxford academic, has shown clearly that what goes on in front of the telly is, in practice, virtually anything.

This research has recently been widely re-publicized in an anti-TV campaign by the Newspaper Proprietors' Association (most of whose members, it was quickly pointed out, use TV aggressively to advertise their own papers).

A further, recent complexity has been added by the widespread use of video recorders. By mid-1992, 65 per cent of UK ITV households had a VCR. While the BARB meters can record whether the VCR or an on-air programme is being watched, there is no way of telling whether people watching a time-shifted programme are cutting out the commercial breaks— or, indeed, what programme they are watching. The spread, too, of remote controls—again, in over 40 per cent of households—enables people to 'zap' commercials or whole commercial breaks. The practice is quite widespread, but no one has achieved any very reliable estimate of its scale, let alone a trend. Yet further complications to TV audience measurements are added by multi-set households (55 per cent of ITV homes have two or more sets), and teletext (Oracle, Ceefax).

According to the National Readership Survey in 1987 nearly 40 per cent of adults claimed to 'skip' ads in normal TV viewing 'almost always' or 'quite often', and 20 per cent said they 'almost always' did so when watching a recorded video programme. The obvious conclusion to be drawn from this is that precise numbers of TVRs accumulated by a campaign according to BARB, predicted at the planning stage, or promised in a package by a TV contractor, have a significant built-in factor of error: precision is mythical. It is, even, a bit of an act of faith comparing two concurrent campaigns' performance. Nonetheless, such is the business world's trust in statistics that analysis of the ratings is done in massive detail, and the results treated like holy writ.

BARB's research shows that the average individual watches around three and a half hours of television per day (and has done so for at least the last 10 years), just over half of this being ITV. There are, of course, variations by the day of the week, and by the season of the year—though the August trough is still over three hours a day, and the December peak under five hours.

Within this overall pattern, too, there are wide variations in the amount of viewing done by different people, and in the proportion of ITV viewing in the total. And, of course, there are very considerable differences in the proportion of people viewing at different times of day: in general, ITV ratings double between 5 pm and 8 pm, which is usually the peak viewing time. ITV ratings for individual programmes can run from under one—less than one per cent of adults viewing—to 40 or 45, and occasionally even higher.

Detailed analysis of the BARB data makes it possible to develop the next, valuable set of information. These are the data which tell the planner how to go about accumulating an audience, and what is needed to achieve given levels of reach and frequency (see page 109). Because of the way the audience is made up, and because of different people's viewing patterns, it requires a very heavy campaign to get anywhere near 100 per cent coverage of the audience. A more typical, fairly niche campaign burst would achieve coverage of perhaps 70 per cent, spread over 30 spots and yielding total TVRs of some 150–200. This gives an average rating per spot of only 5–6, and an average OTS of some 2.5—but a range of OTS from one or two (the majority) up to around 10. This make-up of the audience will be, in fact, as shown in Figure 11.3.

Clearly, your commercial is going to have to achieve some kind of miracle if it is to avoid boring the pants off the heavy viewer and still have some impact on the light viewer.

Data of this kind, to enable media planners to assess their schedules' reach and frequency, are held by AGB, who run the BARB service. The new BARB service offers the agency the ability to carry out a very wide range of detailed analysis—arguably to the point where the analyst becomes totally overloaded with data. A package of analyses under labels like FACETS, REACT, QUASAR, QUARTZ, etc., enable the media planner to identify in detail the demographic make-up of the audience to any spot or programme, either at individual or household level; audience reach and frequency build-up (see Figure 11.3); detailed spot by spot TVRs, by region, for defined audiences; analyses of own and competing brands; spending by region, daypart, day of week, etc.; the performance of individual TV stations; and so on. The whole can be made available in terms of 'live viewing'—the audience seeing the programme when it is transmitted—or 'consolidated viewing', which adds in the people who record the programme and view it later on their VCR. Finally, in contrast to the weekly availability of pre-1991 BARB, it is now possible to get top-line viewing data overnight.

The empty armchair
An obvious extension of head-counting research involves taking the fact that a TV set is switched onto ITV, and finding out whether anyone is actually in front of it watching it. Research has shown—as might be expected—that

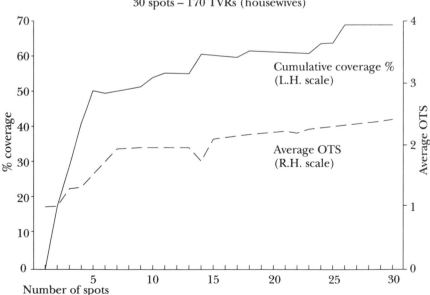

Figure 11.3 The build-up of a TV audience (*Source:* BARB (AGB Special Analysis))

'natural breaks' in programmes allow people to go to the lavatory or brew up a cup of tea rather than watch the commercials. In particular, between-programme breaks tend to favour this, since they are usually longer.

Equally, TV is—though intrusive—not necessarily anywhere near a completely dominating presence. People read, knit, iron, drink, talk, play cards, make love, build matchstick models of the *Queen Mary*... all in front of *Coronation Street* or *News at Ten*.

Unfortunately, there is no systematic, regular measurement available of attention to TV commercials (or, indeed, to TV programmes), so there is no reliable quantification of the 'attention factor', and our knowledge of how it varies by type or audience or time of day (or any other variable) is fairly rudimentary. Work done by J. Walter Thompson in the sixties, and some more recent experimental work by a number of researchers suggest that attention does vary by programme type, and 24-hour commercial recall actually varies by individual programme. A survey by TABS under the title *Cost per Thousand Adults, Or Cost per Thousand Empty Armchairs* indicates the reason for interest in the subject.

Does it work?
This subject was discussed at greater length in Chapter 9. Here, it is sufficient to point out that there are a number of ways of researching a commercial. It can be done before it appears on the air, either in a private room or in a theatre, to a large or small audience; it can be done after it has appeared by personal interview or (as frequently in the USA) by telephone. Similarly, you can set out to assess what the commercial communicates about the product advertised; or simply whether key details are remembered; or whether people like it. All you have to do, with any of these research methods and findings, is to decide which answer (if any) tells you the most about whether the commercial is any good. For discussion of this, see Chapter 9.

12 Press media

Newspapers

UK newspapers can be classified into six distinct groups:

National dailies
National Sundays
Regional mornings
Regional evenings
Regional weeklies
Regional free newspapers

The UK is unusual, in comparison with the USA or Continental Europe in particular, in having a very strong national daily and Sunday newspaper business which provides massive coverage of the country as a whole. In most other countries, even the largest papers, or those with the most prestige, are usually only, at best, semi-national, and the major newspaper market is a local or regional one.

In fact, as an advertising medium, the regional press in the UK is in total value more important than the national papers, and the combined circulation of regional papers is considerably higher than the nationals', but the latter carry greater prestige as media and are generally more attractive to major advertisers—with the notable exception of the retail trade. A large part of the regional papers' advertising is, in fact, classified (see Table 12.1).

National newspapers

The UK's national newspapers consist of 12 dailies and 11 Sundays. After years of decline in number through closures and mergers, the mid-eighties saw dramatic changes, based on the introduction of new technology and the subsequent collapse of the Fleet Street unions' stranglehold on newspaper management—and the dispersal of Fleet Street itself to Wapping and elsewhere. There have been, too, a number of changes in ownership: new 'barons' have emerged.

Both dailies and Sundays are normally thought of in two divisions—'quality' and 'mass market', though the two *Mails* and the two *Expresses*, together with *Today*, can legitimately claim to represent a 'middle-of-the-road' market, in terms of their readers' demographic profiles.

The combined circulations of the national papers have tended to decline, very gradually, over the years, though the fortunes of individual papers have varied; see Tables 12.2 and 12.3. In particular, the *Sun* replaced the *Daily Mirror* as the clear leader in circulation terms, and is—I think—the largest daily in the world apart from Japan's *Asahi Shimbun.* Among Sundays, the *News of the World* has declined rapidly, but still has a massive circulation.

Table 12.1   Newspaper advertising expenditure, 1991

	National £m	Regional £m	Total £m
Display	914	632	1546
Classified	208	996	1204
	1122	1628	2750

(*Source:* Advertising Association).

Table 12.2   National newspapers: circulation and readership trends 1970–1990 (1970=100)

	All national newspapers		National dailies		National Sundays	
	Circulation	Readership	Circulation	Readership	Circulation	Readership
1970	100	100	100	104	100	100
1975	94	92	106	99	88	87
1980	92	88	111	99	80	80
1985	90	87	104	95	80	82
1990	85	74	101	75	76	74

(*Source:* JICNARS, ABC)

In total, circulations of the national dailies have drifted downwards during the eighties, but, within this, the 'quality' papers have gained ground, helped by the strength of the *Guardian* and *The Times* and, most recently, the launch of the *Independent.* Sundays, as a whole, have lost circulation and readership rather steadily, though here again the qualities have done better.

The launch of *Today* in 1986 promised to introduce a new era of colour, both in editorial and advertising, but the quality of the editorial photography left much to be desired. Since then, 'on-the-run' colour has greatly improved, and become available on most national papers, though advertising space tends to be limited.

Alongside the newspapers are a growing number of colour magazines, started by the *Sunday Times,* but now available with the *Observer* and the Saturday issues of the *Independent, Daily Telegraph* and *The Times* among the qualities, as well as the *Mail on Sunday* (*You*), *Sunday Express* and *News of the World* (*Sunday*). While these are distributed with their parent newspapers, they compete, in practice, in the magazine advertising market

The other major feature of recent years has been the proliferation of

Table 12.3   Circulation of national dailies 1961–1992, in thousands

	1961	1971	1981	1986	1992
Daily Express	4321	3413	2160	1786	1511
Daily Mail	2649	1798	1932	1766	1744
Daily Mirror/Record	4578	4384	4191	3859	3602
Daily Sketch	991	–	–	–	–
The Star	–	–	1420	1349	795
Sun/Daily Herald	1407	2298	3882	4057	3553
Today	–	–	–	298	540
Total 'popular'	13946	11893	13585	13115	11445
Daily Telegraph	1248	1446	1372	1146	1038
Financial Times	240	170	201	193	287
Guardian	132	332	402	516	416
Independent	–	–	–	302*	365
The Times	257	340	292	468	377
Total 'quality'	1877	2228	2267	2625	2483
TOTAL	15823	14181	15852	15740	13928

*Q4 only
(*Source:* ABC)

separate sections of (mostly) the 'quality' papers, especially the Sundays, which started the process, and is most exaggerated in *The Sunday Times*. It is a failing of standard readership research (see page 154) that no data are available on the separate readership of, say, the business section of these split papers.

Regional papers
There are 17 regional morning papers, seven Sundays, over 120 evening papers and some 480 local paid-for weeklies in the UK at present, quite apart from over 800 free newspapers, distributed door-to-door. The growth of free newspapers, and of their advertising revenue, is a major phenomenon in the changing regional scene over the last 20 years. By 1991, free papers had not only outstripped paid-for weeklies in number, but had substantially higher coverage (70 per cent of adults against 41 per cent for paid-for papers, according to JICNARS), and had overtaken the paid-for weeklies in advertising revenue. The combined weekly regional press now exceeds the daily (morning and evening combined) regionals' advertising revenue.

    The regional press is a low-interest area for most of the media research fraternity, even though it accounts, in total, for over 20 per cent of advertising expenditure. The result of this, is that, in spite of the efforts of the Newspaper Society and the Association of Free Newspapers (a younger and livelier body), detailed analysis and comment at a technical level is extremely limited.

This applies to all sectors of the regional press, but most especially to the regional mornings: these papers, which are of very considerable importance in their areas, and reach one in eight of all adults on a national level, tend to be ignored by the largely London-based agencies—who are frequently heard deploring the south-eastern bias of national newspapers' strength but rarely go out to buy the *Yorkshire Post* or even the *Scotsman* to compensate. The only regional daily found on most national press schedules is the *Daily Record*, the *Mirror*'s Scottish stablemate.

The local evening press—including the London evenings, which tend, illogically, to be included among national dailies—is a major medium in its own right, reaching nearly a third of all adults. Simply because they are local, these papers are highly important for retail advertisers, as well as being massively used for classified advertising.

A number of surveys show that people say they regard their local paper as a rather good source of advertising information: it has the great merit of being specific to their area, so that they can be reasonably sure, for example, of finding a particular item at their local branch of a store chain, rather than having to look for it at the bigger one in the next major centre.

The local evening press offers a great diversity of size of circulation and quality of editorial and production, though standards in many centres have risen sharply with the introduction of new technology—well in advance of the nationals, in most cases. Evening papers exist in virtually all major cities, though very few now have more than one evening paper.

Apart from the London *Evening Standard*, only 11 evenings appear in the *National Readership Survey*, the press planner's guide to consumer behaviour, and this tends to set them apart from the rest, as they can be included in the more sophisticated forms of schedule analysis (see page 110) on a strictly comparable basis.

This is a major problem for all regional papers, not just the evenings, and the situation is only partly alleviated by the work of JICREG (Joint Industry Committee for Regional Press Research) and the development by the Newspaper Society of the PressAd database. For the advertiser and his or her agent, the regional picture is hardly simplified by the proliferation of groupings and sales houses, since the possibility of buying regional or—even—national 'packages' of publications, however tempting it may look, is not likely to lead to very effective use of the media. Regional papers, more than any other medium, need to be very carefully evaluated on a case-by-case, area-by-area basis.

Local weekly papers account for some £950 million of advertising annually, much of it classified. Free papers take some 65 per cent of this, and are growing in importance, while paid-for papers are static in revenue, and have declined sharply in numbers over the last 10 years. Between them, paid-for and free weeklies have a total circulation of over 55 million copies, with three-quarters of this going to the free papers, which claim 95 per cent coverage of households in their circulation areas, and a very high level of readership. Claims about readership are important to the free papers, since there is a widely-held belief in the advertising business that 'freesheets' are of low editorial quality and treated by their recipients as so much junk mail. In practice, free newspapers, like paid-for weeklies, vary widely in quality and—presumably—in the extent to which they are read.

The scale and fragmentation of the weekly press is far greater than that of the regional evenings, varied as they are. The task of any agency trying to put together a national campaign using local weeklies is formidable: even in a small region like East Anglia, over 40 publications are required to achieve reasonable coverage, and East Anglia has only some 5 per cent of the UK population. As a result, even with the aid of the sales houses, the local weeklies' advertising market tends to be, in reality, very local in character.

How newspaper space is sold

A newspaper is a more or less flexible product, so that, within certain restrictions, the space available for advertising is unlimited. In practice, of course, any editor tries to balance editorial and advertising, lest the readers feel swamped by the ads. Just what is the right balance is a moot point (see Table 12.4).

Media Week, a weekly magazine specializing in detailed coverage of advertising media matters, publishes regular figures for national press pagination. In November 1991—a reasonably typical month—the average national daily had around 65 per cent of its pages as editorial: this represents a slight increase in the figure of 61 per cent shown by an *Admap* study in 1984: compared with 1984, however, there are two conspicuous differences. First, the papers have tended to increase their total number of pages quite considerably (until 1989, the *Daily Mirror* was effectively confined to 32 pages by its presses); and, secondly, the 1991–2 recession has certainly adversely affected the classified market. All papers publish rate cards, and these are all available in summary form in *BRAD*, which usually brings together the essential basic figures for the media planner. (What *BRAD* does not do, however, is provide the other dimension of media planning—readership data, especially the demographics.) The vast majority of papers now sell space on the basis of the column centimetre. While the basic rate is the 'scc' (single column centimetre), the majority of papers have a preference for particular sizes over about 2 cm × 2 col (a 'two centimetre double'), and special rates are available for such spaces as 15 cm × 2 col, 35 cm × 6 col, etc. Some papers, at least in the abbreviated rate cards published in *BRAD*, quote *only* a column centimetre rate.

In general, the larger the space, the lower is the price per cm^2. This reflects the observable, but not exactly proven, fact that the cost effectiveness of press space declines over a certain size: a page is rarely, if ever, twice as effective as a half page, and the price must be discounted accordingly.

Beyond this, however, there is usually a wide variety of special rates available—whether premium rates for special positions in the paper, or reduced rates for those who are not so choosy. Thus, there is usually a premium of around 10 per cent for 'fixing' a position, premiums for solus positions, premiums for 'ear-pieces' (the two small spaces at the top of the front page of the *Daily Telegraph*), premiums for the front page.... Similarly, there are reductions for 'run-of-paper' or 'run-of-week' (which are, I hope, self-explanatory), and, usually, a quantity discount for a given number of pages, or indeed for insertions, over a given period.

Table 12.4   The content of national dailies 1975 and 1991*

	The Times		Daily Mail		Daily Mirror	
	1991	*1975*	*1991*	*1975*	*1991*	*1975*
Issue size (tabloid pages or equivalent	93	48	60	34	47	28
% of total space: Editorial	67	65	62	65	65	63
Advertising:						
Display	24	16	33	27	33	33
Classified:	9	19	5	8	2	4
	100	100	100	100	100	100
% of display advertising in colour	27	na	13	na	27	na

*November
(*Sources: Admap*, April 1985, *Media Week*)

In addition to the basic rate card, too, most papers have developed a series of special promotional programmes. These may involve advertising-based supplements—the *Financial Times* seems to have about two a week, ranging from such exotic subjects as banking in Luxembourg to reviews of office equipment or the economy of the USA. Some of these can be highly informative, but often the editorial is purely a device for filling in the space between the ads, and the value of the whole exercise to the advertiser is liable to be highly questionable. Another common device is the 'Christmas gift' page (or pages) which has a special rate structure favouring the small advertiser. Finally, at the level of national papers, there is a developing pattern of regional space selling. This is by now quite well developed, and it is possible to buy tabloids on a semi-regional basis, but not down to the level of individual TV areas. In addition, the weekly *Daily Mirror 'Xtra'* offers greater regional flexibility. Several of the Sunday colour supplements offer almost complete TV regional breakdowns.

Buying individual regions carries a substantial premium over the equivalent national rate—for example, in *You* magazine, buying a page in all 10 regions individually costs just under twice the national page rate—and this reflects, to an extent at least, the added complexity entailed for the publication, in terms of selling, administration, editorial and production make-up. There is still room for extension of, in particular, the daily papers' regional facilities: this is wanted by many advertisers, and the new technology makes it easier to implement than in the past.

After all this, of course, everything is, at least in theory, open to negotiation. Until the end of the seventies few national newspapers would directly discount their rate cards except in real desperation. Nowadays, this is no longer true, and even the *Daily Telegraph* has begun to deal. Between 1977 and 1986, the *average* discount on national newspapers' display advertising rose from 9 per cent to 26 per cent, according to figures derived from Advertising Association statistics by one of the leading media independents. Even the regional press has started to discount to national advertisers. In addition to straight money-off deals, of course, it is often quite possible to buy premium space at run-of-paper rates, and papers may often be willing to help with extra services—merchandising, mailings to retailers, run-on copies of colour ads, special 'editions' of the paper with a front page devoted to news about the client's business, etc. Sometimes a paper will be prepared to cooperate with, and contribute to, a research programme designed to assess some aspect of the campaign's effectiveness. All of these things can add value to what the buyer is getting for his or her money.

The buyer's task

Buying newspaper space is, like any other media buying task, a matter of balancing reach, frequency, cost, editorial quality and timing against a selected target audience.

Unlike TV, which is a very homogeneous medium in demographic terms, the newspaper business offers a fairly flexible choice of demographics—though with national papers these are a matter of weighting rather than genuine selectivity: to select a specific audience you have to go to magazines (or cinema or radio or direct mail).

Normally, a newspaper campaign—like a magazine campaign—is built up on the basis of an initial selection of newspapers against a specified target group. This is done on the basis of the *National Readership Survey*'s data on the demographic profiles of the various papers' average issue readership. Against the definition of the target audience, weights can be set for each sector. Thus, if you are advertising an expensive car, say a Saab, your primary target audience is likely to be (say) AB men, aged 35–55. These might well be regarded as the only relevant dimensions on which to weight. You then allocate your weights—perhaps as in Table 12.5

This mix of weights is then fed into a computer which holds the NRS data and the latest information on page costs for the various papers, and the computer will provide a listing of papers, giving the coverage of the primary audience and the cost per thousand of the primary audience.

This list provides the planner with the initial basis—no more—for a plan, by pointing out which papers are the most cost-effective for reaching that

Table 12.5 Allocation of weights

Men 2	AB 2	15–24 0
Women 0	C1 1	25–35 1
	C2DE 0	35–55 2
		55+ 0

particular audience. What the list does not do, however, is show how to put them together.

The next stage is to establish targets for coverage of the audience, since this defines the range of publications which will have to be used: you cannot reach more than some 35 per cent of AB men in an average issue of any paper, and although greater frequency will accumulate more of the audience through one paper, others will be needed to extend the coverage significantly.

(In practice, of course, you would be most unlikely to confine this exercise to newspapers alone, and the schedule would include magazines as well, but the principle is the same.)

To cut a long story short, you will end up with a list of perhaps four or five papers, and a number of insertions which, according to your own computer bureau's schedule-optimizing programme, will give you the most cost-effective combination of reach and frequency for your money. The process is complicated, of course, by considerations of space size. In the case of the Saab, you will probably insist on full pages, because these are believed—with some justification—to reflect the product's prestige and, even, contribute to it. For less obviously status-oriented products, however, the same effect can be achieved far less expensively by using spaces which, for all practical purposes, dominate the page—25 cm × 4 cols in a tabloid, or 35 cm × 6 cols in a broadsheet format.

Finally, then, we must end up with a schedule, which sets out, for the campaign period, the following information:

– the publications;
– the space size in each;
– the number and dates of each insertion;
– the total space cost;
– coverage of the primary target audience;
– average OTS for the primary audience.

It may, also, for completeness, include details of production costs and of the cost per thousand of the target audience, for each publication and for the campaign as a whole.

The whole thing will look like the press visual shown in Figure 12.1.

In practice, of course, the planner can, and will, use more than just raw demographic data to plan a schedule. On the one hand, lifestyle or psychographic pictures of the target audience (page 71) may be used as a further control on the publications to be used. On the other, the precise editorial context, for example, Wednesday's *Money Mail* section of the *Daily Mail* for a financial service, may be a key consideration.

Finally, once the schedule has been planned, the planner can use analysis based on the NRS to work out the cumulative reach and frequency achieved by the campaign.

Magazines

There are over 2000 different consumer magazines published in the UK, and their diversity of circulation size, readership and range of specialization is vast. Obviously, to do more than give a rather crude sketch plan of such an area is outside the compass of this book.

Magazines are published at intervals: weekly, two-weekly, monthly, bi-monthly, quarterly, six-monthly and even annually in certain specialized cases. Circulations range from a few hundred to millions, and magazines, more than any other medium, offer the possibility of selecting target audiences by most demographic criteria—with the significant exception, in most cases, of regionality—and by specific special interests. While they offer this degree of selectivity, however, they tend to be less good in terms of overall coverage. With the notable exceptions of the TV programme magazines and the major women's weeklies, it is impossible to build a magazine schedule which provides really mass coverage, though the more specialist groups of publications such as those covering gardening, or DIY, or motoring, can be combined to give very complete coverage of 'serious' gardeners, home improvers or motorists.

In total, then, magazines are an extremely important group of media, accounting in 1991 for advertising spending of over £395 million in consumer magazines and a further £535 million in trade and technical media. Altogether, magazines take in about 14 per cent of UK advertising expenditure. In countries without commercial TV, this proportion is usually significantly higher.

UK magazine publishers produce a range of titles covering most possible areas, though there are apparent gaps, with the result that new launches are frequent. Many of these succeed in establishing a niche in the market, but really major circulations are hard to achieve. A quite recent phenomenon in the magazine market is the launch in the UK of English versions of established successful titles from Europe. Since about 1985, *Prima, Chat, Best, Bella, Take A Break, Marie Claire, Hello!* and *Auto Express* have been successfully launched. The one major failure seems to have been Bauer's *TV Quick*, which has come a poor fourth in the still unfinished battle for the newly-liberated TV listings market, once Bauer started selling the magazine at a realistic price, rather than a promotional 10p.

Magazines with UK circulations over 200000 are common, as Table 12.6 shows. As can be seen from the table, there are a number of groups of publications with these high circulations, and they tend to come high on media planners' lists as they build their schedules.

MEDIA PLAN FOR 1992

LANSDOWNEURO
LANSDOWNEURO LIMITED, ABBEY HOUSE,
215–229 BAKER STREET, LONDON NW1 6YA
071-486 7111 TELEX: 8952286 FAX: 071-486 5310

			J F M A M J J A S O N D		£
TWO SELECTED TITLES					
Sunday Times magazine	6 pages				150000
Observer magazine			<— — —> 1 pg in each per month <— — —> 1 pg in each per month		
COLOUR SUPPLEMENTS					350000
YOU Magazine	2 pages + 1 DPS				
Telegraph magazine			<— — —>		
Independent magazine					
MEN'S INTEREST					
ES magazine	2 pages + 1 DPS				
GQ			<— — —>		
Esquire					
Economist					
WOMEN'S INTEREST	2 pages + 1 DPS				
Good Housekeeping, Harpers & Queen,					
Tatler, House & Garden, Taste,			<— — —>		
Country Living, Options, Marie Claire					
SPECIALS					150000
Recipe cards bound into selected titles			<— — — —>		
OUTDOOR					150000
London & South East	Superlites				
	48 sheets		<—> <—>		
	Cross-track				
TRADE					30000
			GROSS COST		830000
			CLIENT COST		810920
			VAT		140000
			GRAND TOTAL		**952920**

Figure 12.1 A typical press (mainly!) schedule for an upmarket brand

Table 12.6   Magazines with a circulation over 200 000

1992 circulation*	'000s		'000s
Radio Times**	1593	Puzzler Collection	413
Readers Digest	1521	Woman & Home	410
Take a Break*	1433	Family Circle	405
TV Times	1281	Woman's Realm	391
Bella*	1123	Auto Trader	364
Viz	875	Smash Hits	346
Woman's Weekly	827	BBC Gardener's World	333
Expression*	720	Marie Claire	310
Woman	717	House Beautiful	306
TV Quick	709	Puzzler	304
Woman's Own	700	More!	303
Prima	682	Sue	284
Best*	658	Satellite TV Europe	269
Me	595	New Woman	262
BBC Good Food	549	Ideal Home	255
Saga	501	Big!	253
Candis	500	Company	251
Hello!	488	Fiesta	246
People's Friend	484	Looks	231
Cosmopolitan	472	Elle	215
Chat	450	Just Seventeen	205
My Weekly	448	Private Eye	201
Good Housekeeping	446	Slimming	201
Essentials	421	19	200

(Source: ABC July–December 1992)
*Publisher's statement

Programme magazines
Until Spring 1991, *Radio Times* (BBC) and *TV Times* (ITV) were a planner's
bankers for broadscale magazine coverage, between them reaching over 40
per cent of UK adults. The removal of the publishers' monopolies of their
respective detailed listings opened the market to new entrants, and *TV Quick*,
TV Plus and *What's On TV* entered the market. By the end of the year, circulations had still not settled down, but the result of massive promotion and
aggressive advertising and price discounting—notably by *TV Quick*—appeared
to be that both *Radio Times* and *TV Times* had lost over a million copies weekly,
but that *TV Quick* and *What's On TV* combined had barely achieved this total as
a going rate, while *TV Plus* had quickly folded. The main effect had been to
cut sharply the cross-purchasing of *Radio Times* and *TV Times*.

Women's weeklies
The major women's weekly magazines are traditionally the main press media
for reaching a mass housewife audience, though their influence has certainly
been reduced by TV, and their circulations, as a group, have declined

considerably since the early sixties. However, the four IPC weeklies, plus *Bella* and *Best*, can reach over 40 per cent of women, and their editorial content provides an ideal context for advertising to women—whatever importance is attached to editorial context.

'Shopping' magazines

Two major monthly magazines, *Family Circle* and *Living*, are sold primarily through supermarkets rather than the traditional newsagent, and have a similar readership profile to the weeklies. They offer the added possibility of advertising purely to the shoppers of a particular supermarket chain, through customized editions, which can be a potentially useful support for tailor-made promotions. Both are, however, declining due to the practical slant of *Prima*.

Women's monthlies

There is a large group of magazines published monthly for a basically female audience. These range in character from the high fashion of *Vogue* to the overwhelming practical nature of *Prima* or *Essentials*. Within this overall monthly group are a number of titles which are more or less geared to specific age groups—usually, specific *young* age groups. (Second-guessing what precise age group reads a magazine from its title, or, indeed, its editorial is very difficult: the only way of being sure is to look at readership research findings.) Women's monthlies, which in total reach some 45 per cent of all women, are a major area for new titles. Of these, *New Woman* is perhaps the most successful recent example.

Household magazines

A small group of publications—*Ideal Home, Good Housekeeping, House Beautiful,* etc.—make up a very successful and strong group of media with considerable pass-on readership, by both sexes, which have a strong editorial authority concerning everything to do with the home. Their readership profiles are all more or less up-market, and they are widely used to advertise expensive and high quality durable and semi-durable goods.

'Practical' magazines

These are a mixture of weekly and monthly publications on subjects such as gardening, motoring, DIY. They tend to have quite small circulations relative to the total number of (say) car owners in the country, but collectively they reach a large proportion of the people who take these activities seriously. They are, therefore, good media for advertising to the professional or semi-professional, but can be less effective for the mass market, who may make up the majority of the potential market for any but the most specialized products. These magazines, therefore, are to an extent a trap for advertisers, in that they provide something of an illusion of completeness of coverage, and can actually cut them off from a large part of their market.

Men's magazines

Since about 1965, a small group of 'girlie' magazines has more or less success-fully attained respectability, on the back of the success of *Playboy* in the USA and internationally. *Mayfair, Penthouse* and *Fiesta*, together with one or two others, all have substantial circulations and provide good coverage of a young, well-off male audience. Their advertising base, in the UK at least, is still rather limited, and many advertisers are still wary of going into them, though the barriers appear to be coming down slowly. In the later eighties, a new branch of the men's magazine market developed in the form of the so-called 'style' publications—*GQ, Arena, The Face* and others—which were joined in 1991 by an aggressive US import, *Esquire*. In spite of the advertising industry's desire for a strong general men's magazine sector, all of these pub-lications remain quite small, so far.

General weeklies

These are a distinctly mixed bag, especially if, as is often done, the pro-gramme magazines and Sunday supplements are included. Apart from these, the group consists of very few major publications. A significant, unsuccessful attempt to enter this market was that of *Now!* a news magazine modelled on *Time* and *Newsweek*, which failed to meet ambitious targets, and folded at a cir-culation level of some 140 000. Other significant magazines in this group include *The Economist* and the late lamented *Punch*. The fortnightly *Private Eye*—not exactly everyone's choice as an advertising medium—also fits into this group, as, perhaps, does the massively successful fortnightly comic, *Viz.*

General monthlies

This is almost a special category for the *Reader's Digest*, since it is far and away the largest magazine in it—and in all respects uncategorizable. The *Digest* is one of those magazines which media people tend to like, but creative people tend not to: rightly or wrongly, there is a persistent view that the small page size makes it difficult to do justice to creative work. This is the main reason why the *Digest* for some years ran its 'Ten Million Club' scheme as the basis of its promotion to the advertising industry, since it focused attention on suc-cessful creative use of the *Digest* format.

Special interest magazines

This is a vast array of mainly monthly publications, though it includes week-lies in newspaper and magazine formats and, arguably, the racing dailies, *The Sporting Life* and *Racing Post*. These publications vary enormously in quality, coverage (even of the interest they cater to) and editorial authority. Many of them provide at best limited information to the advertiser—not even an audited circulation figure in many cases—and it can be extremely difficult for a newcomer to a particular field such as, say, model railways, to establish the relative merits as media of *Railway Modeller, Model Railway Engineer*, etc. A useful starting point for evaualtion is, quite simply, to see who else is advertising in each of the available publications. If all the more respected names are in one but not in the others, there is usually a good reason. This problem can be greatly exaggerated in a new field: the personal computer explosion of the early eighties led to a host of new titles competing for an uncharted and erratic market, and video games have had the same effect in 1992.

Free magazines

Free magazines, like free newspapers, have seen very rapid growth, and there are now at least 800 titles available, accounting for a substantial advertising revenue. Their combined circulation is well in excess of 1000 million annually. A substantial proportion of these magazines are controlled circulation publications for trade and technical markets, but the growth area has been the consumer market. Major categories, in circulation terms, are airlines' in-flight magazines, London street-distribution magazines like *Ms London* or *Nine to Five*, and financial institutions' mailed magazines like American Express's *Expressions*.

The Association of Free Magazines and Periodicals has joined with the AFN, the Association of Distributors of Advertising Material and the on-line media information service MediaTel to publish the annual A–Z of Britain's free newspapers and magazines, a comprehensive guide to these publications.

Trade and technical magazines

Trade magazines are mainly geared to the retail trade, and most major divisions of retailing are served by one or more such publications—*The Grocer, Hardware Trade Journal, Travel Trade Gazette, CTN, Off-Licence News,* etc. Most of these retail-oriented papers are weekly, with the notable exception of the publicans' daily, the *Morning Advertiser.* Retail magazines are widely used for launch announcements of new products and announcements of new campaigns. Many advertisers tend to regard the retail trade press with some scepticism as a way of talking to the trade, as it is a widely held view that it is not very thoroughly read by most retailers, so that advertising has to be very dramatic or large scale to be noticed, and major campaigns often use inserts, or gate-fold formats to increase their ability to attract attention. It should, however, be made clear that there is very little actual research evidence to support this view of the trade press, and retailers, one survey showed, do tend to think that ads in the trade press show that the advertisers are serious in their approach to the market. In any event, though, the main job of reaching the trade is surely that of the sales force, and advertising has, or should have, very much a supporting role for the manufacturer in selling to retail stockists.

The more technical media have a rather different role, since these publications are used mainly by businesses to sell to other businesses. Here there is a very wide range of available publications covering most significant branches of industry or the service trades. According to *Benn's Press Directory,* there are well over 850 trade and technical publications, with a combined circulation of at least 10 million. The quality is, arguably, not as high as it is in the USA, nor is the variety as extensive, but in both respects the British media are generally superior to those available in Continental Europe. There are, in fact, a number of major industries where the main media internationally are either American or British, and where there is little competition from local sources even in the main non-English-speaking markets.

It is worth noting here, although this book is not primarily concerned with industrial advertising, that industrial advertising is by no means confined to the technical press—indeed, it is appearing more often in general press media and even, increasingly, on TV. Equally, media advertising is normally a small part of the industrial marketer's promotional effort, in contrast to its very substantial share of consumer goods marketing budgets.

How magazine space is sold and bought
The basis of magazine space selling and buying is very similar to that of newspapers. The business operates according to similar categories of space size, special positions, premiums for fixing, series discounts, etc. Colour is far more generally available, and the proportion of colour, at least for sizes over about a quarter page, is generally high. The major problem for the magazine space salespeople, far more than for their colleagues on newspapers, is likely to be to get on the schedule: the choice open to space buyers is very large, and at least part of a wide magazine schedule usually ends up being bought to an extent on the basis of either advertisers' or agencies' (carefully rationalized) prejudices. This is because the available research sources—see page 144—are not so comprehensive as for newspapers; and, especially in the case of more specialized fields, the availability of audited circulation figures, let alone all the candidate titles being on the *National Readership Survey*, is far from certain.

Magazine marketing departments are particularly active, therefore, in carrying out surveys of their public, speculative schedule-building exercises, and other more or less research-based attempts to demonstrate the relevance or, ideally, the indispensability of their publication to a particular advertiser. Some of this material is genuinely useful—for example, the *Businessman Readership Surveys*, now extended to Europe, initially started by the *Financial Times*, have filled a significant gap in advertisers' knowledge. Obviously, however, any analysis produced by salespeople needs to be carefully scrutinized before its conclusions can be accepted—this is not to cast doubt on the integrity of magazine marketing departments: it is just sound common sense. Usually what need to be checked are the basic assumptions: just what has been left out from, or added to, the ideal approach in order to present the salespeople's magazine in the best possible light.

In addition to this area of technical selling points, magazines are often willing or able to offer the advertiser special inducements to advertise: promotions, sampling programmes, PR services, reader reply services, merchandising efforts against particular categories of store. For the creative department, many magazines nowadays are prepared to be very flexible about the shapes of ads—indeed, *Company* actually ran a competition for the most imaginative space bought in the magazine. Certainly, diagonal arrangements of quarter page ads across a DPS, horizontal half pages (even, occasionally, across the middle third of the page) L-shaped and T-shaped ads, are far more frequently seen today than 10 years ago. One innovation that comes and goes in cycles is the microencapsulation of fragrance on the page: it had a brief vogue about 15 years ago and since then has reappeared at regular intervals.

One or two major publishers, notably IPC, are able to offer an advertiser packages linking several publications. This is most common with IPC's four major women's weeklies, but is also done with some groups of teenage publications and even in the IPC 'practical' group, where a commonality of interest across several magazines is rarer. Similarly, the women's weeklies, and one or two other publications, offer limited facilities for regional advertising: the only genuine regional breaks, however, are in the TV programme magazines. An important regional facility, available in a growing number of magazines, is the ability to put inserts—leaflets or brochures—into a limited number of copies, usually within closely controlled distribution areas.

The process of buying magazine space is similar to that for newspapers, but there are some significant differences. The major one of these is that of lead times. Copy dates for colour ads in monthly magazines are, typically, five to six weeks before publication, and so the space has to be booked, in general, a good three to four months in advance, and cancellation dates are often two to three months before copy date. A further difference is in another aspect of the time-scale. With infrequent publication, several insertions in one magazine can cover six months or more very easily. Magazine campaigns, in consequence, tend to be considerably more drawn out than newspaper campaigns, let alone bursts of TV. By the same token, since coverage has to be built up both by extending the list of publications and by frequency of insertion within a publication, a magazine campaign tends to be relatively slow to build its effect. This is less true of the weeklies than of other magazines, of course.

Media buying in magazines—as elsewhere—is subject to a fair collection of myths and rules of thumb, most of them of rather dubious standing. No one, to my knowledge, has successfully established a value, or a conclusive argument in favour, for being on the right-hand rather than a left-hand page; or for being in the front rather than the back of the 'book'; or for facing matter as opposed to another ad. There is a certain amount of evidence from reading and noting surveys for propositions of this kind, but reading and noting surveys are not the most satisfactory of research tools, and there has been virtually no controlled experimentation except by direct response advertisers, who keep the findings very carefully to themselves. Nonetheless, many magazines' rate cards charge premiums for specifying certain positions of this type, and many advertisers subscribe to the various myths. (My personal candidate for the least valuable premium position is the inside back cover.) The whole area is, frankly, ripe for some systematic and scientifically structured research, but apart from one or two articles in *Admap*, there is little sign of any real interest in the problem in the industry, and the technical problems are considerable.

The media buyer's objectives with magazines are, ultimately, the same as for newspapers: to achieve the best possible combination of coverage, frequency and cost per thousand within his or her budget. There is a far wider capability for effectively specifying a target audience and setting weights for it. The only difficulty is that, although the *NRS* now carries over 250 titles, of which 190-odd are magazines, this is a quite narrow coverage of the candidate media for most campaigns. For the other publications there may only be available an audited circulation figure (possibly not even that), and conceivably either data from *TGI* on the reader profile or, perhaps, a proprietor-sponsored survey. None of these data fit very easily into an *NRS*-based computer analysis. The scope for judgement is, therefore, far wider and more varied than with newspapers.

When you go from consumer magazines to the trade and technical field, the situation is even less clear. There is often little research data available from which to establish a 'pecking order' among directly competing publications: many have ABC* circulation certificates, but it is unusual to get from anywhere any assessment of overall readership or the quality of that readership. Within the advertising industry itself, for example, each copy of *Campaign* might be read by four or five people: but of those four or five, possibly only one may be a relevant decision-maker if you are trying to advertise, say, the services of a studio, or a range of business gifts. Among recently developing markets, computers offer the widest and most complex puzzle to the media buyer.

The advertising industry has tried to make the media people's task a little easier in this cloudy area by means of the *Media Data Form*, sponsored by ISBA and the IPA, but this provides, at best, limited information.

Research into press media
The discussion of the media and how they are bought has already outlined the main types of research available into press media.

The national readership survey
The main, basic research source is the *National Readership Survey*, carried out currently by Research Services Ltd for the Joint Industry Committee for National Readership Surveys (JICNARS). This survey is concerned solely with readership, and is based on a survey of 35000 adults carried out throughout the year. Reports, on a cumulative annual basis, are published six-monthly.

'Readership' is defined as 'having read or looked at recently'. If a

*Audit Bureau of Circulation.

respondent has 'last read', in these terms, a publication within its publication interval, he or she is then classified as an 'average issue reader', which is the basic readership category. Further questioning establishes how many of the last six issues of each publication have been read, making it possible to provide estimates of cumulative readership.

The technique has its limitations—chiefly those of memory, which affects monthlies more than dailies or weeklies, and of sheer fatigue: each respondent goes through over 100 titles. There are, too, specific problems with some product groups—women's weeklies and household magazines, in particular—because of title confusion; and problems of so-called 'parallel readership' (if someone has read two or more different issues of a publication in the publication period, readership will be underestimated) and 'replicated readership' (if someone has read the same issue across two or more publication periods, readership will be overestimated).

In addition to readership data, the *NRS* collects an increasing amount of information about the people in its sample, making it possible to carry out at least limited cross-analysis against recent ownership of a range of consumer durables, ownership of credit cards, use of other media, holiday taking, etc.

As far as magazines are concerned, an added complication has been created by a research measurement known as MPX (multiple page exposure). This is based on the premise that at least some magazines, and even newspapers, are read or referred to more than once by their readers. Thus, an ad in *Radio Times*—to take a particular example—may be seen three or four times, while one in *Woman* may only be seen once. While some magazines have tried to make this into a case against other media groups, it carries more weight in comparing individual magazines: this is because an ad in a magazine does not become any more effective *vis-à-vis* (say) TV, just because you suddenly know that it is seen twice as often as you thought it was—if anything, this means that, in the light of past history and experience, it is actually *less* effective. If, however, you are building a press schedule and evaluating it by OTS comparisons between publications (as opposed to referring to past history), a higher MPX may reasonably influence the choice of publication.

TGI

The other major general source on magazine readership is the *Target Group Index*, produced annually by the British Market Research Bureau. This is a very large (25000 adults) self-completion survey which provides data on product and brand usage in a vast variety of product fields and analyses these against readership of over a hundred press media and broad categories of exposure to other media. It is possible to use *TGI* data to identify which magazines or papers are most appropriate to a given brand—or, for the magazine, which products or brands it should try to persuade to become advertisers. This type of media-linked product survey is a valuable guide to media selection, though it is expensive and frequently misused. The important factor to be considered is not only whether the medium has a high proportion of users of the product among its readers, but whether it also actually reaches a significant proportion of the users. An apparently attractive publication may in fact only be able to reach a tiny proportion of your target audience, and add nothing to an overall schedule at rather high cost.

Individual media surveys

Individual publications or groups of publications periodically carry out surveys into their own and competitive publications' readers, usually designed to establish that their magazine's or paper's reputation or editorial authority is superior, or that their advertising is better remembered or valued. These surveys tend to be technically flawed, though their quality has improved in the last 15 years. When faced with such a survey, you need to be very clear about the nature of the sample—American magazines are particularly liable to use postal surveys inserted in the magazine, which are virtually useless—and about the precise questionnaire, which may well involve leading questions or be chiefly of interest for what was not asked.

Reading and noting surveys

Techniques developed by Starch in the USA and Gallup in the UK are used to examine the extent to which a claimed reader of a publication has looked at or studied individual pages—editorial or advertising. A page looked at at all achieves a percentage 'page traffic' in the sample as a whole, and further questioning establishes whether the page was merely looked at, read in full, or read in part.

The technique is clearly vulnerable to problems of memory, as was demonstrated by work by the Agencies Research Consortium, among others, during the late sixties. It can, however, probably provide a reasonable comparative guide to how a particular ad, in a particular position, in a particular magazine, stands up against other, possibly competitive ads in the same magazine. At least, if your ad was not looked at at all, you are probably in trouble.

Other techniques

During the last 10 years, a lot of technical work has been done with eye cameras and similar devices to try to establish the relationship between claimed readership and advertisement recall and actual readership. This work, which is summarized at some length in a booklet published by the Agencies Research Consortium,[*] shows that there are enormous conceptual and technical difficulties in producing meaningful and usable results from reading, noting and recall types of research. A more recent set of papers on readership, which adds some new ideas, but little positive in the way of conclusions, is to be found in *Admap*, June 1985. The problems, and the debates, continue.

---

[*]W. A. Twyman, *The Measurement of Page and Advertisement Exposure—a Review of Progress by the ARC*, ARC, 1972.

13 The minor media

Outside TV and the press, there are three major, if secondary, media: radio, outdoor, and cinema. In addition, there is a substantial business in direct mail which is also discussed in this chapter, and a number of very marginal, lesser media.

Cinema

There are some 1700 cinemas (defined as separate screens) in the UK taking advertisements. Numbers have fallen from nearly 3000 in the late fifties, but the decline bottomed out around 1970, and there has been a sharp increase since the mid-eighties. The cinema industry has been quite active in the last few years in restructuring its 'plant', and many large cinemas have been converted into two-screen or three-screen operations which can offer a choice of films to the same locality at the same time.

Cinemas in the UK are dominated by two major circuits, owned respectively by Rank (Odeon) and Cannon, but a number of minor chains have been built up—with rather mixed results—over recent years.

The cinema as a place of regular mass entertainment was killed after the war by TV, and its current position is far from secure, although the years since 1985 have seen some recovery from the disastrous decline between 1978 and 1984. Nonetheless, at 90 million annual admissions in 1990, the industry was running at only one-fifth of its 1960 level, and was still 35 per cent below 1978.

To a very large extent the cinema has become a refuge for young people: 15–24 year olds are only 18 per cent of the population over age seven, but account for 56 per cent of all cinema visits, according to the regular surveys carried out by the Cinema Advertising Association.

A 15–24 year old is six times as likely to go to the cinema once a month as a 35–44 year old. Children aged 7–14 are, too, more likely to go to the cinema than older adults, in spite of their exclusion from many films rated 15 or 18, and may account for 25–30 per cent of the audience for a popular PG-rated film. As well as this young bias, the audience is quite strongly ABC1 in character, but recent trends in popular films—towards war and Rambo-like violence—have removed any female bias from the audiences.

The cinema is thus a good medium for reaching a young, reasonably well-off audience which is in a mood to enjoy itself: and, for the most part, those

who are outside the dominant 15–24 age group share most of these attitudes—with, presumably, the exception of the select band of middle-aged
men in dirty mackintoshes who make up most of the rather small audience
for such X-rated sagas as *Danish Dentist on the Job.*

As a medium, the cinema is almost infinitely flexible. Advertising can be
bought by cinema, by the week; it can be bought—with a bit of difficulty—
against specific films; it can be bought in units from 15 to 60 seconds or
longer. You can, therefore, use it to advertise a single fast food restaurant in
Romford or a brand of gin nationally. For the small local advertiser, the major
chains provide a service of slides or generalized films with an appropriate
voice over. For the major advertiser, it is possible to top-and-tail a commercial
with the name and details of a local dealer or retailer. In addition, it is now
possible to buy an 'Audience Delivery Package'—equivalent to a TV GHI
package—at a rate of £33 per thousand admissions in London, or £24.20 per
thousand elsewhere.

As a general principle, national campaigns are bought in half of all cinemas—if you do more, you are buying a large proportion of duplication rather
expensively—and rarely two weeks running, because most cinemas run major
films for at least two weeks and audiences fall off—it is, therefore, rather
important that you should be in on the first week of a run.

For a week on 50 per cent of UK cinema screens, a 30-second spot cost
some £48 500 in 1992, but this did not include the cost of either production
of the film or, importantly, the cost of the 800-plus prints required—at an
approximate cost of £35 each. While 30 seconds is quoted as a convenient
comparison with TV, major national advertisers tend to use 60-second films
for preference: 60-second costs are twice as high as for 30 seconds.

Although cinema has become very much TV's poor relation in expenditure terms, accounting for a mere 0.5 per cent of UK advertising spending, it
is creatively an exciting medium, in which far more innovative and high quality work, in relation to spending levels, is being done than in TV. This is for
three reasons.

First of all, the cinema audience is, unquestionably, livelier and more
receptive to visual ideas than the TV audience: it is not only younger, and
therefore more in tune with changing trends in film, it is also an audience
that is quite interested in seeing what is put on the screen in front of it—
that is, after all, virtually the only reason for being in the cinema. Secondly,
because of this key factor about the cinema audience, that it is expecting to
be entertained, cinema commercials *have,* far more than TV commercials,
actually to set out to be entertaining: this does not mean that they have to
be uproariously funny, but it does mean that they must, for example, like
the Southern Comfort drink commercials, be visually attractive. The third
reason is, in fact, related to the presence in the cinema of Southern Comfort. The fact that spirits and cigarettes are allowed to advertise in the cinema gives these very major advertisers their only opportunity to use film for
advertising, and they not only use this chance enthusiastically, but do their

best to get the most out of it. In so doing, they set a high standard for others.

It is, therefore, easy to be self-indulgent in cinema advertising. The key control has to remain the question of whether the commercial is or is not on strategy. It is, however, difficult to use TV commercials in the cinema as they stand: usually, they do not translate well to the larger screen—unless they have been made very explicitly for a younger audience.

In addition to the industry's surveys, limited data on cinema visiting are collected in both the *Target Group Index* and the *National Readership Survey*, so that cinema use can be cross-analysed against other media. These data show that the cinema enables you, over time, to accumulate a very large audience among younger people, but that it takes a considerable time to do so.

Cinema advertising is mainly sold by two major groups: Rank, which covers the Odeon and related cinemas, and Pearl and Dean, which covers the Cannon chain and a variety of other groups. Cinema commercials are sold on the basis of a 15 second rate, which increases *pro rata* for longer spots.

Outdoor

Outdoor advertising covers a variety of individual media in many different locations. The major section of the business consists of the conventional poster, but there are plenty of other possibilities: bus sides and interior panels, railway and underground sites and panels, illuminated signs, 'poster motors', balloons, sky-writing, etc. Even more exotic possibilities exist, of course, ranging from sandwich-men to suitably decorated cattle grazing beside railway lines.

Outdoor and transport advertising accounts for less than 4 per cent of total UK advertising expenditure—this is a similar proportion to that in many other developed markets—and this share has tended to decline since the early sixties. However, the industry has undergone a series of transformations in recent years, and it is now both more concentrated and better organized than ever.

Posters

There are some 120 000 roadside poster sites in the UK of varying sizes and qualities. Since the dissolution of British Posters by the Monopolies Commission in 1981, the industry has gone through a series of mergers and reorganizations, which may still have some life in it. At present, three main groups control some 70 per cent of the business—Mills and Allen, Arthur Maiden, and More O'Ferrall. Poster revenue is quite small in relation to all advertising—3.6 per cent of the total—but is growing, and is worth just over £270 million.

Posters are available in three main sizes: 4-sheet, 16-sheet and 48-sheet (a 4-sheet is 60 in × 40 in, and most of the rest are multiples of that): 12-sheet and 32-sheet sites are also available in small numbers, and there is a growing number of 'Supersites'. 'Supersites' is a generic term for large, often unique sites, that may offer special facilities for tailored, unusual creative treatments. The total number of sites is declining quite steadily, and is 30 per cent smaller than in 1976; while 4-sheets had consistently gained in importance within the whole, largely at the expense of 16-sheets, until the recent development of 6-sheets (see Table 13.1).

Table 13.1   Availability of poster sites, by size, 1991

Size	1991	% change since 1987
4-sheet	47761	– 35
6-sheet	21048	(+ 00)
12-sheet	1092	– 42
16-sheet	7366	– 56
32-sheet	1966	– 9
48-sheet	32486	+ 1
Supersites	2092	+ 24
	114701	– 10

(*Source:* OSCAR/Poster Marketing)

Sites are marketed in three main ways: line by line on an individual site basis; in packages marketed by contractors to meet a fairly simple specification, and in long-running TC ('till countermanded') campaigns held by, typically, tobacco and alcohol advertisers. As recently as 1976, TC holdings accounted for over a third of all poster sales, but they have declined rapidly in recent years. The late seventies saw a rapid build-up of packages, but this process was halted by the break-up of British Posters, and a present two-thirds of sales are made line by line—an altogether more complex process, which tends to be carried out by many agencies through specialist sub-contractors like Portland. These specialists control two-thirds of roadside poster spreads.

Traditionally, posters were sold on a three-monthly basis, but this has changed rapidly and most contractors base their rate cards on either 14 or 28 days. Costs vary according to size and quality of site, and the type of package bought. Line by line, 4-sheets cost up to £75 per month, but for 12 months this is discounted to, say, £50 per month. At the other end of the scale, a supersite on London's Cromwell Road may cost £35000 a month, including production. Some typical costs for packages are given in Table 13.2.

As advertising media, posters provide massive coverage and frequency—as measured by passing traffic—for a very simple message. Except in the London Underground, where it is possible to while away waiting time by reading quite lengthy copy, posters have to be very simple and direct communications. As such, they are ideal for reminder campaigns, and as support and continuation media for TV campaigns, though American research has demonstrated a clear ability to increase recall of particular messages over an inferior performance by TV.

Table 13.2   Costs of typical poster packages, 1993

Group	Package	Size	No. of posters	Cost £'000 per month
More O'Ferrall	Standard	6-sheet	5 000	*
More O'Ferrall	London	6-sheet	1 000	*
British Transport	National Core	48-sheet	300	120
Maiden Outdoor	601	48-sheet	600	286
Mills & Allen	Master 1	48-sheet	1 000	500
National Sales	Classic Red	48-sheet	300	132
Dolphin	London (GLC)	48-sheet	210	95
KMS	Granada	48-sheet	75	24
Mills & Allen	Main City 1	96-sheet	200	340
National Sales	Choice	96-sheet	124	180
More O'Ferrall	270 Network	27' × 10'	500	580

(Source: *Media Week*)
*Seasonal rates

Creatively, the poster offers an opportunity both for design and for writing, and many of the classic British ads have, in fact, been posters. There are some technical problems in designing a poster—a 16-sheet poster is produced in two separate portions, and colour matching across the join may create difficulties. The possibility always exists of overprinting (or, rather, 'overposting') a poster to update it or extend its message, and some of the fancier supersites offer the sort of opportunity, used by the *Observer* newspaper, of keeping a permanent site with a replaceable panel to carry the front cover of the next week's colour magazine.

Research on the poster medium has traditionally been limited. In 1985, however, the Outdoor Advertising Association (OAA) introduced OSCAR (Outdoor Site Classification and Audience Research). Using research by NOP, an audit was carried out of 130 000 sites, which resulted in each site being classified according to eight criteria: visibility, competition (i.e. is the site solus?), angle of vision, deflection, obstruction, height above ground, illumination, and weekly traffic past site. This survey is updated on a continuous basis. Traffic is computed for both pedestrians and vehicles, and a mathematical calculation used to give the site a rating in the form of an adjusted OTS. The location of each site is also described in detail in the *Outdoor Digest*. OSCAR has thus provided the poster buyer with at least a passable equivalent to the research available to other media for planning a campaign. From a different viewpoint the industry has sometimes mounted or sponsored research designed to demonstrate the ability of posters to generate recall. Poster Marketing, the OAA's marketing arm, is the active mover in these exercises.

Other outdoor media

Apart from orthodox posters, the most important outdoor medium is transport advertising, chiefly on buses, where bus sides and backs are marketed on a regional basis by two major contractors: British Transport Advertising and London Transport Advertising—who also, of course, handle London Underground ads, both posters and tube cards. Double-decker sides cost around £55–85 per month, and a London campaign might involve some 500 bus sides, though you can, of course, just buy one or two routes if you have reason to be selective.

London Underground posters, on a line basis, range from some £5 per month for tube cards to £25 per month for escalator panels, and offer very considerable flexibility in terms of choice of station or route; a typical piece of concentrated buying is Barclaycard's monopoly of the escalator panels between London Transport and the main line BR concourse at Waterloo. Airport advertising has grown rapidly in importance in recent years, too.

Beyond these 'orthodox' transport sites, you can now buy taxi door panels and interior panels in major cities all over Britain, as well as ads on vans, trucks and lorries. While some of these offer opportunities for precise, local targeting, others appear—to say the least—speculative.

Football grounds and other sporting venues offer interesting possibilities of getting your poster—usually just a name—on TV, but are hardly reliable media if that sort of coverage is looked for.

Radio

Until 1973, the only commercial radio available in the UK was Radio Luxembourg—very much a specialized minority medium, broadcasting an evening-only schedule more or less nationally. In the last 15 years, however, the Independent Local Radio (ILR) network has been expanded to its present level of some 80 individual local stations, covering between them 90 per cent of UK households.

Most ILR stations have local commercial monolopies, but London's two original stations, Capital and LBC, have been joined by half a dozen more—Kiss FM, Buzz FM, Melody, Jazz FM, WMC—and there are also second stations in Manchester and Belfast, while Capital has split its service between Capital Gold and Capital FM. ILR stations compete, of course, with the five national BBC services, as well as BBC local stations. In addition, although Luxembourg is now only accessible via the Astra Satellite and has effectively ceased broadcasting to the UK, an Irish station, Atlantic 252, has near-national coverage of the UK.

Finally, the Radio Authority has licensed its first national channel, Classic FM, and Virgin 1215 FM opened in May 1993; there are plans for these to be followed by a third, INR3, in 1993.

ILR has not really fulfilled some of the more optimistic hopes for its development as an advertising medium, and the performance of individual stations, both commercially and in terms of audience development, has been patchy. A number of stations have had to be financially restructured or have changed ownership.

As can be seen from the summary table (Table 13.3), the weekly adult penetration varies very considerably from station to station. Nationally, some 52 per cent of adults listen to ILR at all in any one week, and ILR accounts for nearly two-fifths of all radio listening. Obviously, crude figures for overall coverage are a massive simplification. Listening intensities vary considerably, though the latest RAJAR research suggested that the average listener to ILR was listening more.

RAJAR, which replaced the earlier ILR-only JICRAR surveys in 1992, is a quarterly survey that provides audience data both for BBC radio and all ILR stations.

The ILR network is limited to nine minutes of advertising in any hour, and the majority of stations now broadcast 24 hours a day. The major development of the late eighties was the practice of splitting stations' output between AM and FM, so as to allow at least a degree of targeted programming. Of course, a key effect of this is to fragment the audience still further, a phenomenon that is vastly more advanced in the highly-developed US market.

Detailed research evidence on patterns of listening and, hence, audience composition by time segment is quite limited, though it is clear, for example, that the mid-morning audience will be predominantly a housewife one, while morning and evening rush-hour commuter periods have a substantial male audience. The overall ILR audience has a slight male bias, but little difference in age or social class from the population as a whole.

Time on ILR is sold on a spot basis, with the day divided into a number of time segments. Morning and evening rush hours are the peak, and therefore more expensive, segments. Although most air time is purchased selectively, it is possible on some stations to buy what Capital Radio calls 'target rating plans' which provide a mix of spots spread over a seven-day period to provide a guaranteed level of ratings.

Given the variety of programming between different ILR stations it is difficult to buy on a spot basis against a particular audience specification—not least because of the lack of regular, detailed research. This can give the local advertiser a potential advantage, due to his or her theoretical ability to apply local knowledge and buy more selectively. Very little ILR programming is networked, apart from the news service provided by Independent Radio News (IRN) and the Network Chart and Network Album Shows—pop music—on Sunday.

ILR airtime is sold through a small group of sales companies—MSM (owned by Capital Radio), IRS and SIRS—which between them handle all the major stations. A further, small company, RSC, handles two of the newer specialist London stations and Manchester's Sunset radio. The sales companies have tended to put together regional groupings of stations that correspond—broadly—to TV areas, though this picture has become less orderly than it appeared two or three years ago. At present, SIRS has a monopoly in

Table 13.3   UK independent local radio stations 1992: main stations

Station	Area/City	Population served ('000 adults)	% weekly reach (mid-1992)	Sales company
Capital FM	London	9591	29 ⎫ 44	Capital (MSM)
Capital Gold	London	9591	18 ⎭	Capital (MSM)
LBC	London	9591	15	IRS
Mercury	West Sussex/Guildford	1077	21	MSM
Ocean	Portsmouth/Southampton Winchester	1171	33	IRS
South Coast	Eastbourne/Hastings	485	30	IRS
South Coast	Brighton	676	31	IRS
Two Counties	Bournemouth	520	40	IRS
Radio 210	Reading/Basingstoke	768	27	IRS
County	Guildford/West Sussex	1077	10	MSM
Invicta	Maidstone/Canterbury	1238	24	IRS
Thamesmead	Thamesmead	390	4	MSM
Devonair	Exeter/Lyme Regis	451	31	MSM
Orchard FM	Taunton/Yeovil	476	19	MSM
Plymouth	Plymouth	314	37	IRS
Chiltern-East	Luton/Bedford/ Milton Keynes	2522	26	MSM
East Anglia	East Anglia	1089	40	IRS
Essex Radio	Southend/Chelmsford	1080	33	MSM
Mid Anglia	Peterborough/Cambridge	854	27	MSM
Chiltern-West	Gloucester	1056	20	MSM
GWR	Bristol/Swindon	1465	37	IRS
Red Dragon	Cardiff/Newport	869	38	MSM
Swansea	Swansea	533	37	MSM
Severn	Hereford/Worcester	596	13	IRS
Beacon	Black Country	1419	37	IRS
Fox FM	Oxford/Banbury	558	37	MSM
Marcher	Wrexham	694	24	IRS
BRMB	Birmingham	2033	20	IRS
Trent	Nottingham/Derby	1521	17	IRS
Leicester Sound	Leicester	657	16	IRS
Mercia	West Midlands	680	40	IRS
Signal	Stoke	1289	23	IRS
City	Liverpool	2104	29	MSM
Piccadilly	Manchester	2863	39	MSM
Red Rose	Preston/Blackpool	1068	38	MSM
Aire	Leeds	863	34	MSM
Metro	Yorkshire	3571	23	IRS
Metro	Tyne and Wear	2314	42	IRS
Clyde	Glasgow	1867	55	SIRS
Forth	Edinburgh	1049	43	SIRS
Tay	Dundee/Perth	424	38	SIRS
Moray Firth	Inverness	160	53	SIRS
Northsound	Aberdeen	250	55	SIRS
West	Ayr	270	43	SIRS
Downtown	Ulster	1134	49	SIRS

(*Source*: RAJAR Oct–Dec 1992)

Scotland and Ulster, and MSM in Granada. IRS is very strong in most of the rest of the country, but their strength is interrupted by pockets of stations handled by other sales companies, mostly MSM in Anglia, HTV and the south-west. This situation makes it relatively easy to put together radio campaigns covering a TV area, either as a support for TV or as a substitute for it.

As commercial radio has become established in the UK, it has tended to become more and more a local advertiser's medium, and has only attracted a rather limited number of major national advertisers, apart from the big retail multiples. There are several reasons for this. Firstly, it is only quite recently that the network has become more or less fully national; and even then coverage remains well below that on TV. Secondly, the capital cost of a 'national' campaign, using 80-plus stations, is substantial, if the campaign is to achieve reasonable coverage and the level of frequency that the medium is considered to require. Then, the pricing structure, in terms of deals and discounts available, tends to favour local advertisers. Finally, the medium has nothing approaching the level of research data available from BARB on ITV—whatever the question marks that can be attached to the detail of the latter. All these factors have combined to keep radio, so far, as a very peripheral medium.

However, the introduction, originally by the Radio Marketing Bureau, of network radio packages has at least made it theoretically possible to advertise 'nationally' on ILR without having to go through too many individual sales organizations.

At present, there is a limited range of opportunities to buy network radio, through MSM, acting on behalf of the Association of Independent Radio Contractors (AIRC): seven day packages of three spots per day; news packages, of three spots per day adjacent to main news broadcasts; and the Sunday Network Chart Show. In addition, IRS sell 'Newslink' and 'Sportslink' packages, covering all the stations for which they or SIRS act as a sales house.

Radio's virtues as a medium are its localness, its 'news' character, the opportunities for considerable repetition, and its relative cheapness, both for production and for a limited number of contacts with a fairly small audience. Commercials can be produced very cheaply, with the assistance of the station, and very quickly. Indeed, it is perfectly possible to have a straightforward message simply read over the air by the announcer.

At present, radio is a rather unexploited medium in the UK, particularly in creative terms. There is virtually nothing to be heard, in the London area at least, to compare with the best American or Australian commercials, though there is some imaginative work.

While the ILR network has taken over most of the running in any discussion of commercial radio in Britain, two other stations should be remembered. From the past, Radio Luxembourg, which for many years was the only commercial station available to UK advertisers and did much to keep radio in advertisers' minds; and, now, Atlantic 252, based in Eire, which is the nearest thing to a national commercial pop music channel, and has a national weekly reach of 12 per cent of adults, with a strong youth bias.

Direct mail, mail order and direct response

Direct marketing methods, using the postal service, catalogues, coupon ads in the press, and the telephone are a rapidly growing sector of the advertising business.

From an advertising point of view, direct marketing divides reasonably neatly into two halves: direct response advertising, off-the-page in the press or in response to a TV commercial, usually with a freephone number; and direct delivery, whether through the mail or by door-to-door delivery ('door drop').

Direct response advertising, including mail order catalogues' advertising, accounted in 1991 for £204 million of press and TV advertising according to *The Media Register*—roughly 1.5 per cent of all advertising expenditure—and has doubled in value over the past five years. Major categories using direct response are mail order catalogues, 'gifts', fashion, and (though not included in the above figures) financial services such as life assurance and unit trusts. Mail order accounts, in total, for some 5 per cent of all retail sales.

Direct mail is the largest part of the direct marketing business. It is estimated that the industry's value in 1991 was approaching £900 million, equivalent to some 11 per cent of total advertising expenditure, and making direct mail the third largest medium, well ahead of outdoor. The volume of direct mail measured by the Post Office rose by 140 per cent from 1980 to 1990, when the annual total exceeded 2370 million items—equivalent to 110 items per household, though of course much of the material is directed to businesses. Of the total expenditure, nearly 70 per cent is accounted for by the creation and production of the material mailed, and this has grown considerably faster than the cost of mailing. In 1991, total volume dropped slightly, to 2100 million items.

Direct response

A glance through the Sunday colour supplements provides ample clues to the range of goods sold by direct response, as do the 'Saturday bargain' pages of the newspapers—two rather different markets, but ones which use similar techniques. The range of products offered continues to expand rapidly, but they can still be categorized into two broad groups: the more or less basic product offered at a bargain, or apparently bargain, price; and the impulse, semi-luxury, possibly unique 'offer'. It is this latter category, epitomized by the business of Scotcade, which is especially significant in the use of the Sunday supplements as direct response media.

There are a small number of fairly simple 'rules' about direct response advertising, not all of which are universally valid, but which provide a starting point for experiment—for direct response lends itself uniquely well to experiment. It is the only form of media advertising where response is completely measurable. These rules are, in no particular order:

– Put the offer, and ideally the price, in the headline.
– Illustrate the product clearly.

– Concentrate on a single product, even if a range is available.
– Use long, but relevant and clear, copy.
– Always include a coupon.
– Always 'code' the coupon to the individual publication and issue. (This is an absolute 'must'.)
– If possible, offer credit.
– A time limit can help.
– A guarantee is essential.

Beyond this list, obviously, it is vital to make absolutely clear exactly what is being offered, on what conditions, whether there is a limit on quantities, or a discount for quantity, and so on.

For the supplier, there are legal and quasi-legal obligations to be observed (see Chapter 16). Apart from registration with the publication and appropriate copy clearance, key elements are that all direct response ads have to carry the supplier's name and address *outside* the coupon, and the goods have to be available for inspection at the given address; the supplier must be able to supply within 28 days, and be willing to refund the purchaser's money beyond that time; and, on some interpretations of a doubtful piece of legislation, each ad must include the company's registration number (this is not, probably, necessary, but some individual media insist on it).

Direct response is a good way of selling goods. It is, however, much more valuable as a source of future customers. A customer, or even an enquirer, is an address, and a potentially valuable one, for future sales. Ideally, every package dispatched should include a further offer, or a catalogue, with an eye to a further sale, and the mailing list should be used regularly for additional mailings.

Couponed ads provide the advertiser with the perfect tool for evaluation of a campaign as it continues. All direct response advertisers can, if they wish, assess every ad, in every medium, in terms of its response and sales, and so evaluate different media and sizes, and the pulling power of different ads and styles of ad. The collected experience of direct response is, unfortunately, not available to the world: the secrets it contains are too commercially valuable. The sort of indications which emerge from this analysis, however, have led to the formulation of the 'rules' listed above. They show, for instance, that too frequent repetition of an ad in a particular publication leads to rapidly diminishing returns, but that less frequent insertions may enable an ad to pull almost indefinitely; that in newspapers, cost-effectiveness declines sharply with increased size over a certain minimum— but that the minimum may generate insufficient volume to justify itself; that quite small variations in headline or illustration can produce dramatic differences in response; that some individual publications are markedly better than others, both in general terms and for specific products; that, if they appear close together in time, different ads pull better in a paper than repetitions of the same ad; that a TV ad directing a viewer to a coupon in a specific publication is especially effective. In recent years, direct response advertisers have become more experimental in terms of ad formats, using devices such as stick-on coupons to enhance response.

One final rule of thumb: unless the ad can bring in orders worth at least three times its space cost, it is not worth it.

Direct mail

Direct response merges easily into direct mail, since a well-run direct response operation should lead to the development of a direct mail business. Direct mail, however, is a technically rather different activity, and there is no doubt that its techniques are a specialized branch of advertising.

Direct mail depends, primarily, on obtaining and managing effectively a good mailing list.* It is, too, an increasingly costly activity, as postage rates continue to rise. This has been a key factor in the developing interaction between direct mail and media advertising: a concurrent media campaign undoubtedly helps response to the mailings, and the media are still a far cheaper way of reaching a mass audience than is the mail.

Direct mail depends for its effect on its ability to develop real one-to-one relationships with consumers, getting their confidence sufficiently for them actually to buy the product. This is why direct mail goes in for long letters, often over three or four pages, and a whole set of attention-getting and value-adding devices: extra options, special series discounts, bonus offers, contests, and so on. This is quite apart from the use of more or less creative mailing shots involving 3-D and pop-up materials. It is quite possible, for example, to run a two- or three-stage mailing to an industrial customer involving—say—a brochure, a key, a box to be unlocked by the key, etc. The apparently unsophisticated presentation of much direct material—it always seems to come in two or three colours and a variety of type or simulated script faces—has usually found its way through a whole series of tests: direct mail is a virtually perfect test medium, since it can be completely isolated from other influences.

Direct mail can be, and is, used to sell virtually anything, though its consumer market uses tend to be particularly concentrated on book, magazine and record publishing, together with financial services, judging by the lists I seem to be on.

Any company in regular contact with the consumer can use the mail to sell. The only question, really, is whether or not to use an account list (say) to sell—or to sell the list to a possible commercial customer: this can be done either absolutely or in a controlled way. For example, Diners Club in effect market their list as a sort of advertising medium in its own right. This is a list with its own built-in conventional media support, since it can be partly duplicated through Diners Club's *Signature* magazine.

Two recent developments have significantly broadened the scope of direct mail: the belated discovery of customer lists by large retailers, based on the

---

*With the aid of computers, sophisticated analysis and manipulation of customer information justifies the description of a good in-house list as a 'database' and the jargon term 'database marketing'.

more active marketing of store credit cards; and the new scope apparently provided by the Government's privatization programme for selling financial services direct to the 'new' shareholder. For the retailer, there seem to be obvious opportunities, both to reward and cement the loyalty of what are, presumably, their best customers, and to sell new products and services through the mail. The 'new' shareholder, on the other hand, is a considerably less homogeneous target, and somewhat less financially sophisticated— or gullible, or rich—than is assumed by many of the mailings that pursue holders of shares in British Telecom or British Airways.

Direct marketing: an overview

Direct marketing is the catch-all term covering direct mail, door-to-door couponing and leafleting, telephone marketing ('telemarketing') and selling off the page or off the screen. Within the overall communications business, direct marketing is, as the available figures show, a major growth area, and can be expected to continue to grow, for a number of reasons.

The key to direct marketing development is the computer, because efficient management and deployment of mailings (or whatever) depends on knowing a lot of detail about the individuals on your list; and using this database systematically and experimentally over a period of time, updating and refining it as more information becomes available.

Clearly, this 'database marketing' depends on, first, acquiring a good list; and then on working and developing it effectively. This process is subject to the controls of the Data Protection Act (see page 197), and may be further limited under proposals, currently under discussion, from the European Commission. If these follow the strictest possible course—modelled on German practice—it will become extremely difficult even to create a database, let alone use it in an efficient and creative way. The worst will *probably* not happen.

Direct marketing offers the marketer a number of clear advantages: tight control of scale of effort, linked to immediate, precise feedback and measurement of results; more or less precise targeting, with the prospect of refining targeting as experience is accumulated; a direct, more or less 'personal' contact with the individual customer; the opportunity (at least) to develop something approaching a 'dialogue' with the customer; the ability to develop a quite detailed, specific picture of loyal—and disloyal—customers.

It sounds marvellous. Well executed, it can be. But direct marketing does have its limitations. First of all, in spite of the apparent precision of targeting, response rates are not, usually, particularly high: 5 per cent is pretty good, for most situations—and that is a figure for any response, not necessarily an actual sale.

Then, there is no doubt that a significant proportion of consumers are quite negative towards buying *anything* direct; and there is a constant undercurrent, fed by the media, of resistance to 'junk mail', let alone 'junk faxes' and telephone selling. Again, costs of production, postage, etc., make direct mail or direct delivery relatively expensive in cost per thousand terms. Finally, unlike media advertising, direct marketing is basically private: there is no rub-off of brand awareness and brand image to give current non-buyers who are potential customers a chance to begin to form an impression of the brand. What this tends to mean, of course, is that direct marketing works best as *part* of an overall communication, not just on its own. For its effectiveness, it depends quite a lot on the brand (or the brand owner) being known to the customer from other forms of communication.

Point-of-sale, etc.

A final topic which deserves a brief comment is the whole area of advertising at the point of purchase. It does not come into anyone's media budget, as a rule, but it does use advertising messages, and places them in front of consumers in what I am sure we will all gladly call a 'buying situation'. The range of possible p-o-s items is, in theory, vast, especially if you consider the paraphernalia provided by suppliers to pubs, restaurants and the like—ashtrays, beer mats, optics, calendars, dartboards, glasses, drip mats, aprons, trays, openers, illuminated signs, posters, door stops, open and closed signs, umbrellas, doormats... the list goes on.

The great majority of the material produced is, however, produced for the retail trade, where the possibilities are less exotic, and the acceptability of unusual pieces far more limited. The willingness of grocery multiples, for example, to accept manufacturers' display material, apart from some special stands and racks and standard display outer packs, decreases steadily. Often it is only for a promotion that display material is accepted, and that may be only on condition that the retailer designs it. Other branches of retailing are, however, less unreceptive, and the chemist trade, in particular, makes very substantial use of manufacturers' material. (The retail grocery business, of course, uses lots of display material, but it uses it very single-mindedly to promote its own store image, not the manufacturer's brand image.)

Point-of-sale material divides, in practice, into two different categories: the permanent or semi-permanent, and the ephemeral. For a piece to be permanent it has, usually, to perform a recognizable function for the store—as a display dispenser, a store fascia, or perhaps an open-and-closed sign. Into this category, too, come ice cream brands' 'A-boards', the easel-like boards which stockists put out on the pavement to attract customers—one of the few examples of a retailer regularly using a manufacturer's display piece, as opposed to just keeping it in place.

Obviously, the more permanent pieces, except where they can simply be stuck on a door or window, need to be produced in sufficiently tough materials to last. And last they can, as ancient signs on backstreet shops all over the country still make clear.

Other media

There are, of course, still other media: directories, book matches, desk pads,

T-shirts, balloons, sandwich-boards. All of them may have a value to a particular advertiser, for a particular purpose. None of them, however, is of any great importance in the overall advertising scene—though I am sure that the producers of these items make a good living out of doing so. The one exception to this sweeping generalization is directories, a medium worth £500 million annually, most of it going to the big customer directories, *Yellow Pages* and *Thomson*.

14 Production for print media

Designing the advertisement

Print advertisements—and other print materials such as brochures, leaflets, mail shots—start their life as rough designs scribbled by the agency art director on anything from the back of an envelope to a layout pad. The essential elements at this stage are, typically, a very few words—usually a headline—an idea for an illustration, and a rough indication of how the total ad might look. Very possibly, this sort of 'scamp' may be shown to the client to give him or her a preliminary idea, or choice of ideas, and to get an initial response.

For the agency, assuming that the response to the idea, whether from the client or from an internal discussion among the account group, is favourable, the next step is to work the design up in more detail. An artist, very possibly the original designer, but maybe a junior in the art department or even at an outside studio, takes the rough and turns it into a more finished design, working in conjunction with the copywriter. This last is essential, because the headline will be a key element in the design, and there must be discussion between artist and writer about the amount of copy and how it should relate to the picture, and, in addition, to ensure that any extra elements—a special footline, or slogan, or logo—appear in the ad in the right size and weight. Once you have decided, for example, to use a particular logo or sign-off formula, as in Figure 14.1, in your advertising, it can be difficult to fit it into a new layout at the first attempt.

At the same time, the agency creative team should be discussing with the media department what sizes of ad are required. This affects both the amount of copy that can be included in the ad—obviously a vital consideration—and its shape: most ads are formatted for either 'portrait' or 'landscape' and it requires adaptation to move from one to the other. That is why a DPS often does not translate readily into a single page.

The creative team should be talking, too, to their production controller, because the requirements of different publications differ markedly, and, although the art director should be aware of these differences in broad terms, the production controller should be able to give much more detailed advice which can help to avoid problems at an early stage. The advice given may well help in making a decision as to whether to use a drawing or a photograph for an ad, or, more likely, on more technical details like the desirable style or colour balance for a colour ad, or whether or not to reverse out the

Figure 14.1 A complex logo limits the ad designer's freedom

copy (printing white on a dark background, instead of the conventional black-on-white).

Estimates

Once copy and layout for the ad have been approved by the client the next step in the production process ought to be the preparation of an estimate of the cost of producing the ad, or series of ads. This involves a series of further decisions, and some detailed work by, in particular, the agency's art buyer. First of all, the agency has to find models, settings or locations for the ad. It has to arrange for—for example—a home economist to prepare any food for photography, or a make-up artist. It has to find the right photographer or artist, and agree on how much work is involved, and how much it will cost. Costs have to be worked out, then, for all the elements of the process of getting the illustration prepared. Then, it is necessary to estimate costs of typesetting, block or plate-making and any other incidental activities.

All this is set down on an estimate form, which may look something like the estimate in Figure 14.2, and has to be agreed with the client before the agency proceeds to produce the ad.

The pictures

Photography for print ads is in many ways similar to filming commercials, in the sense that it involves a great deal of work getting every detail absolutely right before any film is exposed. The most obvious difference is that, for most jobs, there is one photographer and an assistant—not the small army of bodies involved in TV production. Photographers tend to specialize in particular types of photography—food, close-ups, fashion, etc.—and some have distinctive styles: the almost impressionistic, soft-focus, style used in Cacharel's campaign for Anais Anais (Plate 1), is a particularly striking example.

Where a particular style, as opposed to a particular expertise, is looked for, however, agencies still tend to look for illustrators rather than photographers. It is still undoubtedly easier to achieve a special effect by a careful choice of illustrator than through photography: it is easier to use imagination in illustration, for the obvious reason that, in the last resort, the camera can only photograph what it sees, in spite of the ingenuity that can be used in lighting and processing film, and in subsequent retouching and photomontage.

LANSDOWNEURO

ABBEY HOUSE, 215-229 BAKER STREET, LONDON NW1 6YA 01-486 7111. TELEX: 8952286. FAX: 01-486 5310

ESTIMATE

PLEASE NOTE THIS IS NOT A QUOTATION
PRINT/PRESS PRODUCTION

CLIENT XXXXXXX	JOB NUMBER
	`4 7 7 2`
PRODUCT XXXXXXX	ESTIMATE NUMBER

TITLE PRESS CAMPAIGN – MAIN SHOT (6 PUBLICATIONS)	DATE 22/1/92

CREATIVE PRODUCTION	ESTIMATED NET COST £	P	MECHANICAL PRODUCTION	ESTIMATED NET COST £	P
FINISHED LAYOUTS/MOCK UPS			BROMIDES		
PHOTOGRAPHY	1500	00	LITHO FILM	4500	00
FILM AND PROCESSING	350	00	PRODUCTION CHARGES BY GRAVURE/LITHO PUBLICATIONS		
MODEL FEES	800	00			
MAKE-UP AND HAIR	300	00	EXTRA PROOFS		
STYLIST	250	00			
HOME ECONOMIST			**PRODUCTION TOTAL**	8070	00
PROPS	300	00	PRINT		
SET BUILD					
ILLUSTRATION			EXTRAS		
RETOUCHING			**NET-TOTAL**		
PHOTOCOMPOSITION	600	00	COMMISSION	2848	71
COPY TRANSPARENCIES			DESIGN		
			MISC EXPENSES		
ART TOTAL	4100	00	TRANSPORT/TRAVEL		
TYPOGRAPHY	620	00			
TYPESETTING	490	00			
MECHANICAL ARTWORK	1800	00			
PRINTS/PMT	600	00	**GROSS TOTAL**	10 918	00

N.B. THESE COSTS DO NOT INCLUDE VALUE ADDED TAX OR OVERTIME.

ART BUYER SIGNATURE	PRODUCTION SIGNATURE	ACCOUNT MANAGER SIGNATURE	TRAFFIC SIGNATURE
ACCEPTED: CLIENT		DATE	

NOTE
1 It should be remembered this is an estimate and not a quotation.
2 The company does not undertake to act as principals when dealing with suppliers, and clients are bound by whatever terms and conditions suppliers impose.
3 50% of above costs will be billed in advance, upon approval of this estimate, the balance upon completion.

Figure 14.2   A press production estimate

Producing the ad

Advertisements in print media, and the various print advertising materials such as display pieces, brochures, etc., can consist of print only, or print plus drawings and/or photographs; and the whole can be in black and white (B/W) or in full colour, or merely with an added second colour. Further, they may be reproduced by any one of several different printing methods—letterpress, lithography, gravure, or screen printing. Each of these methods requires material produced in a rather different way, and each imposes its own limitations on the quality of reproduction and on the type of material that can be effectively reproduced.

The printing industry is a curious mixture of very advanced technology and very traditional methods, and it is still possible—in theory, at least—to produce advertising material by methods which would have been totally familiar to Gutenberg, the originator, in the fifteenth century, of movable metal type: conversely, it is theoretically possible—though still difficult in practice—to reproduce colour illustrations completely electronically by a one-stage printing process.

Advertising relies heavily on the skills of the printer, both in the studio and at the production house, for the production of advertisements. For the small advertiser, it is possible, in practice, to leave virtually all the work to the printer. You can give a local newspaper, or a technical magazine—or a block-maker—a rough layout, some copy, and a rough illustration, or a photograph, and tell them to get on with it. The result is likely to be fairly crude, but in a magazine like *Railway Modeller*, for example, where most ads are 'pub. set' (copy set and laid out by the publication), you do not notice the difference that much.

Obviously, by leaving it all to the publication, you lose all control, in effect, over the quality and appearance of the ad. This may not be a disadvantage, but it does, frankly, have to be a fairly simple ad if it is to avoid damage: on pub. set and pub. layout ads, the media are hardly able to be sophisticated. (There is, in addition to the wholly pub. set ad, an option quite frequently used by large advertisers, especially those using dealer support campaigns, where a basic format is supplied to the publication with space for a pub. set message within the ad—this may be, for example, an up-to-the-minute topical message, or a dealer address.)

Type

All classified ads, with very few exceptions, are pub. set, though semi-display ads, especially recruitment, may be typeset by the agency, or at least set in an agency-designed frame. Most display advertisers, however, will use a professional typographer, whether from the agency or from a specialist studio, to choose (in conjunction with the art director) the appropriate type face and to 'cast off' the type. 'Casting off' is the process of deciding on the required size of type for the various elements of the ad, and arranging the blocks of type in accordance with the art director's requirements. The process used to involve careful calculation by the typographer, but has been at least partially simplified by the introduction of computer typesetting. The drawback to this is, however, that while computer setting can be fine for lengthy text or body copy, it is still a somewhat inflexible system for much display type. There is a definite art in arranging display type so as to achieve the optimum effect and readability.

The look of an ad depends quite critically on typography, to an extent of which most outsiders are quite unaware: an ad can be made or destroyed by type choice and layout. It is, in fact, quite possible, in certain instances, to carry out research into the effect of type faces. In designing new signage for Asda stores—a specialized use of type, admittedly—research was carried out into several different type faces which showed clearly that by changing the style of type face used for in-store signs you can give widely different impressions of the store's character and pricing. Undoubtedly, this also happens in advertisements. Similarly, different type faces vary considerably in readability, whether used for headlines or for body copy.

There are innumerable different type faces, in several different 'families' of style, and fashions in type vary over the years. Type can be heavy or light, flowing or staccato, crude or delicate, in conformity with the mood of an ad. The most obvious distinction—to the layman—is between more or less classic type faces with serifs, like Press Roman,

ABCD................. Z,   abc....................z
and those without serifs like, say, Univers:
ABCD.................Z,   abc...................z

The sans-serif types are more modern, and at present more fashionable, and they are especially good for headlines and for signs. They tend, however, to be hard to read if used for body copy. A recent, limited vogue, which still has some life in it, has been for type faces which resemble hand lettering. Another recent fashion—less practical because it is less legible—is to set all the body copy in caps.

Type faces are specified by the typographer by their design, by size and by weight. Size is calculated, in the UK at least, by 'points', the smallest type usually used in ads being six point, while headlines may go up to 24 or 30 point or beyond. Most body copy is set in 10 or 12 point type, with 12 point probably the most popular; but the look of a given size varies from type face to type face, so that a 10 point of one face may read as clearly as a 12 point of another.

Most type faces are available in a variety of different 'weights' from extra light to ultra bold, which can be used to provide stress or emphasis to headlines, sub-heads or individual words. Similarly, most faces are available, too, in an italic form, and many in 'condensed' or 'extended' forms, where the letters are squeezed-up or broadened versions of the basic face.

The vast majority of body copy, and most headlines, are nowadays photoset by sophisticated machines which produce a photographic version of the required material. Modern techniques produce the type matter on self-adhesive film, which can then be cut out and put down onto acetate, to make up the complete type layout. (More traditional methods reproduce the type on to good quality paper, which is then pasted up on board.) This process of pasting up the complete layout is often still done in the agency's art department, usually by a junior, though it can be done by the blockmaker or by an outside studio: art directors are reluctant, however, to leave this part of the production process to outsiders, as they have a built-in tendency to alter layouts fractionally once they see the finished type and illustration together.

In practice, much of the design of print material, especially for leaflets and brochures, can be done entirely by computer, with the help of one of the good proprietary desk-top publishing programs, and a number of print houses have the facility to handle complete layouts on this basis—an invaluable service for major retail advertisers and their agencies, in particular.

Printing processes

Before going on to discuss what happens to the illustrations, it is important to consider very briefly the main printing processes, as their requirements and capabilities are rather different.

As has been said earlier, there are four major printing processes: letterpress, gravure, litho and screen printing. The first three all involve the pressing of a prepared plate or block, suitably inked, on to paper. Screen printing involves printing literally through a prepared screen or stencil.

Letterpress, or relief printing, was the original printing process, and is still used very extensively, by jobbing printers at one end of the scale and a few newspapers at the other. However, it has lost much of its importance in the face of, especially, litho printing. Letterpress has some key advantages as a system, especially in its crispness of type reproduction, but it is more cumbersome than more modern, essentially photographic methods of printing, since it still relies on type cast in metal as its basic ingredient, though even here, modern methods make it possible to produce type matter by etching from a photographic master.

Traditionally, type matter was composed by taking individual strips of type and placing them in a special holder—a 'forme'—with the appropriate spacing material, etc. More modern techniques enable this process to be done more or less mechanically, through the use of machines which are, in effect, typewriters linked to a system of matrices using hot metal to cast the type as it is typed into the machine. This method is still fairly widely used for newspaper copy.

For advertising purposes, it is now perfectly possible, and in fact the general practice, to use filmsetting methods to produce photographic type matter that can be pasted up with any illustrations or other matter onto a single 'flat' ready for making the block as a single piece.

Lithography, or planographic (flat surface) printing is based on the principle that water and oil repel each other. The printing elements of the plate (originally a limestone block) are treated with fatty oils, and the plate is damped with water before printing, so that only the printing areas will take up the (greasy) ink.

Virtually all litho printing is now done by 'offset' printing, where the plate itself never comes into contact with paper. Instead, the plate, which is a positive of the material, prints onto a rubber 'blanket', which thus carries a negative of the material, and it is this which is then brought into contact with the paper to produce the final, printed positive image. Litho has the great advantage over letterpress of printing well on virtually any type of paper, but has a slightly more limited range of tone than letterpress printing.

Litho plates are usually made photographically, by printing onto a sensitized metal plate, of zinc or aluminium, which is then developed so as to leave a water-sensitive surface on the non-image areas. The great majority of newspaper and magazine printing is now web-offset litho, and it was this switch that took the UK's national newspaper industry out of Fleet Street and—it could be argued—into the twentieth century.

Photogravure is a form of intaglio printing—the reverse of relief, or letterpress printing—in which the image is etched into a copper cylinder. In printing, in effect, ink is poured into the etched image, and the printed design is produced by the variations in the depth of weight of ink taken up by the plate. Preparing gravure cylinders is a time-consuming business and corrections are virtually impossible once the cylinder has been made. Gravure is used chiefly for mass circulation magazine printing, since it is an especially good method for long runs of good quality colour work.

Silk screening is a stencil method of printing. In essence, you start with a screen drawn over a frame, on which a stencil is superimposed. Printing is then achieved by running a kind of squeegee loaded with ink over the screen, which is laid on the paper. The image is created by the ink passing through the holes in the stencil. Silk screen was largely confined to packaging and point-of-sale materials, but advances in techniques have led to very sophisticated 4-colour work for posters—most art posters are silk screened.

Illustrations

Returning to the production of ads, the major production element in most ads is the illustration. Illustrations can be either line drawings or drawings, paintings or photographs involving tones. Line drawings are simple to reproduce, but once any sort of tone, whether in B/W or colour, is used, this complicates the issue considerably.

The essential problem which has to be overcome is that of reducing continuous tone to something that can be produced mechanically. This is, in fact, achieved in more or less the same way for all the basic printing processes. In order to achieve a tonal effect in print, you have to break the picture up into a series of areas of tone of different depths. This is done photographically, by taking a picture of the original artwork—be it a photograph or an illustration—through a screen. A screen is a sort of lattice, with the lines across it placed at regular distances, so that, as you take a picture through it, the image is divided into squares. Depending on the lightness or darkness of the picture, each individual square will then be light or dark. When a photograph is taken in this way, and developed, the result is to produce an image consisting of a multitude of dots of varying light intensities.

Different screen sizes are used to suit different types and qualities of paper or, in certain cases, to achieve special effects. It is impossible to print using a fine screen on coarse paper such as newsprint, because the paper is too rough and too absorbent, and the result will be a blur, as the fine dots merge into each other. Screen sizes are measured by the number of lines to the inch, and for newsprint a screen as large as 50 may be needed, though 65 is about average. For better quality paper, a 120 screen is normal, and this is the size usually used for litho work.

By means of this process the illustration is converted from continuous tone to 'half-tone', and can now be made into a half-tone block or plate or, for gravure, a cylinder. This is done by the same method as that used for areas of photo-set type: the image is printed down on a sensitized metal plate, and processed to produce the required result.

Colour
Production of colour illustrations is merely a more complex extension of the basic half-tone process. The great majority of work is done 'four-colour', involving separate plates or blocks for cyan (blue), yellow, magenta (red) and black. Occasionally, more colours can be used, but this is normally only done for fine art reproduction.

In order to achieve effective colour reproduction, the original transparency first has to be tonally corrected to reduce the density range of the original, to allow for the spectral limitations of printers' ink. This is usually done by producing a negative by making a contact exposure of the transparency onto a special photographic film, which is then used as a mask superimposed on the transparency when the colour separation negatives are made.

Colour separation is done by exposing the transparency through an appropriately coloured filter—blue for yellow printing, green for magenta, red for cyan. The black printing is taken through a yellow or tri-colour filter. At the same time, exactly as for the black and white half-tones, a screen is used. The screen is rotated, usually through 30 degrees for each colour, so that the dots of the screens do not merge and produce strange patterns on the eventual print. From the resulting photographs, blocks or plates for printing can be made in the same way as has been described for B/W half-tones. Colour work typically requires very substantial correction and re-touching before it is ready for printing. This is done either on the original negative or transparency or on the colour separation negatives. For letterpress, it is possible to carry out some retouching on the block, but this is not possible for litho or gravure. Colour retouching is a highly skilled business, which can be used to arrive at an almost completely new picture—but to do that is an expensive business, and should, ideally, be unnecessary if the original artwork is good enough (which it should be).

As with the rest of the processes involved in print production, the detailed preparation of illustrations for the printer is now very largely handled by computers, and this applies especially to re-touching, where modern computer screening tends to reproduce the signs of manual re-touching.

Proofs

Once blocks or plates have been made, the printer or print house provides proofs of the job to the agency. In the case of proofs of newspaper jobs these are, typically, on imitation art paper—a far higher quality than the newsprint used in the actual publication—so that it is easy to be misled about the likely eventual appearance of the ad in the medium.

The proofs provide client and agency with the opportunity to make any final corrections to the ad before blocks and plates are supplied to the media for printing. Given the way in which most type matter is produced these days, the final proof is relatively unimportant, since the type will have been available in photographic form as soon as it has been set, but the opportunity to modify the illustration will remain. Sometimes it will be necessary to do further work on the block—or even on the plate, as some limited work can be done on litho plates—but often this is the opportunity for the production team to discuss with the printer any difficult details of inking, which can influence the ultimate appearance of the ad. It is an easily observable fact that two different copies of the same magazine can carry almost totally different versions of the same ad: this is usually due to inking variations.

Material for the press

From this description of the various elements of the printing process, there are, clearly, lots of bits of paper and film flying around. It is the production controller's job to schedule and keep track of it all—and to make sure it is done at reasonable cost by knowing the suppliers. But what of all this does the agency have to give the publication, and in what form? The process all works slightly differently according to the precise format adopted for a given production job. Ultimately, the agency provides a letterpress medium with blocks, which will already have been proofed up by the blockmaker. Where a long run of printing is required, it may be necessary to provide duplicates, which are taken off the original block by a short-cut process leading to the production of an 'electro' or 'stereo'. Blocks have to be supplied, obviously, exactly to size. Regularly-used items such as the client's logo will usually be provided as photo-mechanical transfers (PMTs).

For lithography, the agency can provide a completed plate of the whole job, or, more commonly at present, a set of mechanicals and transparencies, including colour separations. A mechanical is a flat layout marked up with clear instructions for the printer, with copy stripped in position. The publication then makes the final plate, in exactly the same way as the blockmaker would, and provides proofs before publication: this process accounts for the long lead times on much magazine production. Materials for litho need not be s/s ('same size'—i.e., the size the eventual ad will appear), but ought to be close to s/s, ideally.

For gravure, what is required is a set of s/s mechanicals and transparencies. Here, of course, because of the impossibility of correction on the cylinder, there is no proofing stage—it is essential to get everything right on the artwork.

Costs

Just as the early eighties saw a crisis in the industry on TV production costs, so the beginning of the nineties has seen a row about print production. Print costs can—and do—vary enormously, just as the daily cost of a photographer can vary from a few hundred pounds to several thousand. Clearly, a lot of the problem arose from a combination of inadequate attention being paid to estimates and insufficient knowledge of what a job might or should actually cost.

Added to this, however, was the suspicion—probably justified in some cases—that agencies might use production budgets to surreptitiously unload a lot of stray costs they hadn't found any other way of passing onto the client. Most agency contracts with their clients include a commission on bought-in production services, usually charged at 17.65 per cent of the cost, and this (or something like it) is probably reasonable—as long as it is honestly done. What does not exist in most agency creative departments is any positive inclination to watch costs: the art director's aim is simply to get the best possible execution of an idea into print.

Clearly, there is an onus on both client and agency to get good value for production costs: every pound overspent on production is a reduction in the cash available to spend on putting the ad in front of the consumer. To achieve this, requires, it seems to me, a combination of factors: professional production controllers at the agency; an informed client; a proper estimating system; firm control by the agency account executive; and a responsible approach from the agency creative people. Easy!

Conclusion

This is, obviously, an extremely cursory sketch of a most complex area, which is, however, critical to the final appearance of advertising material. It is, really, essential to see the job being done, and to learn directly from the experts— printers, blockmakers, agency production managers. Every agency account or creative person needs to acquire at least a background knowledge of the processes involved, and every client advertising manager or brand manager should, also. Without it, it is very easy to achieve badly produced and, therefore, less than effective advertising; and it is easy, too, for both agency and client to be involved in endless misunderstandings about the quality of reproduction, and the cost of production.

In this short chapter, I have, I must confess, barely scratched the surface of a field in which agencies and clients are all too inclined to remain determinedly ignorant.

15 Getting it together – planning the campaign

So far, I have been talking about advertising in a bit of a vacuum: it is all very well to have a media schedule, and some kind of advertisement to put in it, but this lacks any context. In the first chapter of this book there was some discussion of *why* you might advertise, and of the *role* of advertising within the overall marketing mix. The prime responsibility of the account director in the agency, and his or her counterpart in the client organization, is to plan the strategic framework into which the advertising has to fit—the campaign. Because of the way in which nearly all businesses budget, the basic unit in which campaigns tend to get approached is a single year: and, as we have seen, advertising budgets are rarely going to be large enough to enable us to advertise continuously throughout the year. At the very least, we will have to deploy our advertising money alongside the other elements in the marketing mix, in such a way that they are mutually supporting and able to sustain our sales efforts whether we are actually advertising or not.

In practice, it would usually make sense to approach the planning of a campaign over a longer time-scale than just a year: in most cases, what we are trying to do is to develop a brand that will have real staying power, over a considerable period of time. Accordingly, we should be starting out with at least an outline idea of how we expect the brand to develop, and of how our advertising and other activity can contribute to the process. For example, if we assume the launch of a new brand, which is in many ways the simplest model on which to work, we are going to have to achieve a number of different things, over a period of time, in order to establish a successful brand, with a clearly thought-through future. We will need, for example:

- to launch the product to the retail trade, and ensure that it achieves adequate distribution;
- to introduce the brand to the target consumer audience, so as to create awareness and encourage trial;
- to provide information to enable consumers to understand the brand, so they may decide to try it;
- to provide emotional triggers or reassurance to enable them to try it with confidence;
- to remind people who have already tried it to buy again, and—perhaps—to

provide them with incentives to do so;

- to extend our selling efforts to new target audiences, or to enter new distribution channels, as the first targets are attained;
- to introduce new variants of the original product, or to add supporting or complementary products to the brand range;
- to launch the product into the market in one or more new countries—or simply to extend from a test area in our own country to national distribution;
- to carry out a series of market research projects to evaluate our progress, and to identify any problems that may be impeding success.

All of this is likely to cover a period of not just 12 months, but, very probably, three years or more. It is, obviously, quite important that at least an outline of the whole three year plan is drawn up at the beginning, not just for the company's standard planning processes, but in order to take a sensible and strategic view of how the brand's communication programme, including the advertising, will have to be deployed and developed. The further ahead this development can be plotted, the easier it will be to take sane decisions about the nature and the scheduling of the advertising.

Implicit in all this are a number of very simple but essential points. Of these, the most important, and one which can all too easily be forgotten in the enthusiasm of creating a new advertising idea, is the fact that an advertising campaign can be expected to change and develop over time, and that a one-off idea, that cannot be extended or modified, or adapted to different media, is in most cases going to prove to be a liability—essentially, a dead end. That, if you like, is the creative message or constraint that becomes clear as soon as we start thinking in terms of campaigns. The main lessons, though, are operational:

- before you can start to advertise to the consumer, you have to be sure that the brand is available in the shops for people to buy: this means both that you may need a trade advertising campaign to help sell the product in; and that the start of the consumer campaign will have to be held until there is sufficient distribution;
- there is very likely to be a need—or at least a strong case—for the initial launch to be on a test basis in a small area of the country; or for it to be phased across the country—for example, to enable a new production line to work up to full capacity;
- the role of the advertising (in particular) will tend to change somewhat over time, moving—for example—from the creation of awareness of the brand to the development of a fully rounded brand image;
- the initial burst of advertising is likely to be at an especially heavy weight, in order to achieve a high level of coverage of the target audience and a strong and noticeable impact on that audience;
- given that the effective life of an advertising campaign in the consumer's mind is quite short, nearly any campaign is going to need to have more

than one burst of advertising in the course of a year: it will be something of a waste of effort to blow the entire budget in one single launch burst lasting perhaps six weeks;
- in principle, if a campaign starts on a test or regional basis, it is desirable to repeat it as exactly as possible when new areas are brought in;
- as far as possible, especially with the launch of a new product, research measurements should be in place to enable the agency to assess progress, and to identify problems and areas for possible improvement.

The task of the account director is to take the client's marketing plans, and to integrate the advertising planning with these plans. In many cases, depending a bit on the relationship between the client and the agency, the agency will have been involved in much of the discussion and analysis that lies behind the marketing plan, and this obviously makes the process a lot easier. The account director will be aware of the considerations that affect the scale and timing of activities in the marketing plan, the basis of sales forecasts and targets, and the precise requirements of advertising within the mix. It is probable, too, that the agency will have had the opportunity to make recommendations on the amount of money that will be required to meet the targets set for the advertising—which will probably have been expressed in terms of brand awareness, in the first instance, for a new product. (Whether the client has accepted the agency's recommended level of expenditure, rather than reducing it quite sharply, is quite another question!)

On the basis of this analysis of the client's requirements, the advertising campaign can begin to take shape. Decisions have to be taken, as has been sketched in in various places in the book, that will enable the agency to deploy the budget effectively and to the best advantage. The main areas involved in these decisions are as follows:

- the optimum timing and interval between bursts of advertising;
- desirable and affordable media to be used, for launch and subsequent bursts;
- levels of coverage and frequency to be aimed at to achieve the required targets;
- the inter-relationship between the advertising campaign and other activities in the mix;
- the stage at which it will be necessary to introduce new creative material into the campaign;
- the need—if it exists—to have creative material that is specifically tailored to particular publications within a press schedule;
- the lead-times required to produce creative work to meet the requirements of the proposed schedules. This will include, for example, time required to make changes as a result of key pieces of consumer research.

The process of turning all these and other decisions into an actual campaign plan is a lengthy one, involving a great deal of discussion both within

the agency and between agency and client, if it is to result in a properly
worked-out, coherent plan. A good plan will be logical, coherent and—as far
as possible—economical: it will also, ideally, have at least some touches of
imagination and originality in it, because success in business as elsewhere is
amply helped by a bit of creativity. If we all did everything 'by the book', there
would probably be no progress. Certainly, in business, following the rules
makes it very easy for competitors to guess what will happen next, and set
their strategies accordingly. The easiest way to steal a march on competitors is
to spend a great deal more money than they expect; but this is not exactly an
original way to attack, and tends to lead to trench warfare, when the competitor with the largest purse wins—eventually. It is likely to be much more cost-
effective, for example, to shift a market's seasonality, or to pre-empt a key
media opportunity, or to add a new dimension to the brand's distribution.
From an advertising point of view, of course, the best form of attack is going
to be a genuinely superior new creative approach—it is likely to be far the
most effective way of increasing the leverage of the advertising budget, and it
is also just about the most difficult competitive initiative to combat.

The end-product of the planning process is likely to be quite a thick docu-
ment, containing the detailed rationale for the recommended plans, and a
selection of charts, schedules and time-plans to put the entire operation in
context. I don't intend to try to reproduce a complete campaign plan here,
but Figure 15.1 shows a rather simplified summary chart of the launch plan
for a new brand, to provide an indication of the scope of a fairly typical plan.

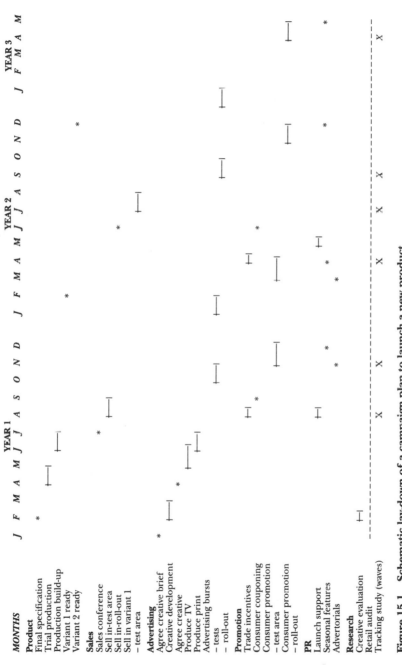

Figure 15.1   Schematic lay-down of a campaign plan to launch a new product

16 Advertising and the law

Like any other aspect of business life, advertising is controlled, constrained and, where appropriate, punished by the law. The law is a complex and apparently capricious subject, which is often open to interpretation, both by learned counsel and by the courts.

For anyone involved in advertising, the most important thing is to be aware of the areas in which the law can affect advertisements or the business of advertising, and to be appropriately cautious. If in doubt, ask a qualified lawyer. This advice, unfortunately, can be easier to give than to follow, since lawyers specializing in the field of advertising are thin on the ground: they can be found chiefly in large agencies and a limited number of large manufacturing companies. The IPA, however, has a legal department which can provide advice and assistance on request, to IPA members and member agencies.

The reason why help is needed with the law is, quite simply, the amount of it. The most recently published, but by now very dated, textbook, *Advertising Law*, by R. G. Lawson,[*] quotes source lists on the following scale:

- 15 pages of cases;
- 143 statutes, going back to 1772;
- 44 statutory instruments.

These are, certainly, the great majority of the laws that affect advertising, but the list only goes up to 1977, and the rate of acceleration in numbers of citations as the list enters the sixties and seventies is formidable. Since 1977, the process has continued.

Voluntary controls

In addition to the legal framework within which advertising operates, there is in the UK a whole structure of voluntary restraints. These operate basically through the British Code of Advertising Practice (BCAP) and related specialized codes.

There are a growing number of Codes of Practice related to the BCAP: the British Code of Sales Promotion Practice has been joined by codes covering—for example—mail order, both off-the-page and catalogue, and, more generally, direct marketing. In addition, the Advertising Association has

*Published by Macdonald & Evans, 1978.

188

sponsored a code on data collection and its use, in line with the Data Protection Act.

Advertising is controlled, in practice, in different ways according to media and, to a limited extent, product field—in particular, the field of medicines is strictly circumscribed by law as well as by the Codes of Practice. The main distinction is between broadcast and other media. Under the Broadcasting Act, the Independent Television Commission (ITC) has a duty to ensure that all broadcast commercials conform to the ITC's Code of Practice. This duty is performed as far as TV is concerned by the ITC through a system of pre-censorship of all commercials (see Chapter 11, page 126). The ITVA vets all scripts and virtually all commercials before they are screened, and imposes its own strict interpretation of the Code on TV advertisers. In particular, the ITVA is accustomed to ask for proof of specific product claims. For radio, the AIRC operates a similar system.

This type of pre-censorship does not occur in other media, at least not on a formal basis, with certain exceptions. In practice, any medium can refuse to run any ad submitted to it, if it believes that it embodies or could lead to an infringement of the law, or if it fails to conform with the relevant Code of Practice. In addition, most media will reject ads if they are likely to offend on grounds of taste—something covered loosely by the Codes of Practice. This is an area where interpretation is very varied, with London Regional Transport—who have a particular problem with graffiti—being notoriously, and occasionally exaggeratedly, strict.

The safety net of the voluntary system which underlies media other than TV is the Advertising Standards Authority. This is a body financed by the advertising industry through a surcharge on display advertising but staffed primarily by people independent of advertising,[*] which has the task of monitoring advertisements' conformity with the Code of Practice, acting as the recipient of complaints about advertisements from the general public, ensuring that offensive or misleading advertisements are withdrawn, and disseminating knowledge of the Code and infringements of it among agencies and advertisers.

The impracticality of pre-censorship of advertising in press media—where the sheer volume of new material appearing daily makes it physically out of the question—places a considerable obligation on advertisers and their agents to ensure that their advertising conforms to both the law and the Code of Practice. The media, too, have a limited ability, at best, to scrutinize ads in advance, especially as copy is often delivered at the last possible moment—or later. The one area in which newspapers, in particular, do systematically exercise a form of pre-scrutiny is in the field of mail order direct response advertising.

Here the Newspaper Proprietors' Association (the NPA) has established a system of vetting of advertisers, a guarantee fund contributed to by all

---

[*]The Council has an independent chairman, and two-thirds of the 12 Council members are independent of any advertising interest.

advertisers, and a policy of examining all direct response copy before it can be run. This is in response to public disquiet both at a number of fraudulent mail order ads and at the sheer inefficiency of many smaller mail order advertisers, and the system was established after detailed consultation with the Office of Fair Trading. A similar, but less stringent, system is run by the Periodical Publishers' Association (the PPA) and the Newspaper Society. Before they can run ads which aim to sell products directly off the page, advertisers have to provide the NPA with very detailed information about their businesses and their ability to meet the likely demand in response to the ad, and must pay a sum related to their prospective media spending into the guarantee fund.

This self-regulatory system of controls is a fundamental feature of the British advertising scene which seems to be in advance of most systems operated elsewhere. It has, certainly, enabled the British agency business to stave off a number of attempts to control advertising by statute and to introduce legal penalties for various misdemeanours. This is in contrast to the situation which prevails in the USA and even more in much of Continental Europe, where the area covered by the British Code of Practice is generally subject to the full rigours of the law, with specific prescribed penalties.

The European Commission in its first draft directive on advertising, sought to impose this sort of system throughout the Community. Subsequent negotiations led to the acceptance in 1984—nearly 10 years later—of a greatly diluted version which recognized the effectiveness of the British system, though a legally-established back-up facility has been put in place through the Control of Misleading Advertisements Regulations 1988. (It is, it has to be said, not immediately clear why it should be necessary to harmonize EC practice in an area where, in the nature of business, virtually all activity is purely national in character, and where advertising *practice*, as opposed to advertising *control*, is not notably in question.)

In the UK a significant breach in the industry's self-regulation has now, however, developed as a result of the 1986 Financial Services Act. The rules on advertising developed by the SIB (Securities and Investment Board) and its self-regulating subsidiaries have the force of law, and place some added restrictions on financial advertisers. A further outside restraint on advertising was unilaterally introduced during 1986 by the City Takeover Panel, which laid down new rules restraining advertising during contested takeover bids.

The voluntary control system undoubtedly offers British advertisers and their agencies a very flexible and responsive set-up which avoids the main need for slow-moving and costly legal proceedings. It is not a perfect system, and the Code of Practice is in a more or less constant state of revision and reinterpretation. Particular areas—for example, the use of children in ads and advertising to children—become contentious and require analysis and attention, as is, indeed, currently going on. What is certainly true is that the vast majority of ads conform to the Code, and, where they infringe it, most infringements are trivial. This was very clearly shown by a major research project sponsored by the Office of Fair Trading, in conjunction with the

Consumers' Association and the ASA, during 1978. This study examined a massive sample of press advertisements from all types of press media, and identified only a tiny proportion of significant breaches of the Code.

A further survey by a Department of Trade Working Party in 1980 also concluded that the system worked well, and a 1987 review of the system by the AA, while admitting that the complexity of controls is a mess, recommended that the basic system should remain as it is.

The Code of Practice

The British Code of Advertising Practice (eighth edition, December, 1988), runs to over 80 pages, excluding the index. The Code is prepared and updated by the Committee of Advertising Practice (CAP), which is composed of representatives of the various associations of advertisers, agencies and media owners, some 20 organizations in all. The CAP issues, from time to time, amendments to the Code and guidance notes on aspects of its interpretation. Advertisers and their agencies are able, if they wish, to submit copy to the CAP for pre-vetting, if they are in doubt about the acceptability or validity of an approach.

In addition to the BCAP and the very similar ITC Code of Practice, there are also specialized codes maintained by the Proprietary Association of Great Britain, the Mail Order Traders' Association and the Association of Mail Order Publishers, all of which include conformity with the BCAP as one of their rules; and there is also the rather different, but related, British Code of Sales Promotion Practice, which is maintained by the CAP.

After an introduction which describes the origins and aims of the Code and how it is administered, a preliminary section defines the Code's scope, sets out some key definitions, and lays down how the Code is to be interpreted. In particular, it is stated:

1. That conformity with the Code is assessed in the light of an advertisement's probable effect, when taken as a whole and in context
2. That the Code is interpreted in the spirit as well as the letter.

The major substance of the Code is contained in Part B, headed 'general rules'. In essence, these rules can be summarized under three main headings, which divide this section into three parts:

1. 'All Advertisements should be Legal, Decent, Honest and Truthful'.
2. 'All Advertisements should be Prepared with a sense of Responsibility to the Consumer and to Society'.
3. 'All Advertisements should Conform to the Principles of Fair Competition Generally Accepted in Business'.

Each of these main headings is qualified and expanded on in some detail, much of which refers, in practice, to legal requirements (relating, e.g., to the use of Royalty and the Royal Warrant, to testimonials, to the format in which prices and offers are quoted, etc.)

A particular area which is increasingly stressed in the more recent version of the Code than in earlier editions is that of the substantiation of factual claims, where there is a clear obligation laid on the advertiser to have, and provide if challenged, adequate substantiation of any claim capable of objective assessment. (This is the position as far as the BCAP is concerned: where advertisements are scrutinized *in advance*, as is done by the ITVA to ensure conformity with the ITC Code of Practice for TV advertising, it is well known to advertisers and agencies that the ITVA will expect such substantiation before a commercial can be aired.)

Part C of the Code sets out specific rules for particular categories of advertisements:

1. Advertisements containing health claims, especially those made for medicinal and related products.
2. Hair and scalp products.
3. Vitamins and minerals.
4. Slimming.
5. Cosmetics.
6. Mail order and direct response advertising.
7. Financial services and products.
8. Employment and business opportunities.
9. Limited editions.
10. Children.
11. Media requirements.
12. Alcoholic drinks.

This detailed section of the Code is followed by an appendix, detailing the 'cigarette code', the text of an agreement between the CAP, ASA and the Department of Health and Social Security, in conjunction with cigarette manufacturers and importers.

The Key Statutes

The various codes do not set out to be a work of legal reference, but a number of Acts of Parliament, Statutory Instruments and European Community directives are cited in the text. A list of some of these illustrates the range of overlap of advertising and the law:

– Broadcasting Act 1988
– Code of Practice for Traders on Price Indications 1989
– Consumer Credit Act 1974
– Consumer Credit (Advertisement) Regulations 1980, 1989
– Consumer Protection Act 1987
– Control of Misleading Advertisements Regulations 1988
– Copyright Designs and Patents Act 1988
– Data Protection Act 1984
– EC Directive on Misleading Advertising 1984

- EC Directive on Food Pricing 1988
- Financial Services Act 1986
- Food Act 1984
- Food Labelling Regulations 1984
- Hallmarking Act 1973
- Mail Order Transactions (Information) Order 1976
- Medicines Act 1968
- Medicines (Labelling and Advertising to the Public) Regulations 1978
- Post Office Act 1953
- Race Relations Act 1976
- Sex Discrimination Acts, 1975, 1986
- Trade Descriptions Act 1968

I am not going to try to summarize these, and the Codes briefly indicate their scope. A broad impression of the areas they cover, however, is an extremely valuable guide to likely problems.

What I do want to do in this section is to discuss briefly some of the legal principles which affect advertising, particularly general areas where care is needed.

Contract

Advertising is subject to the law of contract. This is an extremely complex area of law, but the essentials are reasonably clear. A contract is a legally binding agreement between two parties—you sign and exchange copies of a contract when you buy a house, or when you change jobs. Obviously, in advertising to a mass market, this does not occur, but what does happen, when someone buys a product or service on the basis of claims made in an advertisement, is that a contract is, in effect, concluded. If the product then clearly fails to deliver what has been claimed in the advertisement, the advertiser is in breach of contract. The classic case on which this is based is that of *Carlill* v. *The Carbolic Smoke Ball Company*. A Mrs Carlill bought a 'smoke ball' which was claimed to prevent colds, flu, etc., and promptly caught flu. On claiming the reward offered in the ad, she was refused: and she sued, successfully. Quite rightly you may say, but this was, in fact, a legal breakthrough. (Its logical limit is now being reached, with product liability legislation, both in the USA and in a slightly weaker form, in the 1987 Consumer Protection Act, which in effect extends the scope of a contract of this kind to make a company totally liable for virtually any mishap that may occur to the user.)

For the law of contract to apply, an actual purchase has to be made. A product advertised—mistakenly—in a shop window for a price far below its real value is in no way a contract. It is merely an 'offer to treat'. Similarly, it is under the law of contract that an advertising claim such as 'Washes whiter than white' is held to be 'mere puffery' rather than a serious, verifiable, legally binding claim.

Endorsements and defamation

Endorsements of a product, or testimonials, are extensively controlled by the Trade Descriptions Act 1968, but also in a number of other ways. Under the Trade Descriptions Act, you cannot give the false impression that a product conforms to a set of recognized standards (BSI or DIN, for example); or that a product is of a type supplied to a particular well-known individual or institution; or, indeed, that any individual or institution approves of the product.

A specific special case is that of Royalty. To cut some complicated legal discussion short, you should not claim that a product or service is used by a member of the Royal family unless you have that person's authority to do so. (There are, in addition, very specific rules about the use of the Royal Warrant.)

In addition to being liable under the Trade Descriptions Act for misrepresentation, a spurious endorsement claim can lead to a common law liability for defamation. In general, defamation means 'the publication of a statement which tends to lower a person in the estimation of right thinking members of society generally...'. There are plenty of examples of well-known (and less well-known) figures having been used without their permission in advertisements and suing successfully on grounds varying from having been subjected to ridicule to the real threat of being held to have breached their amateur status. One problem of defamation in relation to advertising is that the use of a fictitious named character in an ad can be held to apply to a real person of the same name, and be found to be defamatory, if the real person can show that he or she has suffered because of the ad. While an unauthorized endorsement may fall under the Trade Descriptions Act, it is not necessarily defamatory.

Passing off

'Passing off' is the misrepresentation of goods or services as those of another trader—by the close imitation or actual copying of a trade mark, brand name or pack design, for example. The counterfeit Levi's jeans produced in various Asian countries are a classic example.

The principle of passing off has been applied—not always successfully—to unauthorized endorsements, for example when 'Uncle Mac' of BBC radio attempted to prevent the marketing of 'Uncle Mac's Puffed Wheat': the established legal principle here seems to be that there has to be a common interest or field of activity (i.e., 'Uncle Mac' would have to have some interest in food manufacturing or marketing) for an action to succeed.

The main historical area, however, is in the field of trade marks and names—a field where the opportunities for trouble are now limited by the controls imposed by the Registration of Business Names Act 1986, which should ensure that there is no conflict between properly registered companies or, indeed, brand names.

There is, however, a whole area of product descriptions which can cause difficulty: the classic cases, perhaps, are actions taken to limit the use of generic regional names such as 'Sherry', 'Champagne', etc., and the continuing efforts of 'household words' such as Hoover, Formica, Pyrex, etc., to retain their status as trade marks. This is a field where the trade mark owner has to tread a very careful path through a minefield which can lead to the loss of an invaluable commercial property. However much it may offend the agency's aesthetic scene to have the symbol® attached to the name at its every appearance, it is, quite simply, essential.*

Copyright

'Original' work, of virtually any kind (including advertisements, which are not always very recognizably 'original') is protected by the law of copyright, now set out in the Copyright Designs and Patents Act 1988. This legislation is matched by similar laws in most countries of the world, and UK copyright confers protection world wide under reciprocal agreements.

For most types of work, copyright protection continues for 50 years from the year in which the author died. To reproduce copyright material, you have to get the permission of the copyright holder and, usually, pay a royalty. (For any reader who feels like copying this book, I should remind you that the Act restricts such copying to single copies, for the purposes of study or research, and limits the amount that can be copied to a single chapter, or no more than 5 per cent of the total!)

The scope of the UK legislation includes technical drawings and advertisement copy or artwork, and it may apply also to circulars, catalogues, commercial letters, etc. It is more doubtful, however, whether copyright applies to slogans or catch-phrases: there has never been a successful claim relating to a slogan or book title—two rather similar uses of words—though this apparent lack of legal protection is surprising.

For most work, copyright is owned by the author of the work, but when an 'artistic, literary or dramatic' work is created by an employee in the course of employment, the employer is the owner of the copyright. This rule does not apply to commercial work, as used to be the case under the old 1956 Copyright Act, and—unless arrangements are agreed to the contrary—the copyright belongs in the first instance to the author of the work. Both advertising agencies' contracts with their creative employees and clients' contracts with their agencies need, therefore, to define clearly where the ownership of copyright should lie.

Trade marks

Trade marks have already been briefly discussed under 'passing off'. The key element in understanding the legal position of trade marks is the system of registration. Trade marks, as defined by Section 9 (1) of the 1938 Act have to have at least one of the following characteristics:

---

*The® is, of course, not the only essential element of good practice in the use of a trade mark. It is just the most obtrusive.

1. Be the name of a company (etc.) represented in a particular manner;
2. Be the signature of the applicant or a predecessor in his or her business;
3. Be an invented word or words;
4. Be a word or words having no direct reference to the character or quality of the goods;
5. Be any other distinctive mark—but a name, signature or word other than as described above is not registrable, except on evidence of its distinctiveness.

In fact, the essential word in all this is 'distinctive'. The major problem facing companies launching new products today is to find registrable names for them.

Under the Trade Marks (Amendment) Act 1984, the scope of trade mark protection was extended to 'service marks'—trade marks applied to, for example, financial service products—as well as to products.

To be fully protected under the law, trade marks have to be registered with the Trade Mark Registry. As with copyright, trade marks are protected by reciprocal international agreements—though there are still parts of the world where these seem, in practice, to be honoured sketchily, if at all: the counterfeit goods industry is still alive and well.

Prices and price comparisons

This is a contentious area, applying primarily to retail advertising and point-of-sale material, where regulations have undergone nearly 20 years of constant change. The latest rules, embodied in the Consumer Protection Act 1987, considerably simplify the previous illogical and almost unintelligible situation that existed.

In essence, the 1987 Act describes a variety of ways in which a price may be misleading—e.g. that it is inaccurate; that it is incomplete; that it is not available for the indicated or implied time period; that it is falsely or misleadingly compared with another price. The Secretary of State then has the option to make specific orders to regulate particular practices as he or she sees fit or the need arises; but the basic thrust of the Act is to allow greater freedom than has recently been the case for advertisers to use prices and price comparisons.

The 1989 Code of Practice for Traders on Price Indications, promulgated by the Office of Fair Trading (OFT), sets out in great detail how prices may (or may not) be presented in retail advertising and at point-of-sale—the main area of contention and confusion. They key principles involved are 'transparency' (ensuring that, if a price is 'reduced', it is quite clear what kind of reduction this is, and from what previous price); 'clarity' (the prevention, as far as possible of sweeping, unspecific and imprecise statements of price and value); and honesty (the rules set out to ensure that where a trader claims to have reduced prices, the earlier price has been genuinely available to customers for a reasonable length of time, either in a specific branch of the traders' stores or in a reasonable proportion of a chain of stores).

Trade descriptions

The Trade Descriptions Act 1968, defines in great detail what a 'trade description' is, and prohibits any person in the course of a trade or business from applying false trade descriptions to goods, or from supplying or offering to supply any goods with a false trade description. An offence is committed whether the false description is deliberate or, with a few exceptions, accidental. For example, genuine mistakes, or 'reliance on information supplied' are allowable defences, and the latter protects advertising agencies, who rely, naturally, on the information provided by their clients. However, the defendant has to be able to show that reasonable precautions have been taken to ensure that a trade description is correct.

Data protection

The proliferation of computers and of personal files held in them led to the Data Protection Act 1984. While the Act's scope is very wide, it has important application to advertisers as the practice of database marketing has become more widespread.

Any business that wants to hold personal data about its customers on a computer has to register with the Data Protection Registrar, and must abide by quite specific and detailed rules which cover how data is obtained, what information is given to the data provider when it is collected, and how the data may be used. In particular, if the data user might wish to pass on a list to another company, the customer has to be given the opportunity to refuse to let this happen.

At the time of writing, the direct marketing industry is greatly exercised by an EC proposal that would place enormous restriction on the industry's ability to collect meaningful data on customers: on past experience, it seems unlikely that any eventual directive will be as stringent as the draft.

Comparative advertising

It is increasingly common for advertisements to compare the product advertised to competitive products to the latter's disadvantage. In much of Continental Europe this is illegal, but there is no law against in in Britain, although several aspects of law touch upon it, and the Code of Practice lays down some guidelines as to what is permissible.

The main essential is that the basis of the comparison is true. Otherwise, a 'knocking' ad could be liable under the common law offence of slander of goods. A more complex set of problems is raised in this area, however, by trade mark infringement. In general, comparison is acceptable, but disparagement is not.

Advertising agents

Advertising agencies are, by long established practice, not legally 'agents' in their dealings with the media, but principals. They are therefore, for example, liable for unpaid bills if one of their clients goes bankrupt or defaults on payment. Because of this, individual media or media associations operate a system of agency 'recognition', under which an agency has to furnish details of its professional and financial capability before it is accepted and allowed to earn commissions from the media.

As far as advertising content is concerned, however, it is normally the advertiser who is prosecuted for a criminal offence, such as a breach of the Trade Descriptions Act, though often both advertiser and agent are liable.

Specific product groups

Food advertising is restricted and controlled chiefly by the Food & Drugs Act 1955, but also by specific regulations concerning particular foods and by the Labelling of Food regulations, which are particularly concerned with nutritional claims, slimming, vitamins, etc.

The advertising of medicines and drugs is under the control of the Medicines Act 1968, which lays down very detailed rules as to what may or may not be said in medicine advertising, especially with regard to claims of efficiency and the involvement of doctors or nurses in advertisements.

As has been noted above, the Financial Services Act 1986, and the SIB rule book derived from it, have led to very specific rules on financial advertising.

The European dimension

This chapter has seen several mentions of EC directives that affect advertising. In addition to the 1984 Directive on Misleading Advertising, which was a considerably watered-down version of earlier proposals, the EC has proposed measures on advertising for a list that includes tobacco products, pharmaceuticals, financial services and foodstuffs; and there are rumours (at least) of proposals relating to toys, sweets, cars, comparative advertising, sexual discrimination in advertising, and so on, in addition to the data protection proposals discussed briefly above.

The relatively bureaucratic and legalistic approach of the EC and the Continental European legal tradition does not fit well with the self-regulating approach of the British, though the advertising industries across the EC tend to have come round to favour self-regulation, and their Brussels lobbying body, the European Advertising Tripartite, works vigorously to promote this type of approach.

A lot of the possible future thrust of EC directives is indicated by Directive 89/552/EEC on TV broadcasting, which sets out the framework under which cross-border TV broadcasting (primarily by satellite) can take place. Apart from specific restrictions on the amount of advertising permissible overall and in any one hour, the Directive bans advertising of tobacco products and prescription drugs; strictly controls alcohol advertising; lays down conditions restricting the nature of advertising directed to minors; prohibits programme sponsorship by tobacco or pharmaceutical companies; and prohibits sponsorship of news or current affairs programmes.

The future development of the EC's approach to advertising may be made simpler and more coherent by the recently announced establishment of a single advertising policy unit within the internal market Directorate General of the EC. This should be an improvement on the present situation, under which any of the 23 Directorates can propose legislation on advertising, leading to piecemeal and controversial proposals.

Conclusion

This brief summary of the main areas of the law's impact on advertising should at least show the extent of the opportunity for finding yourself in court once you get involved in the business. At least, you have been warned.

It is an unfortunate characteristic of this age of consumerism and multinational regulation that the volume of laws and rules and regulations expands continuously. Some new laws are useful and even necessary. Some appear to be produced almost purely for the hell of it, and with little thought to their practicality in a commercial context. The most extreme cases are, in fact, on the edge of advertising itself in the field of product liability, though here there is, I suspect, the risk of advertising claims becoming involved.

If anyone can explain to me how a manufacturer of a hammer can be held liable if a man commits suicide by hitting himself on the head with it—which appears a perfectly possible interpretation of US product liability law—I shall be surprised.

17 Advertising and society

The demon advertising

Advertising, as anyone who works in the industry or is responsible for advertising for his or her employers will find, is blamed for many of the ills of society. Significantly, the word used when a politician—or judge, or social worker, or member of the clergy, or the person next door—accuses advertising of some heinous crime against humanity is always 'advertising'. It is rarely, if ever, 'advertisements', far less 'that advertisement'. The only accusations specifically against individual ads that you are likely to meet are the neat little stickers—themselves a nearly perfect piece of advertising—which appear from time to time on the swimwear and lingerie ads on London Transport escalators saying 'This advertisement exploits women'. (This is arguably true: certainly, a growing number of women feel that this is the case, and that these ads present women as sexual objects in a public place. The fact remains, however, that these products are being advertised *to* women, and the products are—I assume—being bought: the advertisers are presumably not deliberately wasting their money. Of course, if you see the whole capitalist system as exploitation, or women as universally exploited, there's no argument.)

The point, of course, is that if you talk about 'advertising' as a nice vague, amorphous something, you can conjure up fearsome visions of an organized conspiracy, presumably composed of international bankers, multinational corporations, the International League for Cruelty to Children, the Ku Klux Klan, Rupert Murdoch and Saatchi and Saatchi, pointing a dagger at the trembling bosom of the poor downtrodden British family. It is good, vivid stuff, if a little lacking in focus or logic. But it is jolly difficult to see how you could conjure up a vision remotely like that if for 'advertising' you substitute 'that ad for Ragu where they all sing opera music in Italian', or even 'those ridiculously over-sexy ads for Häagen-Dazs'.

The most sinister version of course, in the sense that it can send a nasty shiver down your spine, is the sort of 'mad scientist' vision of brilliant psychologists having discovered all the secret springs of our motivations, and all the necessary tricks of parapsychology and thought transference, so that an apparently innocent ad can be invested with some altogether incredible potency—usually of a rather despicable sexual nature. I could quote a passage from a book that does this *in extenso*, but I cannot really see why I should encourage anyone to read it. So I shall not.

By this stage, you may be beginning to think that I protest too much. I must be hiding something. I have, however, to admit that I am too human for that. If I had anything so powerful to hide, I would be extremely rich, and have long ago retired to Mustique or Mauritius to enjoy my ill-gotten gains. Regrettably (for anyone who hopes to make a fortune in advertising) it is not as easy as that. Nobody in advertising that I know of has any magic insight into human psychology that makes it possible to move human mountains against their will. All that even the most successful people in the business have is an instinct—a salesperson's instinct, on the whole—for what people want to hear. This instinct can, to be sure, be sharpened and refined by market research, but there is nothing magic and effective available to do more than this.

Through the looking glass

Far from turning society upside down, the majority of advertisements, I would suggest, mirror society. It is, however, generally a distorting mirror. As a result, society looks at what it sees in the glass, does not like it, and with a certain justification blames the mirror. Ads are distorting mirrors for two main reasons. Firstly, advertisers, though part of society, are *only* part of it, and not a typical part. The clients, who are usually very normal business-people from the AB or possibly C1 classes—with a dash of upwardly-mobile ex-C2s—are not 'typical'; nor, far more, are the mostly young people (whom I would not dream of trying to categorize in any way at all) who create the ads.

Then, secondly, once an advertisement has struggled through this initial set of distortions, it gets hit by a massive dose of doublethink. Nearly everyone in advertising believes that an ad ought to be something that the target audience can relate to, or perhaps aspire to. There must be some rapport between ad and audience. But if it is too 'ordinary', people will ignore it. So you find people who are already atypical trying to produce typical ads and then to make them a bit less typical.

Nonetheless, the distorted picture usually has something in common with observable reality, even if the people in the ad are too good, or too nasty, to be true. Understandably, though, the world's critics will react in a jaundiced way if they see a world in which housewives worry endlessly about whether they are using the right washing powder, or spotty kids rush around saying 'gimme this' and 'gimme that' all the time, and words like 'pinta' keep coming out of the woodwork. This, surely, is what advertising has done to society? And what you see in the ads is merely reflecting what the ads have achieved?

It is, in fact, quite difficult for many people to accept that advertisements are, individually, merely attempts by individual firms to sell their goods; that they do this by presenting them in ways which, they hope, will strike a responsive chord with their target audience; and that no ulterior motive is in their minds beyond the profit figure on the bottom line. Only a politician or perhaps an Ayatollah would seek to change the world with advertisements, and both Dr Goebbels and Khomeini had to resort to arms eventually—

though I must admit that they had got some way with publicity first.

The problem faced by the COI and the Department of Health in getting people to adopt sensible measures to prevent the spread of AIDS is a clear indication of the difficulties involved in changing people's behaviour, even where there is very widespread associated publicity in the media, and great public concern. In spite of heavy and intensive advertising—both to the public at large and to high-risk groups such as drug users (a difficult market to reach!), gays and young people in general—evidence of widely changed sexual habits and, in particular, of increased use of condoms, is still fairly limited, after several years' effort.

Servant or seducer?

Advertisements are, of course, a means of separating people from their money. Judging from the relative cost per thousand of a 30-second national commercial and a good in-store demonstrator, I am bound to say that the public has probably gained a substantial degree of safety for its collective purse from the substitution of Anthony Valentine's voice on the telly for the blandishments of the snake-oil salesman. The vast majority of ads are at a substantial distance from the actual point of sale, both in physical yardage and in time. What is more, they are clearly and recognizably trying to sell something. And they have to obey the rules (see Chapter 16).

To be sure, much of what the ads display is very enticing. That is what selling is—and always has been—about. There are, of course, plenty of defences against enticements. There is, for example, the good, simple two-letter word 'no', which appears to be much under-rated these days. There is also the rather simple expedient of running out of money—though admittedly sources of credit are still so easy to find these days that that is no longer reliable. The fact is, of course, that salespeople and sales devices have always had a bad name.

It remains true, however, that people do, in fact, want to buy things. They actually do have needs to be met, and sometimes they have to seek quite hard for ways to meet them. One important source of information in this search is advertising. As soon as one talks about ads as information, one runs the risk of raising another philosophical argument—the extent to which ads do, or should, 'persuade' rather than 'inform'. This is an argument which quite misses the point that one person's information is another's persuasion. In this particular area madness lies. The fact remains that advertisements *are* sources of information, at one level or another.

It is actually very difficult to assess how useful ads *are* as information—not least because if you ask people where they heard of something they bought, they rarely say 'advertising'. Nonetheless, if you ask people how they go about looking for, say, a new washing machine, a very substantial proportion will mention ads as one source of information; and if you ask questions obliquely, about—say—the relative merits of ads in different media as sources of information, it is abundantly clear that they have this use very widely. (In fact, I believe you can legitimately argue that even most 'reminder' ads for mass-market grocery products are in fact information more than anything else.)

The brutal persuaders

So, if ads are useful as information—almost regardless of their content—but are also enticers and seducers, what can we make of this? If you put to people in a survey on attitudes to aspects of marketing and advertising the proposition that 'Ads make people buy things they do not need', you will get massive agreement. This is a view which has been picked up by politicians—and moralists—who have painted Dickensian pictures of old age pensioners being forced by compelling ads to waste their hard-earned pensions, meagre as they are, on skateboards and replicas of eighteenth-century carriage clocks. It is, you will find, always other people who are 'forced' by ads to buy things they do not need. As for me, or you, we have our wits about us.

I suppose, in the last resort, all we actually *need* is a roof over our heads—even a cave—some sort of coarse clothing, and a diet of locusts and wild honey. For better or worse, however, most of us live in, and have worked hard for, a rather more elaborately stocked world than that. What people lucky enough to live in the so-called developed world have achieved is a situation of material *choice*. And that choice includes, yet again, the choice not to buy. Advertisements, to be sure, put forward the buying choices: but that is their job, and everyone knows it.

There is, perhaps, an argument which says that you should not dangle diamond necklaces before old age pensioners with low incomes: but it is moderately rare to find such things advertised in media that really poor pensioners see. If the media selection is realistic, the products advertised will rarely be beyond the means of the vast majority of the audience. (Somewhere down this path lies a very complex argument about equality and social justice: but that is really not what we are arguing about. As I said, advertising reacts to and reflects society, and cannot hope to change it.)

In the last resort, there is one very simple refutation (in the proper sense of the word, for once) of the argument that ads force people to buy. Very simply, no ad *could* ever force anyone to buy anything, in any meaningful sense of the word 'force'.

But, of course, ads could lead people into crime by constantly putting before them things they cannot afford, could they not? Yes, of course, they could, in a society where morals do not appear to be very high in anyone's priorities. But is it really the ads that cause all these robberies? If you look at what gets knocked off in the average theft, it is not often heavily advertised goods, except, perhaps, cars, and it is easy to spot the fallacy there: a car is its own advertisement.

Suffer little children

Children, of course, are extremely vulnerable beings, and this includes vulnerability to commercial pressures. As a result, the Code of Practice has an extensive section on advertising to children, and it is a field where there has been considerable discussion over the years by the OFT, consumer bodies and the advertising industry. Children, with regard to ads, are among those classed as 'they'—who are forced by ads, etc…. They are also widely believed, with some justification, to drive their parents mad by wanting 'The one I saw on telly'.

Therefore, say some, ads aimed at children, or screened during children's viewing times, or printed in children's comics, should be banned, and there is growing pressure at EC level for further restrictions.

It is a nice simple solution, but difficult to carry through—how do you prevent a child from seeing a poster? How do you define children's viewing times? How do you define an ad aimed at children? More importantly, though, would it do any good in the long run?

Clearly the short-term results could be less over-spending of pocket money and fewer persecuted parents. In the longer term, however, is anything gained? One of the best controls over dishonest advertising, and one of the best pressures for responsible advertising, is an educated consumer. A process has certainly started, some years ago now, by which children have been learning, at least in school, how to deal with advertisements. This learning process is, surely, considerably assisted by exposure to ads. It would be a pity if this were to be halted. Whatever you may think about our materialistic society, it is the one we have to live in, and learning to deal with one of the more conspicuous aspects of that society seems to me to be a useful part of any child's education. A gullible public is a dangerous public, on any terms, and gullibility in the face of ads is just one aspect of a possibly far wider susceptibility to being taken in.

I do believe, therefore, that while advertisements directed to children should be closely controlled—more closely than other ads— it would actually be counterproductive to ban them. I *want* an educated public that can use ads on its own terms: that way ads can be more responsible—because they have to be. I also believe that if parents let themselves be bullied by their kids into buying things they have seen in the ads, they have only themselves to blame. Once again, 'no' is a very useful word, whether it is used directly with respect to buying something for a child, or indirectly as a refusal to replace squandered pocket money.

Prostitution of the arts

In the world of the artist, commercialism devalues most things. The lofty ideal of artistic integrity is above considerations of pounds and pence. So the fact that advertising uses the language of several arts—writing, illustration, photography, music—is in itself an affront. The further, generally observable, fact that most ads contain neither good writing, nor good illustration, nor good photography, nor good music is merely extra evidence of the parasitism of the industry on the fair face of culture. *Ars gratia artis*, but Ads *gratia* Addis, in fact.

Now there is, obviously, something in this, but I do not think it goes very far. In general, advertisements do not masquerade as works of art, though some come very near it: you have only to look through a magazine like *Graphis*, or collections of DADA award-winners, to see extremely 'artistic' ads. Much advertising photography is of an extremely high standard, and TV commercial techniques have contributed much to film. It is less easy—to put it mildly—to claim much positive benefit to the language from advertising copy.

Quite apart, however, from a very positive contribution to visual arts—and, I suspect, to the visual awareness of the public—there is no doubt that the advertising industry provides an essential social service to much of the artistic world. The majority of students from art college go into commercial work of one kind or another, and many artists pay for their 'genuine' art by working for advertising. Similarly, there is a significant list of writers, both of prose and poetry, who earn their living in advertising—in spite of the constraints of advertising copy.

Thus, although advertising may ape art, and the objectives of art used in advertising are not the objectives of 'pure' art, the advertising industry's contribution to art (or 'the arts') is, on the whole, a positive one.

The environment

Once the idea of pollution became widely accepted, it quickly became applied, more or less metaphorically, to a vast variety of aspects of the world we live in. Quite apart from pollution of air or water or food, we now have aural pollution, visual pollution, even spiritual pollution. Advertisements, naturally, have become pollution—of several kinds—in these terms.

This is a view with which I have some sympathy. There is little doubt, as one finds only too often when trying to devise and place advertising for a client, that the sheer volume of advertisements, in all media, makes it very difficult—increasingly difficult—to find a way of standing out and getting attention. For many advertisers, the only solution has been to increase the volume of their efforts, and so increase the amount of 'noise' their own and others' ads have to penetrate in order to communicate.

The number of ads to which we are potentially exposed every day is vast. If you live in a town, have you ever counted the number of posters you pass as you go about your daily business? The average newspaper or magazine may be 60 per cent or 70 per cent ads. On television, about three minutes of every hour watched in the UK consists of commercials.* Naturally, we attend to only a limited proportion of these ads.

The question of whether ads add to, or detract from, the environment in which we live is, I think, rather more complex than simply to dismiss them as 'pollution', of whatever kind. There is little doubt that our eyes are, in general, accustomed to the presence of posters, and that they do actually tend to enhance the look of a town if they are suitably placed and controlled. The

*Seven minutes of commercials on ITV per hour, and ITV has half the audience.

drabness of most Eastern European cities and, indeed, of many small country towns is due, to an extent, to the absence of posters. (The countryside is another thing: the poet who wrote 'I think that I shall never see a billboard lovely as a tree' was, surely, right.)

In television, the old joke that the commercials are better entertainment than the programmes has more than a little truth in it—most commercials are produced with more technical skill and more imaginative thought than most programmes. In the press, as is well known, the publications could not survive without their advertising revenue. Either you have ads or you have no papers—at least not at prices you can afford. In other words, the ads are not pollution of the environment: they actually *are* the environment.

True pollution, I would suggest, is something which actively damages the environment, and the removal of which would result in a positive benefit. Unless you believe that newspapers and magazines are unnecessary luxuries, or that a reasonable choice of TV programmes is not a desirable thing to have, especially if someone else pays, or that towns really are somehow better without posters, I do not think the pollution charge really stands up. You do not *need* to remove the ads. Nearly always, you can ignore them: the human brain is a marvellous machine for excluding unwanted communications— that is another of advertising's problems.

But there is more to the relation of ads to the environment than simple pollution. The 'green' movements that have sprung up all over the world in the last 10 years or so have, inevitably, influenced manufacturers and their marketing. There has been a rash of products that claim 'green' credentials, with varying degrees of precision or honesty, and their advertising reflects this. Thus, we have 'ozone-friendly' deodorants, organic vegetables, recycled toilet tissue, low consumption washing machines (less powder, less water, less energy), cars with catalytic converters and, now, the more or less recyclable car. To control all this, we will, shortly, have EC-wide labelling regulations (if all the interested parties manage to agree, which seems slightly improbable) and, I expect, restrictions on environment-based advertising claims.

Health and safety

Closely related to environmental considerations are issues of health and safety. The prime battleground here is food, where a whole army of pressure groups is involved in a raft of claims and counter-claims about fats, fibre, sugar, 'additives', 'junk food', and—more broadly—the nature and constitu- ents of a healthy diet. And then there is alcohol, of course. Add to this the possible internationalization of the Japanese fad for so-called 'functional foods', that are designed, for example, to aid digestion, and there is a rich field in which advertising can, and will, be accused of misleading, confusing or—even—poisoning people.

Much of this area already comes well within the purview of the regulatory or self-regulating systems—but it does not stop people being misled and con- fused, especially if they don't know (unlike the advertisers) precisely what claims can or cannot be made, and how a clever copywriter can weasel a way around the rules. This is a field ripe for argument and recrimination, in which advertising will always get, and sometimes deserve, a large part of any blame. Part of the problem, of course, is that the goalposts keep moving: from the viewpoint of (say) 1970, it is hard to credit that the ITVA would refuse—as it does—to accept claims that the milk in milk chocolate is in any sense healthy.

A similar situation occurs in another, quite different but equally contentious area—car advertising—where it has become, quite rapidly, almost completely unacceptable to talk in advertising about a car's speed and acceleration, as this is, allegedly, to encourage dangerous driving. Half of me says this is pious piffle: the other half is prepared to listen.

Sex and sexism

Another strong trend of the eighties was the spread of more or less feminist thinking. Any man writing about women's position in society risks being misunderstood, so please be tolerant!

As far as advertising is concerned, feminism has led to two generally justifiable critiques of the way in which ads portray women and try to sell to them. The first is the use of women purely as sex objects, primarily to sell to men. Outside the small ads in motor trade magazines, this is something that, in its crudest form, has largely disappeared in the UK. These days, perhaps, we are more subtle... (I don't think you can legitimately criticize lingerie ads for showing pretty women in a state of near undress—though you may legitimately question the choice of media, hence the regular complaints at the Hennes retail chain's gratuitously provocative posters on the London Underground).

The second area, which is more difficult to deal with, is sexual stereotyping: women in ads tend to be shown in situations that reflect the 'little woman' housewife roles that disappeared from many women's lives 15 or 20 years ago. This sort of advertising often goes with a tone of voice in which women are talked down to in a very patronizing way. This seems to me to be an area in which women have a legitimate complaint—but in which it is clear that the advertisers have simply got it commercially wrong, if they are hoping to sell to women who subscribe at all to a modern view of women's role in society. The penalty ought to be, simply, low sales.

Certainly, this is an area in which advertisers have to be increasingly careful—and in 10 years' time, the issue may well have disappeared. In the meantime, it can still come as something of a surprise, the first time a research group tells you, loud and clear, that perfume advertising should have nothing to do with attracting men.

African, Asian, black, brown – or just foreign?

Advertising tends to mirror society in its unwillingness to recognize the (significant) presence of racial minorities. Very few British ads have actors of

African or Asian origin in them—Frank Bruno and Lenny Henry are rare exceptions, and I cannot personally remember seeing an adult Asian in any ad without a clear ethnic slant to it (e.g., for a curry powder). Similarly, the specifically ethnic market, represented in media terms by (for example) Choice FM radio (Brixton), the *Daily Jang, Garavi Gujarat*, the *Gleaner, Multi-Mag*, or the *Voice* is an unknown quantity to most people in the advertising business. Yet there are at least 2.8 million members of ethnic minorities in the UK.

In the USA, various pressure groups have succeeded in achieving both recognition and participation for 'blacks' in US advertising, and there are 'black' agencies and agencies specializing in selling to the Hispanic market. In the UK, there is a significant element of Asian staff in most large agencies, but little reflection of this in ads—even on a local basis in large towns and cities such as Slough, Birmingham or Bradford.

This situation will change, but probably only slowly, and primarily in response to the recognition of specific market segments rather than as a reaction to political militancy. The growing presence of 'black' athletes in national sports teams is one key element in raising awareness of ethnic minorities. The fact remains that these minorities are very under-recognized by the market and by advertisers, and a wider use of such actors in ads would probably help enhance their standing.

A benefit to society?
This chapter has discussed, briefly, the main charges laid against advertising for doing some form of damage to society. They are all more or less common, and some are firmly believed by many people. Most of them, on inspection, turn out to be criticisms of society itself—its materialism, its immorality, its indiscipline, its dishonesty—rather than of advertisements. We happen to live in an advanced industrial society, with a particular economic structure which will change only slowly. As it changes, advertising will change, too: it will not change society. It cannot.

There seem to me to be good reasons to dismiss these charges against advertising as being sweeping, generalized, inaccurate, and wrongly directed. I do not believe advertising is Simon Pure, but people recognize this: there is plenty of research evidence to prove it.

I am not so naïve, either, as to argue that advertising is a positive benefit to society in these general social terms—there are some clear benefits, but mostly it seems to me pretty neutral. I do believe, however, that advertising is able to provide at least some economic benefits. These are discussed in the next chapter.

18 Advertising and economics

pIn this chapter, I want to discuss briefly the role of advertising in economic life, and the effects advertising can have, in economic terms.

Advertising in the economy
Advertising in the UK became in the eighties a substantial growth industry, both in absolute terms and relative to the economy as a whole. This is in marked contrast to the experience of most of the seventies, when it was safe to say in the first edition of this book that advertising was—surprisingly—a declining business. The data set out in Table 18.1 show the way in which expenditure rose to new heights in relation both to the gross national product (GNP) and, possibly more relevantly, to consumers' expenditure and then slipped back as the recession took over.

As can be seen, advertising represents a very small proportion indeed of total consumer spending—just over one penny in the pound. So when people complain that they are paying for all that advertising in the cost of the goods they buy, it is helpful to keep that in perspective. (It is true, however, that in certain categories of goods they may be spending rather more, as is shown by Table 2.1, page 19).

Similarly, the advertising industry is, itself, a small one. No one, as far as I know, has set out to calculate the total numbers involved in advertising, including those responsible for advertising in client companies (which is often only a part-time task for a brand or marketing manager), and workers in art studios, TV commercial production companies and printers, and on the advertising side of the various media. As far as agencies are concerned, the IPA publishes statistics for membership of IPA agencies, which probably account for 85–90 per cent of total agency employment. These figures show that numbers employed in agencies fell from a peak of over 18 000 in the mid-sixties to a low point of some 13 000 in 1976, and have moved erratically since then: the figures for the end of 1991 show the IPA agencies back at the 1976 level.

Advertising, then, is not a major factor in employment, but it is a fairly significant one in the economy as a whole, especially as it represents a large part of the marketing expenses of companies. As such, it can have an important relationship with, and effect on, company profits.

Companies' profitability is determined by a very wide variety of factors— notably the state of the economy, rates of inflation, developments in wage costs, and the level of interest rates. The overall state of the economy, in particular, affects sales levels and the ability to achieve those sales at a reasonable profit margin—both because lower sales mean less efficient use of capacity, in manufacturing and distribution, and because the competition in a weak market produces intense pressure on prices.

Table 18.1   Advertising expenditure, display advertising, consumer expenditure and GDP 1961–1991

	Advertising expenditure (1)	Display advertising (2)	(1) as % of		(2) as % of	
			GDP	Consumers' Expenditure	GDP	Consumers' Expenditure
1961	338	260	1.38	1.89	1.06	1.45
1965	435	313	1.37	1.90	0.99	1.37
1971	591	409	1.19	1.68	0.82	1.16
1975	976	730	1.01	1.48	0.76	1.10
1981	2884	2271	1.31	1.86	1.04	1.46
1985	4609	3558	1.49	2.12	1.16	1.63
1986	5322	4114	1.61	2.21	1.26	1.70
1987	6055	4591	1.67	2.29	1.28	1.73
1988	7044	5216	1.75	2.35	1.31	1.75
1989	7827	5734	1.78	2.39	1.32	1.75
1990	7885	5773	1.66	2.26	1.22	1.66
1991	7577	5654	1.51	2.86	1.13	1.54

(*Source:* Advertising Association)

It is an observable fact that advertising expenditures, in the aggregate, tend to be closely related to company profits: when profits fall, so does advertising spending, and vice versa. This reflects the equally observable fact, common to the experience of all advertising agencies and advertising managers, that when there is pressure on a company's profits, its natural instinct is to cut the advertising budget.

This is an illogical response, perhaps: logic says that when times are difficult, both for you and your competitors, you will win if you can fight that much harder. But there are few marketing directors with the strength and standing in their companies to win an all-out battle over budget cuts. What is more, advertising is especially easy to cut: unlike all other elements in the company's operations, it involves virtually no use of physical resources—at least, not of physical resources belonging to the company. You can cut the advertising budget without laying off any employees, or mothballing vans or lorries. What is more, there is a lot of evidence—for example, from the 1979 ITV strike—to show that a month or two without advertising is unlikely to harm your business; or, it if does, it is virtually impossible to prove it until far later.*

*The ITV strike, of course, tends to prove only that if you remove all significant advertising from a market, you do little harm, since most TV advertisers' main competitors also use TV.

(All this constitutes an interesting set of rather cynical reasons why an agency should aim to achieve two specific objectives in relation to its clients: it should aim to have clients with a mixture of financial year ends; and it should aim to get those most prone to cutting their budgets onto a minimum income agreement.) The corollary of this relationship with profits is that advertising tends to thrive when things are going well with companies and the economy. Advertising, therefore, is used in practice more to support success than to fight adversity. In terms of its possible role in the marketing mix (see Chapter 1), this *may* be a correct approach, but there is sufficient evidence from markets where individual brands have successfully kept on advertising when others have stopped to suggest that advertising's defensive values are greater than might be expected.[*]

Advertising and the company

It has already been pointed out that advertising is quite a small, though significant, part of the average company's overall expenses. It is, however, an important part of the business of selling the company's products, and it is this that focuses attention on advertising's economic role in the company. (This argument is usually applied to advertising alone: it is more realistic to look at overall marketing costs.)

The basic mechanisms by which marketing activity affects company economics are two. The most obvious one is that increased sales volumes typically lead to economies of scale in manufacturing and distribution. This makes it possible for the company either to sell its products more cheaply, thus strengthening its hold on its market *vis-à-vis* competition; or to sell its products more profitably. Either way, the process makes it easier for the company to invest in new equipment and in research and development for new, better products.

The other mechanism involved in the operation of effective marketing affects profitability. If the company's marketing of its products is more effective than that of its competitors, it is able either simply to be more profitable at equal prices to competition or, alternatively, to sell at a premium price, reflecting the quality 'added' to the product by the brand values attached to it by good marketing and advertising. Again, this clearly puts the company in a stronger position for the future.

It is quite easy to argue that, if advertising enables the company to achieve higher profitability, it is going to lead to increased prices for the company's customers. On the face of it, it is easy to believe that this might be true. In practice, although the evidence is by no means conclusive, a study by Reekie[†] for the Advertising Association makes it reasonably clear that advertising does not lead to raised prices—indeed, it very often leads to lowered prices. This is both because it happens to be an effective weapon of competition, and because of the economies of scale it can lead to. Certainly, Reekie is able to

[*]See, for example, S. Buck and A. Roberts: *Television Advertising in a Recession*, AGB International, Information For Decision Makers, No. 3, April 1991.

[†]W. Duncan Reekie: *Advertising & Price*, Advertising Association, London, 1979.

produce a wide range of examples to illustrate the way in which advertising can lead to reduced prices.

Monopoly

Monopoly is a particularly dirty word among economists, and anything that tends to create a monopoly is suspect. With this in mind, economists often suggest that advertising can be used to develop monopoly power and, once this is achieved, to maintain that position and, by inference, to exploit customers. As a number of investigations into heavily advertised markets by the Monopolies Commission and others have shown, these markets tend to be highly competitive, and prices charged are by no means inflated: advertising does offer economies of operation.

Similarly, there is no quantifiable evidence to suggest that advertising is the major force in establishing or even in maintaining monopolies. Certainly, large companies with high market shares use advertising—as they use advanced distribution systems, economies of scale in production and buying, more efficient administration through the use of expensive computers—to defend themselves against competition.[*] There are, nonetheless, plenty of examples of apparent monopolies or very dominant market shares being attacked and significantly eroded. Reasonably recent ones include Gillette (a classic), Oxo's partial loss to Bovril cubes, and IBM's dominant position in data processing, eroded by competitors' development of personal computers. Ten years ago no one seemed to have regarded those two substantial technical monopolies, BL and Ford, as exercising monopoly power in the car market. Reasonably, too, as it turned out. In fact, the possibility open to new challengers of using media advertising, with its rapid coverage of mass audiences, tends to make monopolies more, rather than less, vulnerable to attack.

The media

The media provide the advertising industry's market, and the *only* genuinely economic transactions undertaken in the course of advertising spending are the purchase of space and time from the media, and the payment of the costs of advertisement production. (When economists, who should know better, say that customers are paying for the advertising when they buy a product, they are guilty of a false analysis—unless they also say that the customer is paying for the sales force, the delivery vans, the warehouses and the order clerks.)

Recently, this has been confirmed by a number of studies in the USA and the UK of the effects of deregulation of advertising on the prices charged by various professions. In particular, the US Federal Trade Commission has shown that opticians' prices in deregulated states are 30–40 per cent lower than those in states where opticians cannot advertise. Similarly, in the UK,

*It is worth remembering that very few companies have a real monopoly in any large market: UK monopolies legislation defines monopoly—arbitrarily—as a market share of over 25 per cent. Similarly, few monopolies are invulnerable to indirect competition: look at British Rail.

the partial relaxation of controls on advertising by lawyers has led to a sharp reduction in prices of standard procedures, such as the drawing up of wills, and this has been publicly recognized by the OFT. Essentially, this demonstrates the direct value to consumers of advertising as information that enables them to compare competing offers. Evidence on this is summarized in detail in a booklet published by the Advertising Association.*

The media owner's sales of advertising make it possible for the paper or magazine or TV or radio programme to be provided for the public at a significantly lower cost than would otherwise be the case. Thus, although the advertising transaction is nothing to do with the consumer, there is significant, if indirect, benefit to the consumer from the existence of advertising.

Consumer benefits

In fact there are, clearly, added benefits beyond this. Advertising is an input into the efficient production and marketing of goods and services. Without it, there is little doubt that the vast majority of advertised goods or services— and many unadvertised goods and services too—would be more expensive to buy and more difficult to purchase than they are.

On the debit side, advertising is, clearly, a cost in the production process. But, given the competitive pressure on firms to reduce their costs, it is a reasonable inference that most of the time it is a substitute for a higher cost, and you cannot treat it in isolation from the other input costs. Customers do not buy advertisements, they buy products—or, indeed, brands.

There may, too, be a cost to some people in terms of aesthetic or moral distaste. However, research studies have consistently shown that few people are concerned about advertising to the extent that any cost-benefit analysis would attribute a significant value to this and, as has been argued elsewhere (page 205), advertising actually has some clear, if concealed, benefits in the aesthetic area.

Conclusions

Advertising has a quite small but significant part to play in the national economy, as measured against GNP. It offers clear benefits to companies, as an aid to more efficient use of resources and reduction in overall selling costs. It provides the financial basis by which the cost to the consumer of advertising media is kept within reasonable bounds. It enables the consumer to buy many goods and services more cheaply and conveniently.

It carries some cost (in 'welfare' terms) in aesthetic and moral terms, and it can be accused of bolstering monopoly. In both cases there are, to say the least, offsetting factors.

---

*M.J. Waterson, *Advertising, Brands and Markets*, Advertising Association, London, 1984.

19 International, multinational, global advertising: why?

So far, this book has been primarily concerned with UK advertising, though I have aimed to refer in passing to differences and similarities between the UK and both the USA and Continental Europe. At the same time, enough has been said to suggest that even in a small, compact, crowded country like the UK, it may be desirable to vary advertising approaches by region, especially in Scotland, which has a unique advertising sub-culture of its own. In the USA, regional variations of this kind are almost the rule, and there are also large sub-sectors of the media and the advertising industry targeted specifically at the major ethnic sub-groups. Clearly, from what was said about targeting and target audiences in Chapter 7, advertisers ought to pay careful attention to the cultural differences between national, regional and racial groups.

It is, therefore, something of a paradox to find major advertisers and agencies increasingly working to develop more or less common coordinated campaigns on a multinational scale; at the same time, it is clear that 'international' advertising is a long-established and accepted phenomenon. There are a number of historical strands to this development, and there is still a substantial debate in the advertising industry as to how best to approach transnational communications, both managerially and creatively.

The growth of multinational agencies

Advertising agencies have been international since the twenties (or, even, a little earlier). Typically, they spread overseas from the United States, as the USA produced the first generation of modern multinational corporations: General Motors, Ford, Chrysler, Procter & Gamble, Kelloggs, Quaker Oats, and so on. To take a specific example, J Walter Thompson agreed to open an office to service the General Motors account wherever GM required them to; and other US agencies followed JWT's example.

On the European side, there seem to have been fewer aggressive international marketing companies, but Unilever's international interests led to their house agency, Lintas, establishing offices all over the world, including— naturally —much of the old British Empire. Similarly, SH Benson, with much Unilever business, also put down roots all over the world.

After the Second World War, the rapid development of consumer goods marketing and the enormous increase in advertising expenditures led to the beginning of a process of mergers, acquisitions and in-filling of networks, primarily—again —by US agencies such as JWT, Grey, McCann-Erickson, Young and Rubicam, Leo Burnett, SSCB (which merged with Lintas in the seventies), BBDO, FCB, Ted Bates, Ayer, Ogilvy and Mather, etc. During this period a number of strong local agencies, especially in the smaller European markets, but even, eventually, large and established firms such as SH Benson, were acquired by international networks.

It was not until the seventies that Europe effectively hit back. The prime movers were Saatchi and Saatchi, who 'went international' when they acquired Garland Compton, and then went on to buy Ted Bates and BSB. By now, too, the French had started to flex their muscles with TBWA, Publicis and Havas starting to develop international networks, followed, significantly, by the media specialists, Carat. Last and by no means least, in 1987, a small and rapidly growing marketing services group headed by ex-Saatchi finance director Martin Sorrell, WPP, astonished the industry by buying J Walter Thompson; Sorrell then repeated the exercise, and—arguably—overreached himself financially, by buying Ogilvy and Mather, to create the world's largest agency group, in terms of billings, displacing Saatchi.

By 1991, about 30 big agency groups could claim to provide a genuinely international—or even global— service to those clients who wanted it. While the majority are, still, American, changes in ownership have led to a wider distribution of the balance between the USA and Europe, and one of the more dynamic groups, Chiat Day Mojo, is Australian in origin. The sleeping giants of the multinational agency market are the big Japanese agencies, Dentsu and Hakuhodo. In the UK, Dentsu has a significant minority share in Collett Dickinson Pearce, but neither group has shown much aggression outside Japan: if anything, Hakuhodo seems more active, though their European client list seems to be exclusively Japanese.

As can be inferred from the preceding couple of pages, it is clear that most multinational advertising networks have been created by a mixture of start-up subsidiaries and acquisitions; and most of the successful subsidiaries have in fact, grown by virtue of being relatively independent of 'head office', and gaining local, domestic business. J Walter Thompson's London and Frankfurt offices are good examples of this. Obviously, if an agency network is to operate and cooperate effectively in handling international business, it helps if there is a common managerial and operational culture and philosophy. This is much easier to achieve through start-up operations than through acquisition, but it still requires a high level of cooperation and sensitivity, for reasons that will become clear in a moment.

Most agencies do not have the long history or the financial strength of the big, established groups; yet to handle the prestige international accounts, they have to be able to point to appropriate networks. The alternative to merger and acquisition is the formal—or, even, informal— 'club'. These more or less loose associations of agencies have their origins in the older practice of 'correspondent' agencies, which still operate in many smaller and third world markets. Few large networks could justify a chain of individual subsidiaries in—say—each of the countries of Africa, the Middle East or, even, Latin America: instead, to handle their multinational business they would set up an agreement with a local agency who (with luck) would competently handle media planning and buying and the physical production of the advertising.

A sophisticated version of this system is now operated by a number of groups of European agencies that do not have offices outside their home countries. I am not sure that any of these work especially well, because of a combination of the absence of common systems and philosophies, and the relative unimportance of most of these relationships, in comparison to the demands of the individual agencies' home markets. Most of the groups are best described as 'dining clubs', rather than business associations.

Multinational advertising: why?

'Global marketing' was invented, as a concept, by Harvard Business School professor Theodore Leavitt, in the seventies. In principle, the theory of global marketing suggests that it should be possible, in many product markets, to successfully exploit economies of scale in R&D, manufacturing and marketing, so as to dominate the world's markets through common, unified marketing activity. The implied corollary of this, which was enthusiastically picked up and promoted by Saatchi and Saatchi (in particular), is that global *marketing* should be supported by global *advertising*.

Indeed, there are a number of examples of products and advertising campaigns that appear to support this analysis: IBM, Coca-Cola, Pepsi-Cola, Marlboro, Levis and McDonalds all appear to exemplify what Leavitt (and Saatchi) were talking about. Benetton, British Airways and a host of other airlines rapidly joined the club.

Interestingly, about there—at least as far as consumer products are concerned—it seems to stop. Why?

Of course, the situation is not as simple as this. And that is where the global marketing-global advertising link begins both to collapse and to make sense. Again, we have two essentially conflicting propositions trying to work together: the advertising planning philosophy that says—to my mind rightly—that advertising should be created to appeal in the most appropriate way to a specific, quite narrowly defined target audience; and the essentially product-based view of the homogeneous *brand* (which may, in practice, be an infinitely variable *product*) sold world-wide. In communication terms (which is what advertising is about) what are we trying to sell?

It seems to me clear that there are only—ever—a limited number of really creative selling ideas in a given product market. It is, equally, clear that a lot of creative ideas in *entertainment* travel quite effectively around the world: look at the film industry and its close relative, television. Why can't we produce commercials or ads that work just as well? I think that we are, in practice, being deluded by a form of cultural imperialism: it is true, certainly, that

American (mostly) films sell successfully all over the world. It is equally true that most American films are only fully understood in the USA: a lot of Hollywood productions lose a great deal in just crossing the Atlantic to Britain where (it is widely believed) the language is the same. By the time the same films have been translated and subtitled or dubbed into German, French, Czech, Urdu or Mandarin, they will have lost, I suggest, a significant proportion of whatever creative qualities they had. They may still be good entertainment, but the nuances of the ideas they use, whether verbal or visual, will have disappeared as cultural and linguistic boundaries are crossed. Even the simplest selling message—a poster with a single line of copy—can be transmogrified by its social context.

What this means, I believe, is that the universal, global advertising campaign is bound to be a very rare creature. It must be either very simple (I think 'the United Colours of Benetton' is probably such an idea, but even then I am not sure ...), or it has to be, in itself, a form of cultural imperialism, inflicting its own legend on the target audience, whether they like it or not. I believe that McDonalds, Coca-Cola (the origin of Coca-colonization), Marlboro and Levis are all, in their way, examples of this: all, in fact, are selling various, very similar, aspects of the 'American way of life', and using the brand as a symbolic representation of that way of life.

Tribes and witch doctors
If 'global' advertising is so inherently difficult, why do we look for it and how can we justify the search? There has to be a market-based rationale (I would assume).

There are, certainly, a number of more or less world-wide phenomena, at least in the industrial world, that suggest the sort of homogeneity, among some groups of consumers, in relation to some products, that can justify global advertising. There is a 'tribal' theory, originally popular in the seventies, that describes teenagers (a loose group aged from about 8 to 27) as a tribe without national boundaries. They are (we should believe), all over the world, interested in the same music; keen on wearing the same clothes; wanting to drink the same drinks, and chew the same gum; aspiring to look the same, live the same, love the same. A similar analysis creates a very different 'tribe', of internationally-travelling business executives. This group eats the same food; drinks the same (expensive) brands of spirits; uses the same airlines; enjoys staying at the same executive hotels; wears the same watches ....

At this point, tribal analysis, as such, seems to run out. More subtly, social attitude studies such as VALS and RISC (see page 71) seem to suggest a commonality of 'trends' in attitudes: the leading trends for the nineties are, we are told, towards caring, 'green' consciousness and self-realization. But then, only perhaps 15 per cent of the population of any one country is 'on trend'. Everyone else is, one way or another, out of step.

In short, the consumer end of the analysis that leads to global advertising is, to say the least, somewhat limited. There is remarkably little real evidence to suggest that real consumers in different countries will respond in the same way to similar advertising stimuli. This is true even for countries as culturally close as France and Belgium or Britain and the USA: how much more so, if we take say Sweden and Spain, or Germany and Japan?

It is abundantly clear to anyone who goes to international advertising festivals—or, even, gets their view of world advertising from TV personalities like Clive James or Jasper Carrott— that most significant advertising markets have their own fairly distinctive styles (especially as regards humour and the use or abuse of sex), based on what appear to be almost purely local frames of reference. The international advertiser can, it seems to me, approach this fact from two alternative points of view: as an obstacle to be circumvented or demolished; or as a set of tools and raw materials with which to work. The latter alternative seems to me to be what marketing should be about. To quote a specific example, it does not seem to me to be very useful for an executive from a German agency to put forward the argument that, since Germany is a major economic power in Europe, and since German consumers like their advertising to be straightforward, factual and informative, therefore other Europeans ought to adopt this type of advertising. If he had added 'when they advertise in Germany', I would have no quarrel with the argument. In effect, national witch doctors should stick to doctoring their own tribes.

'Think global, act local'

In spite of the market logic that goes against global advertising, there are a number of very real pressures that favour it. I have already mentioned the fact that there are very few really creative selling ideas. Then there is the sheer cost of production, be it for film or stills. There is the effort in managerial time involved in managing the creation of good advertising for the same brand in 17 or 57 different countries, and the corresponding time spent by the advertising agencies. There is the economy of scale in dealing with one agency, and having centralized media buying.

All these factors, plus the growing internationalization of management (as opposed to consumers), encourage the desire on the part of managements to have, at least, coordinated campaigns running around the world. This managerial view is further encouraged by the increasing centralization and simplification of many large companies' chains of command. One of the by-products of the computer revolution has been a significant slimming of most companies' marketing departments, and a shift up the command chain in the key communications decisions. In short, top managers increasingly like the idea that they take the advertising decisions; and, on an international scale, that the decisions can be made for entire regions, hemispheres or, even, the world.

At this stage, the practical problems begin to arise. First of all, on the client side of the equation, local operating companies tend to resist head office initiatives that represent specific interference in 'their' markets. Because advertising is—or is thought to be—one major area of managerial decision-making that can be, by its nature, highly specific and totally flexible, local marketing managers will, and do, fight to retain autonomy. With some justification, they can claim that head office does not understand the nuances and subtleties of their market; they can point to the (quite common) fact that whereas the brand is a mass market product in its home market in the USA, it is an exclusive luxury, or an idiosyncratic niche product, in Britain or France or Italy. For example, Kellogg's breakfast cereals are regarded purely as breakfast cereals in the USA, Britain, Australia; but in Continental Europe they are—variously—snacks, children's desserts, cooking ingredients, etc. Similarly, in the UK, Yardley Lavender is an old-fashioned scent for granny; in France, it is distinctly unisex in character; in Latin America, it is used by archetypically macho men.

Then, what about the agency? It is (regrettably, perhaps) characteristic of agencies that they tend to think very little of other agencies' work: respect has to be genuinely earned. So, almost any agency worth its salt will regard a 'foreign' campaign as something to be looked on with suspicion or, even, contempt; and will immediately want to make radical changes in the campaign. Agencies, too, subscribe enthusiastically to a NIH ('not invented here') view, even if the work comes from a sister company.

The difficulty for management—both of the multinational client and the multinational agency—is that the locals' instincts have a better than average chance of being right, simply because of the real differences between consumers in different countries, even when the target markets remain basically the same. As a result, using a single, unified, multinational campaign is very likely to be a distinctly sub-optimal strategy in most of the markets it tries to cover: and, given the fact, pointed out in Chapter 9, that the influence of different creative approaches can be the key factor that gives a brand's advertising success or failure, this is clearly crucial.

The upshot of all this is that the most sophisticated international marketing companies have adopted—long before Leavitt thought of global marketing—a distinctly flexible approach to their international advertising. They recognize the value of a really powerful creative idea, but they adapt and modify it to fit individual markets. Unilever, for example, tends to coordinate very tightly its brand and market positionings on an international or global scale; but the brand names for a given positioning may well vary by country, and the detail of creative executions will, usually, be tailored to the individual market. In a phrase, Unilever 'thinks global, acts local'.

It is, too, very noteworthy that the Japanese firms who are perhaps the most successful modern global marketers mostly make little or no attempt to coordinate their advertising across different major markets: as far as advertising is concerned, they actually 'think local'.

The 'how' of coordination
The fact remains that an increasing number of advertisers, and their agencies

with them, are committed to more or less detailed international coordination of their advertising.

Conditions for success
There appear to be a number of necessary pre-conditions for this to have a chance of working. These concern, first, the product and its market:

1. A specific need or set of needs common to end-users in many or all of the company's markets, that can be satisfied by a common brand.
2. Given (1), a reasonably homogeneous target-market segment in all the markets concerned.
3. Common key customer criteria both for buying the product category and for distinguishing between brands in all the markets concerned.
4. Competitive positions for the brand in all markets concerned that are at least recognizably similar (e.g. it is not a low quality 'price' brand in one market and an exotic luxury in another).

Second, there are considerations about the advertising:

1. An effective, original idea that is capable of being accepted, in cultural terms, in all the target markets.
2. Advertising that can be effectively translated into all relevant languages, without losing its force (i.e. advertising copy that does not depend on plays on words in its original language, since these are usually untranslatable).
3. An advertising idea that can be equally effective in all main media—TV, press, outdoor, radio—since in no multinational campaign will the same media mix be available in all countries.
4. An advertising idea that is legally acceptable in all the target markets.

Finally, there are some critical factors relating to the client and his or her agency:

1. The client's managers in the individual markets must be prepared to accept, cooperate with, and work together to improve the central campaign development.
2. Client's central advertising management must have the experience and the sensitivity to recognize and cater for the existence of real differences between countries and national psychology (quite apart from being able to recognize and deal with phoney differences).
3. The agency must be able to deliver comparable levels of understanding and cooperation from its local offices in the target markets.

These conditions will not always be met.

How to achieve success
Even with all these conditions, you still need a system that will lead to the development of a good campaign in the first place. Here again, there seem to be a number of key elements, that combine to make the process a relatively drawn-out one:

1. A clear, written brief needs to be developed in consultation between client and agency, and this process should involve at least the main countries in which the campaign will be run. Everybody important should be given the formal opportunity to argue: once they have bought into the brief, they are then committed.
2. The agency should aim to develop its strategy and its creative work as far as possible internationally. Language problems will tend to preclude mixed-country creative teams, though this is becoming a little easier; but the agency should, at least, set out to develop work in two or three different centres.
3. The agency needs to agree on its proposed campaign(s) internationally, before presentation to the client: at the very least, this means agreeing the basic creative concept, key pieces of copy (e.g. headlines and slogans or footlines), and the basis of the visual treatment.
4. Detailed execution has to be the task of the creative team who developed the winning campaign; but copy translation has to be done at the local level, and, as far as possible, double-checked,
   (a) to ensure that it embodies the spirit of the original, and
   (b) to ensure that it is correct usage and idiom in the language of the user country.

It is this last condition that causes the most problems, though less with advertising, which is usually very carefully checked, than with collateral material: copy on packaging, instruction leaflets, guarantee cards, brochures, and so on. A simple rule of thumb is that if you can detect the language from which a piece of copy has been translated, it is—for most purposes—an inadequate translation. Read the instructions for most Japanese and Italian electrical goods, and you will see what I mean: 'English as a foreign language' is all very well, but it is best not used to try to sell to the British.

Conclusions

Global, or at least, multinational campaigns are a feasible possibility. Yet they seem to remain limited to quite narrow categories of product or service, and the successful campaigns are creatively very simple in conception.

This is not, of course, to say that it makes no sense for—say—Ford to work world-wide with JWT and Ogilvy, or Kodak with JWT and McCann. There may be, and almost certainly are, very good commercial reasons (like a reduced overall rate of commissions or fees) why multinational advertisers align their business with just one or two multinational agencies. Certainly, such an arrangement has the effect of keeping commercial secrets within a relatively narrow group of agencies, and should ensure a fruitful exchange of knowledge across the agency network. But the existence of this form of agency alignment does not dictate a requirement for a common, global advertising campaign. Nor should it—unless *all* the conditions are right.

20 The future: where do we all go from here?

Any attempt to look ahead in the advertising business tends to get embroiled in considerations of the structural development of large multinational groups. This is interesting to people working in large multinational groups, but not much to anyone else. So I will ignore this area—except to say that there will, inevitably, be more mergers and acquisitions, initiated from 'non-traditional' sources, such as Continental Europe, Japan, Australia, rather than the USA or UK. It is more interesting to consider what clients will increasingly be looking for from their agencies; how they will balance the elements of the marketing mix; and how these demands will relate to developments in the media and in the attitudes and responses of consumers.

Clients' requirements
The last 10 or 15 years have seen the progressive emergence of two conflicting trends in advertisers' requirements. On the one hand, the need to integrate the elements of the communication mix into a common creative strategy has become increasingly recognized—or, at least, lip service is paid to it. On the other hand, managers have felt a need to shop around for marketing services, and this pressure has fuelled the massive growth in the share of media advertising taken by media independents. Related to these trends is the tendency—very clear in fmcg markets in the USA for several years—for marketers to rely more on essentially short-term promotional activity.

Coupled to the design revolution of the seventies and eighties, this last trend tempted some analysts in the mid-eighties to believe that advertising's importance within the overall marketing mix would be steadily and surely eroded. The WPP Group's annual report for 1986—the year before Martin Sorrell bought J Walter Thompson—is a sort of *locus classicus* for this thinking. What is certainly true is that the balance between media advertising and other elements in the mix will, inevitably, change over time; and that as 'old' markets for advertising lose their importance, 'new' markets will develop. In the UK, for example, the eighties saw a massive rise in the importance of financial service advertising, both relative to advertising expenditures as a whole and within financial institutions' marketing mix. A rapidly developing, but so far small, 'new' area in the market is Europe-wide advertising by the European Commission, and this can be expected to grow vastly as some form

222

of federal structure inevitably evolves in Europe. Big agencies are already lining up plans to pitch for the introduction of the single currency!

For both clients and their agencies, the possibility of using a single source for their marketing communications requirements is probably the major issue that affects the development of advertising as a business. Working in a medium-sized agency with a strong 'through-the-line' tradition, I certainly see a growing number of clients who say they are looking for a single source—at least creatively, (media is another matter). The logic of this search seems to me irrefutable, but few agencies are genuinely geared up to meet the requirement—especially if it includes public relations, which is not a traditional part of advertising agency services in the UK, in contrast to the situation in much of Continental Europe.

Agency structures

The difficulty for most agency groups in dealing with this client demand is both structural and historical. Historically, 'below-the-line' has been the poor relation in most agencies: as a result, those agency groups that have tried to move into this area have established separate units or companies to specialize in promotions, packaging, print, etc., and then set out to cross-sell, taking a profit at every turn. This is very hard to get to work satisfactorily, and, for the client, it is actually little more convenient than buying each service separately. While there is, certainly, a growing number of small or medium-sized 'through-the-line' agencies in the consumer field—and industrial agencies have always worked like this—most big consumer agencies will have to think very hard about their structure and culture if they are to find a satisfactory way of dealing with this aspect of their clients' requirements.

The simplest piece of single-sourcing is, of course, the most traditional: creative and media. In spite of the strong growth of media independents, and the likelihood that media broking and sponsorship services will add to the specialized character of the media business, I believe the nineties may see a switchback of at least some significant budgets from media independents to full-service agencies. I have no doubt that having media and creative together in the same agency is the most satisfactory arrangement, simply because a close inter-relationship between the core account group—which includes media—should lead to more creative use of the media and genuinely fruitful collaboration between media and creative. Once it becomes realistic, as it already has, for full-service agencies to start winning business back from independents, this has the inevitable effect of distancing the two parties in any split-source relationship: and it means that the full-service agencies, under the influence of pressures on margins and costs, have become sufficiently competitive to undermine the media shops' key selling point – price.

That said, the increasing fragmentation and complexity of the media scene means that there is a rising size threshold for an effective media department, whether in an agency or as an independent. Even with the benefit of sophisticated computers (which require investment spending), it is almost impossible to cover adequately the full range of media with less than five or six media specialists: a rule-of-thumb guide, based on IPA agency personnel statistics, suggests that agencies with less than 50 people, in total, will be pushed to provide an adequate media service across all media.

An issue related to this is the development of direct marketing. If you listen to the apostles of direct marketing (and many of them are almost aggressively evangelical), by the year 2000 media advertising will have given up most of its market to direct marketing. This seems to be, at least, mildly optimistic. There is, to my mind, no question that direct marketing has a significant and potentially important role in the mix for suppliers of a very wide range of goods and services, and it lends itself very readily (for example) to financial services, a wide range of durables and some retail operations. It is, however, far from convincing as part of most fmcg products' mainstream activities, in spite of one or two well-publicized American examples. Quite apart from the increasing probability that EC regulations will significantly limit the compilation and use of databases, the success rate of even quite well-targeted cold mailings is far from brilliant, and the direct marketing industry suffers from a degree of self-delusion when it oversells their technique's ability to establish a 'dialogue' with the consumer: it takes two to hold a dialogue.

The consumer

People change, times change, attitudes and concerns change. All the available evidence suggests that—very broadly—consumers in the nineties, in most industrialized countries, at least, will approach life rather differently from their behaviour and attitudes in the eighties. Part of this is, of course, a continuation of already established trends.

Key elements in this will continue to be the strength of a growing range of health concerns; the importance of at least protecting the environment; and elements of feminism. Each of these three major trends has a variety of different strands, and each is subject, to a greater or lesser extent, to regulations and legal or voluntary controls that affect advertising. These controls are likely to intensify.

For the advertiser, this will mean an ever-increasing need to be vigilant and sensitive to the development of issues in this area. It is very clear, for example, that women have become very sensitive to suggestions that a perfume or a brand of cosmetics is worn primarily to interest men: whatever the underlying truth, they mostly do not wish to have this suggested to them in advertising, (or so they say).

More broadly, evidence from VALS-type studies (see page 71) suggests that there is a gradual but broadly based shift in consumers' attitudes going on on a more or less pan-European scale. Interpreted in UK terms, what is happening can best be described as a quite sharp retreat from the explicit values of the Thatcher era, with its emphasis on ostentatious, aggressive self-advancement. In the nineties, it appears, people will be less concerned with affluence for affluence's sake, and more interested in self-realization. If this (much-simplified) view has any validity, the implications for advertising are—obviously—interesting and complex. This sort of change should have the effect of making the stylistic symbols and motivations of the eighties largely irrelevant, at least for those consumers who are more or less on the major trend—though these symbols may still be relevant for trend-laggers. After all, 'medallion man' still survived in places long after he had become a complete joke for the majority.

The other much talked-about aspect of developing consumer trends is—of course—ageing populations. This is a media cliché, but describes, in fact, an extremely gradual process. In the UK at least, the numbers involved in this trend are for marketing purposes, remarkably limited, in the sense that the number of say, 45–64-year-olds in the population is only going to grow from 21.6 per cent to 24.9 per cent between 1991 and 2006. The big proportional increase is among the over-75s, who are a very small part of the population, but have a disproportionate impact on health and welfare services and, inevitably, tend eventually to place a burden of caring on their younger relations.

At the other end of the age scale, the mid-eighties saw the start of a sharp decline in the 15–25 year old age group: by the mid to late nineties, this will translate into a sharp fall in the number of births—unless something quite unexpected happens.

Regulations and controls

One of the inevitabilities of life seems to be that if it moves, it's regulated. As Chapter 16 has shown, advertising is not an exception. The nineties will see an increasingly uncertain combination of the spread of EC regulation (as opposed to merely national legislation) and the increased lobbying activity of special interest groups—the single interest pressure group has already started to cross the Atlantic into Europe: there will be more of them.

Where there are lobbies, there will be draft directives from the EC, and, inevitably, some of these will affect advertising, simply because it is easier to prevent or control advertising than most other aspects of product marketing. Basically, it is not difficult to foresee both areas in which there will be pressure to ban advertising (alcohol, toy advertising to children); and where there will be pressure to limit or define the content of advertising (health claims in food advertising; consumer credit; 'green' claims; aspects of car advertising). On the past record, many of the first draft proposals will make no obvious logical, commercial or political sense; but, on the past record, some at least will come into force, albeit in modified form. This will certainly make the lives of advertising agencies and their clients more complex and difficult, and in some instances lead advertisers to shift their budgets into other—usually—less cost-effective marketing activity. So here, of course, 'consumer protection' will have the ultimate main effect of raising the price of the goods to the consumer: a consequence the pressure groups prefer to ignore.

The media

The 'known' changes in the media—especially in TV—have been outlined in earlier chapters. We can be reasonably certain that there will be others. It seems at least a fair bet, for example, that advertising will be providing at least some of the finance for the BBC by the end of the decade.

Simply because of the ability of national or supra-national governments to control most of the airwaves, plus the cost of putting satellites into orbit, TV will remain quite firmly controlled both nationally and internationally, as far as Europe, at least, is concerned. Nonetheless, we can expect an increasing proliferation of channels to become at least theoretically available to view, assuming the consumer takes the trouble to acquire the necessary combination of satellite dish, cable receptor, multi-channel TV set, decoder or descrambler, etc., plus, in a growing number of cases, an appropriate system to pay for programmes as they are taken off-air.

An example of things to come was the announcement in December 1991 of a new channel broadcasting in Hindustani off the Astra satellite, to provide Britain's half-million plus Asian households with a regular supply of Bombay-originated blockbuster films.

Radio, where the availability of FM and AM channels and reasonably tightly controlled small marketing areas has already led to a proliferation of stations broadcasting both very locally and—increasingly—nationally, should see still more development. Here, perhaps the most potentially interesting developments lie in the embryo pan-European services, but language problems are going to inhibit this development as anything more than an exclusive, specialized group of media for the foreseeable future.

Press media are, inevitably, more localized—on the basis of language: but the logistics of data collection and dissemination, and the growing similarities, at least at a superficial level, between countries in Europe will certainly encourage the already evident multinationalization of the magazine market; and this is likely to extend into more immediate press media such as weekly magazines and newspapers, following the examples of the *Financial Times European Edition*, the *International Herald Tribune* and the so far ill-starred *European*. This is likely to move rapidly beyond the example of the *Guardian*, with its cooperative venture with selected continental newspapers. As, and if, major newspapers go international in this way, it seems likely that there will be something of a nationalist backlash, either at the level of chauvinist national papers (it is difficult to see the *Sun* changing its spots) or, even, at a regional level: people will start looking for a more human and familiar scale of news and information.

The media opportunities

One of the factors underlying the growth of media independents has been the increasing complexity and fragmentation of media, allied to the Continental European practice of media broking and what the French call 'sur-commissions'—overriding discounts for volume. On top of this, the nineties will, undoubtedly, see a substantial rise in TV programme sponsorship and similar 'sub-media' deals: already in the UK there are calls for a code of practice to control the more elaborate forms of 'advertorial'.

Add to the very wide range of 'orthodox' media already available the almost limitless possibilities of direct marketing through electronic mail and similar systems (look what use the French make of Minitel), and it is inevitable that media use will have to become more carefully planned and targeted than ever.

What is liable to be forgotten in all this, I believe, is the importance—real or potential—of editorial environment. It is one thing actually to reach a target customer through one medium or another: it is altogether different if you can reach them in an appropriate context and an appropriate frame of mind.

As the numerical or statistical side of targeting becomes more difficult, this qualitative side of media selection will become more important: the question 'cost per thousand *what?*' will become increasingly important in the way the more intelligent and imaginative clients control their budgets, and agencies will have to respond with appropriately sophisticated modes of understanding and analysis.

This view of the media seems likely to favour the continuing strength of press media, even in an increasingly un-literate world: special interest magazines continue to proliferate (video games are the latest UK boom area), because the ability of audio and audio-visual media to cover special interests in depth is extremely limited, and increased leisure and affluence continue to create new fields for publishers of magazines to occupy; and these new publications generate, in turn, opportunities to reach very specific target groups. Mostly, of course, these groups are advertised to by advertisers who live off the specific special interest: but there is potentially considerable scope for the non-specialist advertiser who can identify appropriate synergies of interest.

Towards the year 2000

In conclusion, the advertising business is heading towards the end of the millenium in a familiar state of frenetic re-development around an established pattern. The need will remain, for the foreseeable future, for suppliers of goods and services to advertise their wares, and they will undoubtedly continue, with few exceptions, to use specialized agencies to create and place their advertising. In doing this, they will, increasingly, be seeking more precise targeting, greater cost-efficiency in the use of the media, and more positive results.

The agencies, in turn, will find themselves—still—short of adequate tools to evaluate the results they achieve. It is an unfortunate but indisputable fact that the measurement and assessment of the effectiveness of advertising remains extremely primitive for all but a small minority of advertisers and agencies; and that, in spite of the good example of the IPA Advertising

Effectiveness Programme, the progress made over the past 20 years has been desperately slow. It is tempting to conclude that both clients and agencies have a joint vested interest in maintaining the partly justifiable view that advertising is mostly art and only a little science; but both sides must realize that in this they are living in something of a fool's paradise.

The information technology revolution may, so far, be more about technology than about information, but it is only a matter of time before the full power of data analysis begins to focus on advertising effects, and most marketing departments and most agencies will immediately become very vulnerable, unless their activities are underpinned by a very clear understanding of their objectives, the methods by which these objectives are achieved, and how to measure the results. The one positive aspect of this, from an advertising agency viewpoint, is that once the first purely quantitative phase of this almost inevitable war has been completed, analysis should shift to creative quality. The limited available evidence shows clearly that really good creative work does deliver markedly better results than mediocre work.

Perhaps, like most people in the business, I am being over-optimistic. With luck, I am right.

Further sources of information

1. Education

General education for advertising—CAM
Advertising education in the UK is organized by the CAM (Communications, Advertising and Marketing) Foundation, a body set up in 1969 by the AA, IPA and IPR to take over the educational programmes and professional qualification schemes of these three bodies. In the early eighties, however, the IPA withdrew from CAM. CAM is now recognized by more than 20 advertising and marketing trade associations.

CAM administers two levels of professional qualification by examination, the CAM Certificate and the CAM Diploma, leading to the ultimate qualification of MCAM, which is awarded to those suitably qualified people in the business who, in addition, have demonstrated their professional capability in a business context.

Courses leading to the CAM qualifications are available from colleges of further education up and down the country, and also from correspondence courses.

Full details about CAM can be obtained from: CAM Foundation Ltd, Abford House, 15 Wilton Road, London SW1V 1NJ. Tel: 071-828 7506.

IPA
The IPA decided to withdraw from CAM because the CAM Diploma course had become too broad to be of benefit to people wishing to be educated specifically in aspects of advertising. The IPA, therefore, now runs its own seven-stage education and training programme, involving a mix of evening classes and seminars and residential courses.

Details can be obtained from the IPA at 44 Belgrave Square, London SW1X 8QS. Tel: 071-235 7020.

Copywriting
CAM and, indeed, IPA courses are primarily suited to people on the business and administrative side of advertising. In spite of one or two claimants, no one seems to have achieved any recognized basis for training copywriters except through on-the-job activity—though an experimental course has recently been started for direct response writers.

Art
Agency and commercial studio artists are usually recruited from the commercial art courses of art schools. It is probably fair to say that few people in the agency business regard art school training, however commercial its bias, as more than a basis for further training in how to work in an agency context. The technical content and skills developed at art school are essential, but the right working methods need to be learned in an agency.

Market research
The Market Research Society organizes regular courses and seminars for differing levels of skill and experience. Details can be obtained from the society, at: 15 Northburgh Street, London EC1V 0AH. Tel: 071-490 4911.

Miscellaneous
There is a wide variety of courses, conferences and seminars, on an *ad hoc* basis, promoted by a variety of organizers, covering most aspects of the business. Details of these are usually published in the trade press—*Campaign, Marketing, Marketing Week* or *Admap.*

The Chartered Institute of Marketing
The Chartered Institute of Marketing is the only other major trade association concerned with communications which is not involved in CAM. The Institute has its own college, at Moor Hall, Cookham, Berks, SL6 9QH. Tel: 06285-24922. The Institute's range of courses extends, obviously, well beyond advertising, but some of its activities include a significant advertising and advertising-related content.

2. The trade press
There are a large number of journals which cover the advertising business in the UK and elsewhere, on levels ranging from gossip to highly technical. The ones most likely to prove useful include:

UK publications
Admap—NTC Publications, monthly. Media and research: technical, but informative.
Advertisers' Annual, British Media Publications, annual. Directory of the advertising business.
Advertising & Marketing, Business Pubs Ltd, quarterly. Semi-technical, chiefly industrial advertising topics.
British Rate & Data (BRAD), Maclean Hunter, monthly. Complete listing of all UK press rates.
BRAD Advertiser & Agency List, three times yearly. Directory.
Campaign, Haymarket Campaign Mags, weekly. The ad-agency newspaper.
Creative Review, Centaur Communications, monthly. Review of advertising and related creative trends.

The Creative Handbook, annual. Guide to creative personnel and services.

Direction, Haymarket Campaign Mags. Monthly review of creative developments in advertising and graphic design.

European Journal of Marketing Research, Bradford Univ., quarterly. Technical,
research techniques and findings.

International Journal of Advertising, Cassell, quarterly. The official journal of
the AA.

J. Market Research Society, MRS/NTC publications, quarterly. Technical, MR
techniques and findings.

Marketing, Haymarket Business, weekly. Journal of Institute of Marketing:
general marketing articles, information summaries.

Marketing Week, Centaur Communications, weekly. Similar to *Campaign*, but
geared more to clients than agencies, marketing as well as advertising.

Media Week, weekly. Review of media news, statistics and gossip.

Precision Marketing, Centaur Communications, weekly. News magazine of
direct marketing.

US publications

Advertising Age, McGraw-Hill, weekly. Detailed news and technical discussion
on advertising topics.

J. Advertising Research
J. Marketing } monthly. Both very technical.

Trade Associations
The IPA and ISBA produce a regular series of leaflets and booklets covering a
variety of topics.

3. Trade associations, etc.

This is an incomplete list of relevant associations and (very briefly) their
aims. The complete list can be found in *Advertisers' Annual*.

Advertising Association, Abford House, 15 Wilton Road, SW1V 1NJ. Tel: 071-
828 2771. Joint Industry body (clients, agencies and media).

Advertising Creative Circle, 43 South Molton Street, W1. Tel: 071-408 1617.
Creative standards, education, interchange of ideas.

British Direct Marketing Association, Grosvenor Gardens House, Grosvenor
Gardens, SW1. Tel: 071-630 7322. Promote direct mail, exchange ideas.

CAM Society, Abford House, 15 Wilton Road, SW1V 1NJ. Open to CAM
'graduates'. Essentially social. Tel: 071-828 7507.

Chartered Institute of Marketing, Moor Hall, Cookham, Berks SL6 9QH. Tel:
06285-24922. Marketing management: professional qualification, training.
Regional branches.

Designers & Art Directors Association, 12 Carlton House Terrace, SW1Y 5AH.
Tel: 071-839 2964. Improve design standards, promote talent.

Incorporated Society of British Advertisers Ltd, 44 Hertford St. London W1Y
8AE. Tel: 071-499 7502. Advertisers: protect and advance advertising
interests.

Institute of Practitioners in Advertising, 44 Belgrave Square SW1X 8QS. Tel: 071-235 7020. Agencies: safeguard and promote interests. Education, information.

Institute of Public Relations, Old Trading House, 16 Northburgh Street, London EC1V 0PR. Tel: 071-253 5151. Enhance status, standards.

International Advertising Association UK Chapter, 39a London Road, Kingston, Surrey. Tel: 081-546 4809. Communications network.

Market Research Society, 15 Northburgh Street, London EC1V 0AH. Tel: 071-490 4911. Education, discussion.

4. Further reading

There are a vast number of books in existence covering different aspects of advertising.This is a selection of those which I have found useful.

General

Bulmore, Jeremy, *Behind the Scenes in Advertising*, NTC Publications, Henley, 1991.

Douglas, Torin, *The Complete Guide to Advertising*, Macmillan, London, 1984.

Mayer, Martin, *Madison Avenue USA*, Penguin, Harmondsworth, 1961.

Ogilvy, David, *Confessions of an Advertising Man*, Longman, Harlow, 1963.

Packard, Vance, *The Hidden Persuaders*, Penguin, Harmondsworth, 1956.

Rapp, S. and T. Collins, *Maxi Marketing*, McGraw-Hill, New York, 1987.

Smelt, Maurice (ed), *What Advertising Is*, Pelham Books, London, 1972.

Thompson, J. Walter, *The Case for Advertising*, JWT, London, 1975.

Branding

Cowley, Don (ed), *Understanding Brands—By Ten People Who Do*, Kogan Page, London, 1992.

King, Stephen, *Developing New Brands*, Pitman, London, 1973.

Careers

Hart, N. and N. Waite (eds), *How to Get on in Advertising*, 3rd edn, Kogan Page, London, 1987.

Taylor, Felicity, *Careers in Marketing, Public Relations and Advertising*, Kogan Page, London, 1987.

Creativity

Baker, Stephen, *Systematic Approach to Advertising Creativity*, McGraw-Hill, New York, 1979.

Koestler, A., *The Act of Creation*, Pan, 3rd edn, 1964.

Roman, K. and J. Maas, *How to Advertise*, St. Martins' Press, New York, 1976.

Media

Adams, James R., *Media Planning*, 2nd edn, Business Books, London, 1977.

Barwise, P. and A. Ehrenberg, *Television and Its Audience*, Sage Publications, 1989.

Broadbent, Simon, and Brian Jacobs, *Spending Advertising Money*, 4th edn, Business Books, London, 1984.

Broadbent, Simon, *The Advertising Budget*, NTC Publications, Henley, 1989.

Advertising Management

Morgan, Eric, *Choosing and Using Advertising Agencies*, Business Books, London, 1974.

Webster, Eric, *Advertising for the Advertiser*, John Murray, London, 1969.

Law

Circus P. and A. Painter, *Sales Promotion Law: A Practical Guide*, Butterworth, London, 1989.

Lawson, R. G., *Advertising Law*, Macdonald & Evans, Plymouth, 1978.

Economics

Broadbent, Simon and Charles Channon (eds) *Advertising Works* (biennial series), IPA, London, 1981, 1983, 1985, 1987, 1989, 1991.

Chipton, Brian and Brian Sturgess, *The Economics of Advertising*, 2nd edn, Advertising Association, London, 1985.

Reekie, W. Duncan, *Advertising & Price*, Advertising Association, London, 1979.

Production

Cory, Peter, *Graphic Design and Reproduction Techniques*, 2nd edn, Focal Press, London, 1972.

Murray, Ray, *How to Brief Designers and Buy Print*, Business Books, London, 1983.

Peacock, J., C. Berrill and M. Bernard (eds), *The Print and Production Manual*, Blueprint Publishing Ltd, London, 1986.

Printing Reproduction Pocket Pal, 4th UK edn, IPA, London, 1979.

Market Research

Birn, R., P. Hague and P. Vangelder (eds), *A Handbook of Market Research Techniques*, Kogan Page, London, 1990.

General Information

NTC Publications in Henley publishes a collection of 'Pocket Books' that are a mine of information on both the UK and Continental European markets. NTC Publications Ltd, PO Box 69, Henley-on-Thames, Oxfordshire RG9 1GB. Tel: 0491-574 671.

Index